Analytics Engineering
with SQL and dbt
Building Meaningful Data Models at Scale

Rui Machado and Hélder Russa

Beijing · Boston · Farnham · Sebastopol · Tokyo

Analytics Engineering with SQL and dbt

by Rui Machado and Hélder Russa

Copyright © 2024 Rui Pedro Machado and Hélder Russa. All rights reserved.

Published by O'Reilly Media, Inc., 1005 Gravenstein Highway North, Sebastopol, CA 95472.

O'Reilly books may be purchased for educational, business, or sales promotional use. Online editions are also available for most titles (*http://oreilly.com*). For more information, contact our corporate/institutional sales department: 800-998-9938 or *corporate@oreilly.com*.

Acquisitions Editor: Michelle Smith	**Indexer:** nSight, Inc.
Development Editor: Angela Rufino	**Interior Designer:** David Futato
Production Editor: Christopher Faucher	**Cover Designer:** Karen Montgomery
Copyeditor: Piper Editorial Consulting, LLC	**Illustrator:** Kate Dullea
Proofreader: Sharon Wilkey	

December 2023:   First Edition

Revision History for the First Edition

2023-12-08:   First Release

See *http://oreilly.com/catalog/errata.csp?isbn=9781098142384* for release details.

The O'Reilly logo is a registered trademark of O'Reilly Media, Inc. *Analytics Engineering with SQL and dbt*, the cover image, and related trade dress are trademarks of O'Reilly Media, Inc.

The views expressed in this work are those of the authors and do not represent the publisher's views. While the publisher and the authors have used good faith efforts to ensure that the information and instructions contained in this work are accurate, the publisher and the authors disclaim all responsibility for errors or omissions, including without limitation responsibility for damages resulting from the use of or reliance on this work. Use of the information and instructions contained in this work is at your own risk. If any code samples or other technology this work contains or describes is subject to open source licenses or the intellectual property rights of others, it is your responsibility to ensure that your use thereof complies with such licenses and/or rights.

978-1-098-14238-4

[LSI]

Table of Contents

Preface

In the ever-evolving business world, a captivating concept known as *analytics engineering* has emerged. It quickly became the talk of the town, in demand by managers, presented by IT companies, and admired by users who marveled at the possibilities it offered. But amid the excitement, many didn't know what analytics engineering was about. They thought it was about creating data pipelines, designing stunning visualizations, and using advanced algorithms. Oh, how wrong they were!

You can imagine this extraordinary world of analytical engineering as a cross between the meticulous investigator Sherlock Holmes, representing the analytical side, and the genius engineer Tony Stark, better known as Iron Man, representing the engineering side. Imagine the remarkable problem-solving skills of Sherlock Holmes combined with the cutting-edge technologies of Iron Man. This combination is what defines the true power and potential of analytical technology.

But beware: if you thought analytics engineering was limited to data pipelines and visualizations, you missed the deep deductive thinking that Sherlock Holmes, as a representation of a data analyst or business analyst, brings to the equation. This field is where analytical investigation crosses with the techniques of a software engineer or data engineer, represented by Tony Stark.

Stop for a moment and think about the importance of data in your business. Why do you seek it? The answer lies in the pursuit of knowledge. Analytic technology is used to transform raw data into actionable insights that serve as the basis for informed decisions. It's a powerful support system that provides facts illuminating your business's reality. However, it doesn't make decisions for you but instead provides you with the information you need to make your business a success.

Before you dive into creating an impressive Iron Man suit of analytics technologies, embrace the wisdom of Sherlock Holmes. Use his keen observational skills to identify and understand the core of your challenges. Refrain from succumbing to the lure of visualizations and algorithms just because others are fascinated by them. Remember that analytics engineering is more than just technology: it's a management tool that will be successful only if it's aligned with your organization's strategies and goals. Ensuring that your key performance indicators are aligned with the reality of your business will ensure that the results of your analytics engineering efforts are accurate, impactful, and won't disappoint you.

The great adventure of analytics engineering doesn't begin with building data pipelines or selecting advanced algorithms. No, my friend, it starts with a thorough introspection of your organization's knowledge gaps. Figure out why that knowledge is important and how it can be leveraged to drive your business to success. Use the transformative power of analytics as your compass, pointing the way to success amid the vast sea of data.

In your pursuit of analytics engineering, always remember the story of Sherlock Holmes. Avoid building an extravagant aircraft when a humble bicycle would suffice. Let the complexity of the problem and its contextual nuances guide your efforts. Remember that analytics isn't just about technology; it's a beacon of management, an invaluable tool that must be used with purpose and precision. Let it become your constant companion on the road to success.

Why We Wrote This Book

In today's era of abundant information, it is not uncommon for vital knowledge, concepts, and techniques to become obscured amid the rapid growth of technology and the relentless pursuit of innovation. During this dynamic transformation, several essential concepts can sometimes be inadvertently overlooked. This oversight doesn't stem from their diminishing relevance but rather from the swift pace of progress.

One such fundamental concept that often falls by the wayside is data modeling in the context of data management. It's worth noting that data modeling encompasses various approaches, including Kimball, conceptual, logical, and physical modeling, among others. We recognize the pressing need to emphasize the significance of data modeling in this diverse landscape, and that's one of the key reasons we've crafted this book. Within these pages, we aim to shed light on the intricacies and various dimensions of data modeling and how it underpins the broader field of analytics engineering.

Over time, the importance of data modeling in guaranteeing a solid data management system has gradually faded from general awareness. This is not because it became outdated but rather due to a shift in the industry's focus. New words, tools, and methods have emerged, making the fundamental principles less important. A transition occurred from traditional practices to modern solutions that promised quickness and efficiency, sometimes resulting in a loss of foundational strength.

The rise of analytics engineering led to a resurgence. It was not just a trend filled with fancy words but also a return to the basics, echoing the principles of the business intelligence sector. The difference is that modern tools, infrastructure, and techniques are now available to implement these principles more efficiently.

So, why did we feel the need to document our thoughts? There are two primary reasons. First and foremost, it is crucial to underscore the enduring value and significance of well-established concepts like data modeling. While these methodologies may have been around for a while, they provide a robust foundation for the development of modern techniques. Our second intention is to emphasize that analytics engineering is not a standalone entity but rather a natural progression from the legacy of business intelligence. By integrating the two, organizations can construct a more resilient data value chain, ensuring that their data is not just extensive but also actionable, ultimately enhancing its utility.

This book is not just a sentimental trip down memory lane or a commentary on the present. It's a blueprint for the future. Our goal is to help organizations revisit their foundations, appreciate the advantages of old and new technologies, and integrate them for a comprehensive data management approach. We'll dig deeper into data modeling and transformation details, explain its importance, and examine how it interacts with modern analytics engineering tools. We aim to provide our readers with a complete understanding, enabling them to strengthen their data management processes and utilize the full potential of their data.

Who This Book Is For

This book is designed for professionals, students, and enthusiasts dealing with the complex world of data management and analytics. Whether you're an experienced veteran reminiscing about the basic principles of data modeling or an aspiring analyst keen to understand the transformation from business intelligence to contemporary analytics engineering, our storytelling assures clearness and direction.

Organizations seeking to strengthen their data processes will discover immense value in the combination of well-proven principles and modern tools discussed in this book. In summary, if you wish to take full advantage of your data by combining the strengths of the past with the innovations of the present, this book will guide you.

How This Book Is Organized

We've structured the book into six chapters:

Chapter 1, "Analytics Engineering"

This chapter traces the evolution of data management from traditional SQL-based systems to innovative tools such as Apache Airflow and dbt, each changing how we handle and view data. The analytics engineer role bridges data engineering and analytics, guaranteeing that our insights are reliable and actionable. Despite the changes in tools and roles, the importance and value of data remain paramount. Nevertheless, challenges endure, such as data quality and efficient storage, as well as optimizing compute resources for tasks like load balancing on platforms such as Redshift or designing efficient jobs with appropriately sized warehouses on Snowflake. Data modeling, which involves structuring data to reflect real-world scenarios, is at the core of these solutions.

Chapter 2, "Data Modeling for Analytics"

This chapter delves into the critical role of data modeling in today's analytics-driven landscape. We will investigate how it aids in structuring data for efficient analysis and explore the significance of data normalization in reducing duplicity. While we emphasize the importance of normalization, it's worth noting that various modeling methodologies, such as Kimball and One Big Table, advocate for different approaches, including denormalization, depending on specific use cases. By understanding these basic principles and considering the broader spectrum of modeling methodologies, analysts can effectively explore the data, ensuring substantial insights and informed decisions. Devoid of a robust data model, whether normalized or denormalized as per the context, the analytical process can be inconsistent and inaccurate.

Chapter 3, "SQL for Analytics"

This chapter explores the enduring strength of SQL as a premier analytics language. We will start by outlining the basics of databases and how SQL serves as the primary language for interacting with databases. Our journey will cover the usefulness of views in streamlining queries, the powerful features of window functions for advanced computations, and the flexibility of common table expressions in refining complex queries. We will also discuss SQL's role in distributed data processing and conclude with an exciting application of SQL in machine learning model training.

Chapter 4, "Data Transformation with dbt"

This chapter provides a detailed exploration of dbt beyond an initial introduction. We will examine dbt's crucial role in the data analytics lifecycle and demonstrate how it transforms raw data into structured and accessible models. Our exploration will navigate the dbt project structure, addressing features such as model building, documentation, and testing while providing insights into dbt artifacts, including YAML files. At the end of this chapter, you will have a comprehensive understanding of dbt, enabling you to seamlessly incorporate it into your analytics workflows.

Chapter 5, "dbt Advanced Topics"
In this chapter, we'll dig into the advanced aspects of dbt. Beyond just views or tables, we'll discuss the range of model materializations in dbt, including the use of ephemeral models, data snapshots, and the implementation of incremental models to sidestep constant full data loads. Additionally, we'll elevate our analytics code, focusing on optimizing its efficiency with techniques such as Jinja, macros, and packages to keep it DRY (Don't Repeat Yourself). Finally, we will also introduce the dbt semantic layer, which plays the key role of acting as a bridge between raw data and meaningful insights.

Chapter 6, "Building an End-to-End Analytics Engineering Use Case"
This concluding chapter consolidates everything you have learned about analytics engineering using dbt and SQL. After deepening the concepts, techniques, and best practices in prior chapters, we now pivot toward a hands-on approach by crafting a complete analytics engineering use case from scratch. dbt and SQL's capabilities will be harnessed to design, implement, and deploy an all-encompassing analytics solution. Data modeling for varied purposes will be in the spotlight. The goal is to illustrate a holistic analytics workflow, spanning from data ingestion to reporting, by merging insights from prior chapters. During this process, we will overcome prevalent challenges and provide strategies to navigate them effectively.

Conventions Used in This Book

The following typographical conventions are used in this book:

Italic
Indicates new terms, URLs, email addresses, filenames, and file extensions.

`Constant width`
Used for program listings, as well as within paragraphs to refer to program elements such as variable or function names, databases, data types, environment variables, statements, and keywords.

`Constant width bold`
Shows commands or other text that should be typed literally by the user.

`Constant width italic`
Shows text that should be replaced with user-supplied values or by values determined by context.

This element signifies a tip or suggestion.

This element signifies a general note.

Using Code Examples

If you have a technical question or a problem using the code examples, please send email to *bookquestions@oreilly.com*.

This book is here to help you get your job done. In general, if example code is offered with this book, you may use it in your programs and documentation. You do not need to contact us for permission unless you're reproducing a significant portion of the code. For example, writing a program that uses several chunks of code from this book does not require permission. Selling or distributing examples from O'Reilly books does require permission. Answering a question by citing this book and quoting example code does not require permission. Incorporating a significant amount of example code from this book into your product's documentation does require permission.

We appreciate, but generally do not require, attribution. An attribution usually includes the title, author, publisher, and ISBN. For example: "*Analytics Engineering with SQL and dbt* by Rui Machado and Hélder Russa (O'Reilly). Copyright 2024 Rui Pedro Machado and Hélder Russa, 978-1-098-14238-4."

If you feel your use of code examples falls outside fair use or the permission given above, feel free to contact us at *permissions@oreilly.com*.

O'Reilly Online Learning

O'REILLY® For more than 40 years, *O'Reilly Media* has provided technology and business training, knowledge, and insight to help companies succeed.

Our unique network of experts and innovators share their knowledge and expertise through books, articles, and our online learning platform. O'Reilly's online learning platform gives you on-demand access to live training courses, in-depth learning paths, interactive coding environments, and a vast collection of text and video from O'Reilly and 200+ other publishers. For more information, visit *https://oreilly.com*.

How to Contact Us

Please address comments and questions concerning this book to the publisher:

O'Reilly Media, Inc.
1005 Gravenstein Highway North
Sebastopol, CA 95472
800-889-8969 (in the United States or Canada)
707-829-7019 (international or local)
707-829-0104 (fax)
support@oreilly.com
https://www.oreilly.com/about/contact.html

We have a web page for this book, where we list errata, examples, and any additional information. You can access this page at *https://oreil.ly/analytics-engineering-SQL-dbt*.

For news and information about our books and courses, visit *https://oreilly.com*.

Find us on LinkedIn: *https://linkedin.com/company/oreilly-media*

Follow us on Twitter: *https://twitter.com/oreillymedia*

Watch us on YouTube: *https://youtube.com/oreillymedia*

Acknowledgments

I want to send a special message to my wife, Ana, and my two wonderful daughters, Mimi and Magui. You inspire me every day to believe in myself and to pursue my dreams unwaveringly because what I achieve for me, I achieve for us. Above all, I want to show my daughters that anything is possible when we set our minds to it. Lastly, I need to thank Hélder, friend and coauthor, for keeping this dream alive and having levels of resilience I have never seen before in anyone.

— *Rui Machado*

I want to thank my (future) wife for always being by my side. Her patience and words were my rock in the toughest times. Also, a special thank you to my parents. Without them and their efforts to allow me to continue my studies and pursue my dreams, certainly this book wouldn't be possible. Again, my genuine thank you to them. Finally, to all my anonymous and not-so-anonymous friend(s) and coauthor, Rui, who stood by my side with their positivity and constructive feedback, and substantially enriched the content of this book.

— *Hélder Russa*

CHAPTER 1
Analytics Engineering

The historical development of analytics includes significant milestones and technologies that have shaped the field into what it is today. It began with the advent of data warehousing in the 1980s, which created the foundational framework for organizing and analyzing business data. Bill Inmon, a computer scientist who continued to publish throughout the 1980s and 1990s, is widely regarded as providing the first solid theoretical foundation for data warehousing.

A subsequent wave of development occurred when Ralph Kimball, another leading contributor to data warehousing and business intelligence (BI), published his influential work, *The Data Warehouse Toolkit*, in 1996. Kimball's work laid the foundation for dimensional modeling, marking another crucial milestone in the evolution of analytics. Together, the contributions of Inmon and Kimball, spanning the late 20th century, played pivotal roles in shaping the landscape of data warehousing and analytics.

In the early 2000s, the emergence of tech giants like Google and Amazon created the need for more advanced solutions for processing massive amounts of data, leading to the release of the Google File System and Apache Hadoop. This marked the era of Big Data Engineering, in which professionals used the Hadoop framework to process large amounts of data.

The rise of public cloud providers like Amazon Web Services (AWS) revolutionized the way software and data applications were developed and deployed. One of the pioneering offerings from AWS was Amazon Redshift, introduced in 2012. It represented an interesting blend of online analytical processing (OLAP) and traditional database technologies. In its early days, Redshift required database administrators to manage tasks like vacuuming and scaling to maintain optimal performance.

Over time, cloud native technologies have continued to evolve, and Redshift itself has undergone significant enhancements. While retaining its core strengths, newer versions of Redshift, along with cloud native platforms like Google BigQuery and Snowflake, have streamlined many of these administrative tasks, offering advanced data processing capabilities to enterprises of all sizes. This evolution highlights the ongoing innovation within the cloud data processing ecosystem.

The modern data stack, consisting of tools like Apache Airflow, data build tool (dbt), and Looker, further transformed data workflows. With these advances, the term "Big Data engineer" became obsolete, making way for a data engineer's broader and more inclusive role. This shift was recognized in the influential articles of Maxime Beauchemin—creator of Apache Superset and Airflow and one of the first data engineers at Facebook and Airbnb—particularly in his article "The Rise of the Data Engineer" (*https://oreil.ly/Sc-94*), which highlighted the growing importance of data engineering in the industry. All of these rapid developments in the data field have led to significant changes in the role of data professionals. With the advent of data tools, simple tasks are becoming strategic tasks.

Today's data engineers have a multifaceted role that encompasses data modeling, quality assurance, security, data management, architectural design, and orchestration. They are increasingly adopting software engineering practices and concepts, such as functional data engineering and declarative programming, to enhance their work-flows. While Python and structured query language (SQL) stand out as indispensable languages for data engineers, it's important to note that the choice of programming languages can vary widely in this field. Engineers may leverage other languages such as Java (commonly used for managing Apache Spark and Beam), Scala (also prevalent in the Spark and Beam ecosystem), Go, and more, depending on the specific needs and preferences of their projects. The combination of languages like Java and SQL is also common among data engineers at large organizations.

Organizations are increasingly moving toward decentralized data teams, self-service platforms, and alternative data storage options. As data engineers are forced to adapt to all these market changes, we often see some taking on a more technical role, focusing on platform enablement. Other data engineers work closer to the business, designing, implementing, and maintaining systems that turn raw data into high-value information as they adapt to this accelerated industry that is bringing new tools to market every day and spawning the fantastic world of analytics engineering.

In this chapter, we provide an introduction to the field of analytics engineering and its role in the data-driven decision-making process. We discuss the importance of analytics engineering in today's data-driven world and the primary roles of an analytics engineer. In addition, we will explore how the analytics engineering lifecycle is used to manage the analytics process and how it ensures the quality and accuracy of the data and insights generated. We will also address the current trends and technologies shaping the field of analytics engineering, from history to the present, touching on emerging concepts like data mesh, and discussing the fundamental choices between extract, load, and transform (ELT) and extract, transform, and load (ETL) strategies as well as the many data modeling techniques being adopted around the world.

Databases and Their Impact on Analytics Engineering

For a long time now, data has increasingly become the focus of interest for companies that want to stay one step ahead of the competition, improve their internal processes, or merely understand the behavior of their customers. With new tools, new ways of working, and new areas of knowledge such as data science and BI, it's becoming increasingly difficult to fully survey and understand the data landscape these days.

The natural progress of technology has caused an oversupply of data analysis, visualization, and storage tools, each offering unique features and capabilities. Nevertheless, an accelerated deployment of those tools has resulted in a fragmented landscape, requiring individuals and organizations to remain up-to-date with the most recent technological developments while at the same time having to make prudent choices on how to use them. Sometimes this abundance creates confusion and requires a continuous cycle of learning and adaptation.

The evolution of work practices is accompanied by a diversification of tools. Dynamic and Agile methodologies have replaced traditional approaches to data management and analysis. Iterative practices and cross-functional collaboration introduce flexibility and speed to data projects, but they also pose a challenge in harmonizing workflows across diverse teams and roles. Effective communication and alignment are crucial as diverse facets of the data process converge, creating a need for a comprehensive understanding of these novel work practices.

Specialized areas such as data science and BI have increased the complexity of the data field as well. Data scientists apply advanced statistical and machine learning techniques to detect complex patterns, whereas BI experts extract valuable information from raw data to produce practical insights. Such specialized areas introduce refined techniques that require regular skill development and learning. A successful adoption of these practices necessitates a dedicated commitment to education and a flexible approach to skill acquisition.

As data spreads across the digital domain, it carries with it unforeseen amounts, varieties, and speeds. The flood of data, along with the complex features of present-day data sources, such as Internet of things (IoT) gadgets and unorganized text, makes data management even more demanding. The details of incorporating, converting, and assessing data precision become more apparent, emphasizing the need for strong methods that guarantee reliable and precise insights.

The multifaceted nature of the data world compounds its complexity. As an outcome of converging skills from various domains, including computer science, statistics, and field-specific proficiency, a cooperative and communicative strategy is necessary. This multidisciplinary interaction accentuates the significance of efficient teamwork and knowledge sharing.

But that has not always been the case. For decades, spreadsheets were the standard technology for storing, managing, and analyzing data at all levels, both for business operational management and for analytics to understand it. However, as businesses have become more complex, so has the need for data-related decision making. And the first of these came in the form of a revolution called databases. *Databases* can be defined as an organized collection of structured information or data, usually stored electronically in a computer system. This data can be in the form of text, numbers, images, or other types of digital information. Data is stored in a way that facilitates access and retrieval using a set of predefined rules and structures called a *schema*.

Databases are an essential part of analytics because they provide a way to efficiently store, organize, and retrieve large amounts of data, allowing analysts to easily access the data they need to perform complex analyses to gain insights that would otherwise be difficult or impossible to obtain. In addition, databases can be configured to ensure data integrity, which guarantees that the data being analyzed is accurate and consistent and thus makes the analysis more reliable and trustworthy.

One of the most common ways to use databases for analytics is the data warehousing technique, that is, to construct and use a data warehouse. A *data warehouse* is a large, centralized data store designed to simplify data use. The data in a data warehouse is typically extracted from a variety of sources, such as transactional systems, external data feeds, and other databases. The data is then cleansed, transformed, and integrated into a single, consistent data model that typically follows a dimensional modeling technique such as the star schema or Data Vault.

Another important use of databases in analytics is the process of data mining. *Data mining* uses statistical and machine learning techniques to uncover patterns and relationships in large datasets. In this way, trends can be identified, future behavior can be predicted, and other types of predictions can be made.

Database technologies and data scientists have thus played a crucial role in the emergence of data science by providing a way to efficiently store, organize, and retrieve large amounts of data, enabling data scientists to work with large datasets and focus on what matters: gaining knowledge from data.

The use of SQL and other programming languages, such as Python or Scala, that allow interaction with databases has enabled data scientists to perform complex data queries and manipulations. Also, the use of data visualization tools such as Tableau and Microsoft Power BI, which easily integrate with database engines, has made it easier for data scientists to present their findings in a clear and intuitive way.

With the advent of Big Data and the growing demand to store and process vast datasets, various database technologies have emerged to meet diverse needs. For instance, data analysts often rely on databases for a wide range of applications, including data warehousing, data mining, and integration with BI tools like Tableau.

However, it's important to delve deeper into these use cases to understand the need for analytics engineering. When connecting BI tools directly to operational databases (online transaction processing [OLTP] replicas), performance and scalability can be limited. This approach may work well for smaller datasets and simple queries, but as data volumes grow and the complexity of analytics increases, it can lead to performance bottlenecks and suboptimal query response times.

This is where analytics engineering comes into play. Analytics engineers are experts in optimizing data workflows, transforming and aggregating data to ensure it's in the right format for analytical tasks. They design and maintain data pipelines that ETL data from various sources into optimized data warehouses or data lakes. By doing so, they help organizations overcome the limitations of direct OLTP connections, enabling faster and more efficient data analysis with tools like Tableau. In essence, analytics engineering bridges the gap between raw data and actionable insights, ensuring that data analysts and scientists can work with large, complex datasets effectively.

Cloud Computing and Its Impact on Analytics Engineering

In recent decades, the world has faced a series of complicated challenges with significant technical implications. Economic downturns have driven innovations in financial technologies and risk management systems. Geopolitical tensions have required advances in cybersecurity to protect critical infrastructure and sensitive data. Global health crises have underscored the importance of advanced data analytics and predictive modeling for disease surveillance and management. In addition, the urgent need to combat climate change has driven the development of cutting-edge renewable energy technologies and sustainable engineering solutions to meet climate goals.

Amid these challenges, the pursuit of profit and growth remains a key driver for businesses worldwide. However, the value of human labor time has taken on a new dimension, leading to significant changes in the way businesses operate and how cloud computing accommodates them. This change is reflected in the increasing adoption of managed and serverless offerings that reduce reliance on full-time support staff such as database administrators.

As companies adapt to this changing landscape, innovation, differentiation, and sustainability of business models and strategies have become essential considerations for companies seeking to succeed in a rapidly changing world. The information technology and systems industry found in this context a good opportunity to grow its capabilities in helping organizations overcome this world of uncertainty and pressure. The rationalization of operating models has become urgent, requiring a re-evaluation of data centers and pricing structures. In addition, product and service offerings must focus primarily on ease of use, lower latency, improved security, a broader range of real-time tools, more integration, more intelligence, less code, and a faster time to market.

Organizations have recognized the importance of investing in innovative tools, driving digital transformation, and adopting a data-centric approach to decision making to achieve greater agility and competitive advantage. To achieve these goals, many are focusing on leveraging well-curated data from internal and external sources. This carefully structured data can provide valuable insights into business performance.

In the industry, the practice of creating, visualizing, and analyzing interconnected business data in an accessible format is commonly referred to as *data analytics*. Historically, it has also been known as *business intelligence*, and the two terms are closely related. While BI is a subset of analytics and focuses on business-oriented decision making, data analytics encompasses a broader spectrum that includes product analytics, operational analytics, and several other specialized areas. Both BI and data analytics play pivotal roles in helping organizations gain a competitive edge through data-driven insights.

Although data analytics offers numerous benefits for improving and reshaping business strategies and monitoring performance, it requires significant financial investment in servers, software licenses, and specialized staff such as data engineers, data scientists, and data visualization specialists. In times of economic crisis, the high up-front and operational costs associated with IT hardware, software, and specialists can be perceived as impractical and unattractive.

As a result, on-premises solutions, where the infrastructure for data analytics is set up and managed on a company's own premises, often lose their appeal. This is especially true for newcomers to analytics who are unfamiliar with the concept. On-premises solutions typically require significant investment in hardware, software, and ongoing maintenance. They are also less flexible and scalable compared to cloud-based data analytics solutions. This shift in preferences is clearing the way for new cloud-based data analytics solutions that meet similar business needs as traditional data analytics. However, instead of relying on on-premises servers and software, cloud-based solutions leverage cloud computing services to accelerate deployment and minimize infrastructure costs.

The increasing adoption of cloud computing in various industries has led software vendors such as Microsoft, Google, and Amazon to develop advanced tools for data analysis and data warehousing. These tools are designed to operate in the cloud computing paradigm and leverage shared network resources to enable greater accessibility and streamlined deployment. A vivid example of this trend is Microsoft's comprehensive data analytics platform, Microsoft Fabric.

In parallel, dbt from dbt Labs, which we discuss in more detail later in this book, stands out as a versatile hybrid product. dbt, like Hadoop, is an open source solution that gives users the flexibility to deploy it according to their specific needs, whether in the cloud or on premises. In its cloud version, dbt integrates seamlessly with leading cloud platforms, including Microsoft Azure, Google Cloud Platform (GCP), and AWS. This open source nature gives organizations the ability to customize their deployment to their unique requirements and infrastructure preferences.

While cloud-based data analytics solutions and platforms are a global trend and a central concept of the modern data platform, it's important to recognize that cloud computing solutions bring both benefits and risks that shouldn't be overlooked. These risks include potential security issues, the physical location of servers, and the costs associated with moving away from a particular provider.

Nonetheless, cloud technologies are currently changing the way organizations deploy and construct information systems and technology solutions, and data analytics is no exception. That's why it's essential to recognize that moving to the cloud will soon no longer be an option but a necessity. Understanding the benefits of analytics solutions in the form of services is important. Otherwise, providing timely information to decision-makers with on-premises solutions that lack flexibility and scalability could become increasingly challenging if this transition isn't addressed.

However, although cloud technologies bring several benefits, such as economies of scale and flexibility, they also bring information security issues. The concentration of data in cloud infrastructures makes them attractive targets for unauthorized attacks. To succeed in the cloud in the data context, organizations must understand and mitigate the risks associated with cloud computing. Key risks include data privacy, loss of control, incomplete or insecure deletion of data, unauthorized internal access, data availability, and complex costing.

Data privacy is a significant concern because it's challenging to verify that vendors are handling data in compliance with laws and standards, even though public audit reports from vendors can help build trust. In nonintegrated scenarios, data security risks multiply as data flows among various systems and data centers, increasing the risk of interception and synchronization. Another important risk is vendor dependency, which occurs when responsibility for data management rests solely within one service provider in such a way that it limits the ability to migrate to other solutions. This kind of dependency ends up limiting an organization's control over decision making and authority over data. While these are just a few known risks, we can already understand that organizations need to get a handle on these risks to effectively reap the benefits of cloud-based data analytics solutions. This requires careful consideration, adherence to security standards and best practices, and ongoing cost control to measure the return on investment.

If all risks are correctly addressed and mitigated in a proper data strategy that outlines how an organization will manage its information assets, including the cloud strategy, technology, processes, people, and rules involved, an organization can gain a substantial competitive advantage when compared to one that doesn't have a data strategy. By focusing on cloud computing and leveraging a cloud data platform, organizations can transform raw data into meaningful insights, accelerating the process of building a solid data foundation. This enables efficient sourcing, structuring, and analysis of relevant data, and it even supports the adoption of AI technologies while driving value in less time and at a lower cost than traditional methods.

Interestingly, the relationship between a cloud data platform, analytics, and AI is symbiotic. Implementing a cloud data platform accelerates the adoption of an analytics-driven architecture and enables the full operationalization of AI initiatives. It empowers organizations to use all relevant data, gain enterprise-wide insights, and unlock new business opportunities. By eliminating the need to manage multiple tools, organizations can focus on data modernization, accelerate insight discovery, and benefit from existing technology partnerships, thereby advancing their AI journey.

This is why it's fair to say that cloud computing has been a core component of both modern data platforms and the cloud-based analytics and AI platforms that continuously grow in volume every day and thus contribute to the disruption of this industry.

The Data Analytics Lifecycle

The *data analytics lifecycle* is a series of steps to transform raw data into valuable and easily consumable data products. These can range from well-managed datasets to dashboards, reports, APIs, or even web applications. In other words, it describes how data is created, collected, processed, used, and analyzed to achieve a specific product or business goal.

The increasing complexity in organizational dynamics directly impacts how data is handled. Numerous people must use the same data but with different goals. While a top executive might need to know just a few top-level key performance indicators to track business performance, a middle manager might need a more granular report to support daily decisions.

This highlights the need for a governed and standardized approach to creating and maintaining data products based on the same data foundation. Given the many decisions an organization must make regarding its data governance, technologies, and management processes, following a structured approach is fundamental to documenting and continuously updating an organization's data strategy.

The data analytics lifecycle is, therefore, an essential framework for understanding and mapping the phases and processes involved in creating and maintaining an analytics solution (Figure 1-1). It is an essential concept in data science and analytics and provides a structured approach to managing the various tasks and activities required to create an effective analytics solution.

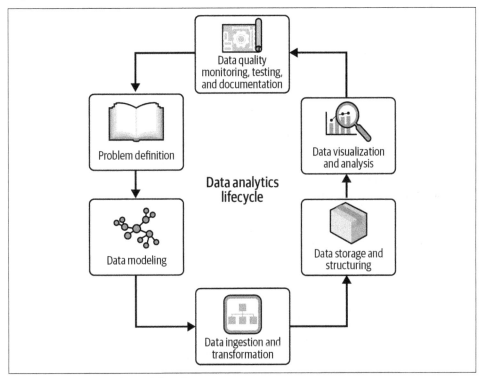

Figure 1-1. Data analytics lifecycle

The data analytics lifecycle typically includes the following stages:

Problem definition
> The first phase of the analytics cycle is about understanding the problem that needs to be solved. This includes identifying the business objectives, the available data, and the resources needed to solve the problem.

Data modeling
> After the business requirements are identified, and an assessment of data sources is completed, you can begin modeling your data according to the modeling technique that best meets your needs. You can choose a diamond strategy, a star schema, a Data Vault, or even a fully denormalized technique. All these concepts will be discussed in Chapter 2.

Data ingestion and transformation

The next phase is to ingest and prepare the data that's coming from the source systems to match the models created. Depending on the overall information architecture, you can opt for a schema-on-write strategy, where you put more effort into transforming the raw data directly into your models, or a schema-on-read strategy, where you ingest and store the data with minimal transformations and move heavy transformations to the downstream layers of your data platform.

Data storage and structuring

Once the data pipelines are designed and potentially implemented, you need to decide on the file formats to use—simple Apache Parquet or more advanced formats like Delta Lake or Apache Iceberg—as well as the partitioning strategies and storage components to use—a cloud-based object store like Amazon Simple Storage Service (S3) or a more data warehouse–like platform like Redshift, BigQuery, or Snowflake.

Data visualization and analysis

Once the data is available, the next step is to explore it, visualize it, or create dashboards that directly support decision making or enable business process monitoring. This phase is very business oriented and should be created in close coordination with business stakeholders.

Data quality monitoring, testing, and documentation

Although illustrated as the final phase of the analytics lifecycle, data quality should be an end-to-end concern and ensured by design across the whole flow. It involves implementing all quality controls to ensure that stakeholders can trust your exposed data models, documenting all transformations and semantic meanings, and ensuring proper testing along the pipelines as the data continues to flow.

With dbt, several of these components are deployed more easily and efficiently because it allows us to build them in parallel and across the lifecycle. Documentation, testing, and quality become common tasks performed in parallel. This will be extensively elaborated in Chapter 4.

The analytics lifecycle is a key concept that enables organizations to approach data engineering, science, and analytics processes in a structured and consistent manner. By following a structured process, organizations can ensure they are solving the right problem, using the right data, and building data products that are accurate and reliable, ultimately leading to better decision making and better business results.

The New Role of Analytics Engineer

As mentioned in previous sections, data scientists and analysts can now easily access the data they need to perform complex analyses and gain insights that would otherwise be difficult or impossible to obtain. However, as the amount of data stored and analyzed continues to grow, it is becoming increasingly important for organizations to have data specialists to help them manage that data and provide the infrastructure needed.

The recently created branch of specialized data engineers, called *analytics engineers*, plays an integral role in developing and maintaining databases and data pipelines, allowing data scientists and analysts to focus on more advanced analytics tasks. Analytics engineers are responsible for designing, building, and maintaining the data architecture that enables organizations to turn data into valuable insights and make data-driven decisions.

In addition, the move from traditional ETL processes with enforced schemas-on-write to an ELT with schema-on-read approach means that data now ends up in the data repositories before it has been transformed. This is an opportunity for super-technical analysts who both know the business very well and have the technical skills to model the raw data into clean, well-defined datasets—analytics engineers. If you were looking for these types of skills in the world of data warehouses and the ETL paradigm, there would need to be specialists with both software engineering and data analytics skills—which would be much harder to find.

The analytics engineer acts as a bridge between data platform engineers, focused on building the technical infrastructure to enable data platforms, and data analysts, focused on converting data into insightful data products. Their job is to create well-tested, up-to-date, and documented datasets that the rest of the organization can use to answer their own questions. They are technically savvy enough to apply software development best practices such as version control and continuous integration and continuous deployment (CI/CD) but also need to be able to communicate effectively with stakeholders.

We can draw an analogy to civil engineering: data platform engineers are the foundation of an analytics project, responsible for ensuring that the infrastructure is robust, including plumbing, electrical systems, and the structural foundation. They lay the groundwork for everything to come.

Analytics engineers can be likened to architects. They take the solid foundation created by data engineers and design structures that align with the business model, constructing everything from exceptional dashboards to valuable data models. They bridge the gap between the technical infrastructure and the business objectives.

Data analysts, in this analogy, serve as interior designers. They step inside the constructed buildings, not only ensuring that the content is aligned with users but also making it user-friendly and tailored to the specific needs of data consumers. Together, these roles collaborate to create a holistic and functional analytics environment.

Looking at the data analytics lifecycle, data platform engineers build platforms and ingest raw data into enterprise-wide data stores. On the other hand, analytics engineers take the raw data and transform it to match the analytical data models the business needs to support decision making.

Responsibilities of an Analytics Engineer

The role of an analytics engineer is becoming increasingly important as both the volume and complexity of data, as well as its diverse applications, continue to grow. This includes everything from designing and implementing data storage and retrieval systems, to creating and maintaining data pipelines, and developing and deploying machine learning models. In this dynamic landscape, analytics engineers play a vital role in harnessing the increasing data resources and maximizing their value across a wide range of applications.

Based on the latest role trends, one of the main responsibilities is to design and implement efficient data storage and retrieval systems. This includes working with databases and data warehousing technologies to design data models and structures that can handle large and complex datasets. Another immediate responsibility is creating and maintaining data pipelines that extract data from various sources, transform it, and load it into a central repository for analysis.

For most analytics engineers, the development and use of machine learning models is somewhat less observable but still happening. This includes working with data scientists to understand their requirements, selecting and implementing the appropriate algorithms, and ensuring that the models are properly trained and deployed with the correct set of training and testing data. When this is not the case, analytics engineers collaborate on building the proper data pipelines to continuously feed data scientists with proper training and testing data.

In addition, analytics engineers are responsible for monitoring and maintaining the performance of machine learning models, both by helping to structure offline evaluation and by combining model-specific metrics with business metrics for online monitoring.

An analytics engineer is typically proficient in programming languages and tools such as Python, R, SQL, and Spark to implement data pipelines, data models, and machine learning models. They should also be familiar with cloud computing platforms like AWS, GCP, or Azure to deploy and scale their solutions.

When observing the responsibilities analytics engineers have in several companies, they can include the following:

- Design and implement data storage and retrieval systems, such as databases and data warehouses, that can handle large and complex datasets. Create and maintain data pipelines to extract, transform, and load data from various sources into a central repository for analysis.

- Ensure data is accurate, complete, consistent, and accessible by performing data quality checks, tracking data flows, and implementing data security measures.

- Leverage cloud computing platforms such as AWS, GCP, or Azure to deploy and scale analytics solutions, as well as scalability, security, and cost optimization of data infrastructure.

- Optimize the performance of data storage and retrieval systems, data pipelines, and machine learning models to ensure they can handle the volume and complexity of data.

- Use programming languages and tools such as Python, R, SQL, and Spark to implement data pipelines, data models, and machine learning models.

- Collaborate with data scientists to understand their requirements, select and implement appropriate algorithms, and ensure machine learning models are properly trained and deployed. Monitor and maintain the performance of machine learning models and troubleshoot and optimize as needed.

- Keep up-to-date with the latest technologies and trends in data engineering, machine learning, and analytics, and continually seek opportunities to improve the organization's data infrastructure and analytics capabilities.

The role of an analyst is broad and requires a combination of technical skills, problem-solving skills, and an understanding of business needs. Analytics engineers must be comfortable with data science's technical and business aspects and should be able to bridge the gap between data scientists and IT.

Enabling Analytics in a Data Mesh

A *data mesh* is a modern framework outlining an organization's data strategy. It enables business domain teams to take ownership of their data and the services that provide access to it instead of relying only on a central data team. It decomposes a monolithic data architecture into a set of independent, autonomous data services, enabling finer scaling, more autonomy, and better data management. It provides more flexibility in handling different types of data and enables a culture of experimentation, innovation, and collaboration. With a data mesh, enterprises should be able to move faster and respond more quickly to changing business needs.

The emergence of data mesh methodology as an architectural pattern has revolutionized the way analysts interact with data infrastructure. By decomposing a monolithic data architecture into a series of independent, autonomous data services that can be developed, deployed, and operated independently, teams can address the challenges of scalability, manageability, and autonomy of the data architecture in a more granular and effortless way.

With this novel approach, teams can scale their data infrastructure more granularly, reducing the risk of data silos and duplication. Each business domain team also has more autonomy, allowing them to choose the best tools and technologies for their specific needs but leverage centrally offered services to manage the whole data lifecycle. This permits them to move faster, be more agile, and respond quickly to changing business needs. In addition, a data mesh approach provides more flexibility in handling different types of data, such as structured, semi-structured, and unstructured data. It also enables better data governance practices by breaking down the monolithic data architecture and enabling clear mapping of data services.

An analytics engineer can deliver value in a data mesh organization by focusing on building and maintaining independent, autonomous data services that support the needs of multiple teams and applications, such as shared data models, well-governed and documented to ensure effortless data discoverability, accessibility, and security.

Another meaningful aspect of working on a data mesh is ensuring data governance and security, which can include implementing data policies and procedures, such as data access controls, data sequencing, and data quality checks, to ensure that data is secure and of high quality. In addition, analytics engineers should work with data owners and stakeholders to understand and comply with all data storage and management regulatory requirements.

Working in a data mesh requires a different mindset than in traditional monolithic data architectures. Analytics engineers must move away from the notion that data is a centralized resource and consider it as distributed autonomous services that various teams can use.

Data Products

Another concept we have been using that is important to define is that of a *data product*. These are accessible applications providing access to data-driven insights that will support business decision-making processes or even automate them. Internally they may contain components for retrieving, transforming, analyzing, and interpreting data. Another important aspect is that data products should expose their data in such a way that it can be accessed and used by other internal or external applications or services.

Some examples of data products are as follows:

- A REST API that allows users to query a specific business data model
- A data pipeline that ingests and processes data from various sources
- A data lake that stores and manages large amounts of structured and unstructured data
- A data visualization tool that helps users understand and communicate data insights

Data products can also consist of microservices. These are small, independent, and focused services that can be developed, deployed, and scaled independently. They can be accessed via an API and reused across the enterprise.

dbt as a Data Mesh Enabler

dbt is an open source tool that helps data engineers, analytics engineers, and data analysts build a data mesh by providing a way to create, test, and manage data services. It allows teams to define, test, and build data models and create a clear and well-defined interface for these models so that other teams and applications can easily use them.

The dbt features that support the creation of a data mesh include the following:

Data modeling capabilities
Data modeling capabilities allow teams to define their data models by using a simple and familiar SQL-based syntax that makes it easy for data engineers and data analysts to define and test data models together.

Data testing capabilities
dbt provides a testing framework that allows teams to test their data models and ensure that they are accurate and reliable. This helps identify errors early in the development process and ensures that data services are of high quality.

Data documentation
dbt enables data models and services to be documented so that they can be easily understood and used by other teams and applications.

Data tracking capabilities
Data tracking capabilities allow teams to trace the origin of data models. This makes it easy to understand how data is used and where it came from.

Data governance capabilities
Data governance capabilities make it possible to enforce data governance policies such as data access controls, data lineage, and data quality checks, which help ensure that data is secure and of high quality.

While the primary focus of analytics engineering is on designing and implementing data models, it's important to note that data tracking and governance capabilities can significantly enhance the effectiveness of analytics engineering processes. These capabilities can be particularly valuable in scenarios where data models need to trace the origin of data and adhere to stringent data governance policies. Adoption of such practices and governance models, including a data mesh, may vary depending on the specific needs and complexity of the data environment. Many successful dbt deployments start with simpler single-star schema data models and may explore advanced concepts like data mesh as their data needs evolve over time.

The Heart of Analytics Engineering

Data transformation converts data from one format or structure to another to make it more useful or suitable for a particular application or purpose. This process is necessary because it enables organizations to transform raw, unstructured data into valuable insights that can inform business decisions, improve operations, and drive growth.

Data transformation is a critical step in the analytics lifecycle, and it is important that organizations have the tools and technology to perform this task efficiently and effectively. Some examples of data transformation include cleaning and preparing data, aggregating and summarizing data, and enriching data with additional information. The use of dbt is widespread for data transformation because it allows organizations to perform complex data transformation tasks quickly and easily, and it can be integrated with other tools, such as Airflow, for end-to-end data pipeline management.

dbt is the *gemba* for analysts and enterprise stakeholders. The value to businesses and stakeholders comes when data is transformed and delivered in an easy-to-use form.

Gemba is a Japanese term meaning "the real place." In the corporate world, gemba refers to the place where value is created.

In an ETL strategy, data transformation is typically performed before the data is loaded into a target system, such as a data warehouse or data lake. Data is extracted from various sources, transformed to match the structure and format of the target system, and then loaded into the target system. This process ensures that the data is consistent and usable across systems and applications.

In contrast, an ELT strategy represents a newer and more flexible approach to data processing. In this strategy, data is first extracted and loaded into a target system before undergoing transformation. ELT offers several advantages, including increased flexibility and the ability to support a wider range of data applications than the traditional ETL paradigm. One significant benefit is its versatility in accommodating various data transformations and real-time insights directly within the target system. This flexibility empowers organizations to derive actionable insights from their data more rapidly and adapt to changing analytical needs.

However, it's important to acknowledge that ELT can come with higher storage and ingestion costs, given the storage of raw or minimally transformed data. Many businesses find these costs justifiable because of the substantial value—in particular, the flexibility it brings to their operations. Therefore, ELT has gained popularity, especially with the emergence of cloud-based data warehousing solutions and the improved data transformation and processing capabilities they offer.

Regardless of the strategy used, without proper data cleaning, transformation, and standardization, data may end up inaccurate, incomplete, or difficult to use, resulting in poor decision making.

The Legacy Processes

Traditionally, legacy ETL processes were often complex, time-consuming, and required specialized skills to develop, implement, and maintain. They also typically required significant manual coding and data manipulation, making them error-prone and difficult to scale.

In addition, these processes were often inflexible and could not be adapted to changing business needs or new data sources. With the growing volume, variety, and velocity of data, legacy ETL processes are becoming increasingly inadequate and, so, are being replaced by more modern and flexible approaches such as ELT.

In the past, ETL was usually performed using custom scripts or specialized visual-based ETL tools. These scripts or tools extracted data from various sources, such as flat files or databases, performed the necessary transformations on the data, and then loaded the data into a target system, such as a data warehouse.

An example of a legacy ETL process would be using a combination of SQL scripts and programming languages such as Java or C# to extract data from a relational database, transforming the data using the programming language, and then loading the transformed data into a data warehouse. Another example is using specialized ETL tools such as Oracle Data Integrator or IBM InfoSphere DataStage to extract, transform, and load data across systems. These legacy ETL processes can be complex, challenging to maintain and scale, and often require a dedicated team of developers.

Using SQL and Stored Procedures for ETL/ELT

In the past, specific data platforms used stored procedures in a relational database management system (RDBMS) such as SQL Server or Oracle for ETL purposes. *Stored procedures* are prepared SQL code that you can store in your database engine so that the code can be used repeatedly. Depending on whether it is a data inflow or outflow, the scripts are executed either in the source or the target database.

Suppose you want to create a simple stored procedure to extract from a table, transform the data, and load it into another table, as shown in Example 1-1.

Example 1-1. SQL procedure to extract data

```
CREATE PROCEDURE etl_example AS
BEGIN
    -- Extract data from the source table
    SELECT * INTO #temp_table FROM source_table;

    -- Transform data
    UPDATE #temp_table
    SET column1 = UPPER(column1),
        column2 = column2 * 2;

    -- Load data into the target table
    INSERT INTO target_table
    SELECT * FROM #temp_table;
END
```

This stored procedure first uses the SELECT INTO statement to extract all data from the source table and store it in a temporary table (#temp_table). Then it uses the UPDATE statement to change the values of column1 to uppercase and double the value of column2. Finally, the stored procedure uses the INSERT INTO statement to load the data from the #temp_table into the target_table.

> Don't be afraid if you aren't familiar with the SQL syntax. Chapter 3 is fully dedicated to giving you the foundations to working with it.

It is important to note that this is an elementary example and that actual ETL processes are often much more complex and involve many more steps, such as data validation, handling null values and errors, and logging process results.

Although it is possible to use stored procedures for ETL processes, it is essential to note that using them may have some implications, such as the need for specialized knowledge and expertise to write and maintain those procedures and the lack of flexibility and scalability. In addition, using stored procedures for ETL can make it challenging to integrate with other systems and technologies and troubleshoot problems that arise during the ETL process.

Using ETL Tools

As previously mentioned, ETL tools are software applications that accelerate the process of building ingestion and transformation pipelines by providing a visual interface, a software development kit (SDK), or a programming library with prepackaged code and artifacts that can be used for extracting, transforming, and loading data from various sources into a target, such as a data warehouse or data lake. They are generally used in many organizations to automate the process of transferring data from various systems and databases to a central data warehouse or data lake, where it can be analyzed.

Airflow is a popular open source platform for managing and scheduling data pipelines. Developed by Airbnb, it has gained popularity in recent years because of its flexibility and scalability. Airflow allows users to define, schedule, and monitor data pipelines using Python code, making them easy for data engineers and scientists to create.

Example 1-2 presents a simple Airflow DAG. A *directed acyclic graph* (DAG) is a directed graph with no directed cycles.

Example 1-2. An Airflow DAG

```
from airflow import DAG
from airflow.operators.bash_operator import BashOperator
from datetime import datetime, timedelta

default_args = {
    'owner': 'me',
    'start_date': datetime(2022, 1, 1),
    'depends_on_past': False,
    'retries': 1,
    'retry_delay': timedelta(minutes=5),
}

dag = DAG(
    'simple_dag',
    default_args=default_args,
    schedule_interval=timedelta(hours=1),
)

task1 = BashOperator(
    task_id='print_date',
    bash_command='date',
    dag=dag,
```

```
)

task2 = BashOperator(
    task_id='sleep',
    bash_command='sleep 5',
    retries=3,
    dag=dag,
)

task1 >> task2
```

This code defines a DAG named `simple_dag` that runs every hour. It has two tasks, `print_date` and `sleep`. The first task executes the `date` command, which prints the current date and time. The second task executes the `sleep 5` command, which makes the task sleep for five seconds. The second task has the number of retries set to 3. So if it fails, it will retry three times before giving up. The two tasks are connected by the operator `>>`. This also means `task2` depends on `task1` and will be executed only after `task1` completes successfully.

Airflow is a productive tool for scheduling and managing ETL pipelines, but it has some limitations. First, Airflow can be very complex to set up and manage, especially for large or complicated pipelines. Second, it is not explicitly designed for data transformation and may require additional tools or custom code to perform certain types of data manipulation.

 dbt can address these Airflow limitations by providing a set of best practices and conventions for data transformation and a simple, straightforward interface for performing and managing data transformation. It can also be integrated with Airflow to supply a complete ETL/ELT solution that is easy to set up and manage while providing high flexibility and control over data pipelines.

The dbt Revolution

dbt is an open source command-line tool that is becoming increasingly popular in the data analytics industry because it simplifies and streamlines the process of data transformation and modeling. On the other hand, Airflow is a powerful open source platform for programmatically creating, scheduling, and monitoring workflows. When dbt is integrated with Airflow, the data pipeline can be more efficiently managed and automated. Airflow can be used to schedule dbt runs, and dbt can be used to perform the data transformation tasks in the pipeline.

This integration enables teams to manage the entire data pipeline from data extraction to loading into a data warehouse, ensuring that data is always up-to-date and accurate. The integration makes it easier to automate data pipeline tasks, schedule and monitor the pipeline, and troubleshoot issues as they arise.

To illustrate the simplicity of building a simple dbt model, imagine that you want to build a model that calculates a company's total revenue by adding the revenue for each order. The model could be defined using a dbt model file specifying the calculation's SQL code and any required dependencies or parameters. Example 1-3 presents what the model file could look like.

Example 1-3. A dbt model

```
{{ config(materialized='table') }}

select
    sum(orders.revenue) as total_revenue
from {{ ref('orders') }} as orders
```

One of the main advantages of dbt is that analytics engineers can write reusable, maintainable, and testable code for data transformations in a simple high-level language that eliminates the complexity of writing SQL. This facilitates team collaboration on data projects and reduces the risk of errors in the data pipeline.

Another benefit of dbt is that it enables more efficient data pipeline management. By integrating with orchestration tools like Airflow and others such as Dagster or Prefect, as well as dbt Labs' own dbt Cloud product, dbt empowers teams to effectively plan, schedule, and monitor data pipelines. This ensures that data remains consistently up-to-date and accurate. The synergy between dbt and orchestration tools like Airflow allows for seamless data refresh and the deployment of new logic, akin to CI/CD practices in software engineering. This integration ensures that as new data becomes available or transformations are updated, the data pipeline can be orchestrated and executed efficiently to deliver reliable and timely insights.

Overall, dbt is becoming widespread for organizations looking to improve their data analytics capabilities and streamline their data pipelines. Although it is still a relatively new technology, it is being used by many companies and is considered a valuable tool for data professionals. Chapter 4 will provide a more in-depth view of dbt and its capabilities and features.

Summary

In recent decades, the field of data management has undergone profound transformations, transitioning from structured methods of data storage and access, such as SQL-based stored procedures, to more flexible and scalable workflows. These modern workflows are supported by powerful tools like Airflow and dbt. Airflow facilitates dynamic orchestration, while dbt elevates analytics code to the level of production-grade software, introducing innovative approaches to data testing and transformation.

Amid this dynamic environment, new roles have emerged, with the analytics engineer standing at the intersection of data engineering and data analytics, ensuring the delivery of robust insights. Despite the evolution of tools and roles, the intrinsic value of data remains unchanged. However, data management is evolving into a discipline that focuses not only on data itself but also on the professionals who wield it.

Even with these advancements, the core challenges persist: acquiring critical data, maintaining the highest data-quality standards, storing data efficiently, and meeting stakeholder expectations in data delivery. At the heart of the data value chain lies the revitalization of data modeling. Efficient data modeling goes beyond data gathering; it structures and organizes data to reflect real-world relationships and hierarchies. Chapter 2 will delve into data modeling and its pivotal role in analytics engineering.

Throughout this chapter, we have explored the evolution of data management, the emergence of the analytics engineer role, and concepts like data mesh and the distinction between ELT and ETL strategies. This diverse set of topics aims to provide a comprehensive overview of the data landscape.

## CHAPTER 2

Data Modeling for Analytics

In today's data-driven world, organizations rely more and more on data analytics to gain valuable insights and make informed decisions. Data modeling plays an imperative role in this process, providing a solid foundation for structuring and organizing data to support effective analysis. In addition, understanding the concepts of data modeling and normalization is essential to realizing the full potential of analytics and gaining actionable insights from complex datasets.

Data modeling is about defining the structure, relationships, and attributes of data entities within a system. An essential aspect of data modeling is the normalization of the data. *Data normalization* is a technique for eliminating data redundancy and improving data integrity. It involves breaking data into logical units and organizing them into separate tables, which reduces data duplication and improves overall database efficiency. Normalization ensures that data is stored in a structured and consistent manner, which is critical for accurate analysis and reliable results.

Regarding analytics, data modeling provides a solid foundation for creating analytical models. Analysts can design effective models that capture relevant information and support the desired analytics objectives by understanding the relationships among entities and data structures. In other words, a well-designed data model enables analysts to perform complex queries, join tables, and aggregate data to produce meaningful insights.

Understanding data modeling and normalization is critical to practical data analysis. Analysts may have difficulty accessing and correctly interpreting data without an appropriate data model, which can lead to incorrect conclusions and ineffective decisions. In addition, a lack of normalization can lead to data anomalies, inconsistencies, and difficulty aggregating data, hindering the analysis process.

In this book, we highlight SQL and dbt as two core technologies to sustain an effective analytics engineering project, and this is also applicable to designing and implementing an effective data model. The reason behind this is that SQL equips users with the ability to define tables, manipulate data, and retrieve information through its robust query capabilities. Its unmatched flexibility and versatility position it as a great tool for constructing and sustaining data models, empowering users to articulate intricate relationships and effortlessly access specific data subsets.

Complementary to SQL, dbt plays a central role in this narrative, taking the art of data modeling to a whole new level. It serves as a comprehensive framework for constructing and orchestrating complex data pipelines. Within this framework, users can define transformation logic, apply essential business rules, and craft reusable modular code components known as *models*. It's worth noting that dbt goes beyond standalone functionality: it seamlessly integrates with version control systems, making collaboration a breeze and ensuring that data models maintain consistency, auditability, and effortless reproducibility.

Another crucial aspect of SQL and dbt in data modeling is their emphasis on testing and documentation, although with some distinctions that are worth clarifying. In the context of data modeling, testing involves validating the data model's accuracy, reliability, and adherence to business rules. While it's important to note that dbt's testing capabilities differ from traditional unit testing in software development, they serve a similar purpose. Instead of traditional unit tests, dbt offers validation queries that are comparable to what analysts are accustomed to running. These validation queries check data quality, data integrity, and adherence to defined rules, providing confidence in the model's outputs. Furthermore, dbt excels in documentation, serving as a valuable resource for analysts and stakeholders alike. This documentation simplifies the understanding of the underlying logic and assumptions that drive the data model, which enhances transparency and fosters effective collaboration.

Together, SQL and dbt empower data professionals to create robust, scalable, and maintainable data models that drive insightful analytics and informed decision making. By leveraging these tools, organizations can unlock the full potential of their data, fueling innovation and gaining a competitive advantage in today's data-driven landscape. Combining both in the same data architecture and strategy brings significant advantages to data modeling.

A Brief on Data Modeling

In the world of database design, creating a structured and organized environment is vital for storing, manipulating, and leveraging data effectively. Database modeling plays a relevant role in achieving this objective by providing the blueprint for representing a specific reality or a business and supporting its processes and rules.

However, before we dive deep into creating this blueprint, we should focus on comprehending the nuances of the business. Understanding the business's operations, terminology, and processes is essential for creating accurate and meaningful data models. By gathering requirements through interviews, document analysis, and process studies, we gain insights into the business's needs and data requirements. During this gathering process, we should focus on natural communication—written language. By expressing business facts in unambiguous sentences, we ensure that representations of the business are accurate and free of interpretation. Breaking complex sentences into simple structures with subjects, verbs, and direct objects helps concisely capture business realities.

In addition to these essential practices, it's worth noting that experts in the field, like Lawrence Corr in his popular book *Agile Data Warehouse Design* (DecisionOne Press), advocate for further techniques such as whiteboarding and canvassing during this initial phase of data model design. These additional strategies can add nuance to the process, allowing for a more comprehensive exploration of business requirements and ensuring that the resulting data models align seamlessly with the business's objectives and intricacies.

Once the understanding phase is complete, we move to the three basic steps of database modeling:

- Conceptual phase
- Logical phase
- Physical phase

These steps form a journey to creating a robust and well-organized database structure. Let's use the example of a book publisher to illustrate the process.

The Conceptual Phase of Modeling

The *conceptual phase* of database modeling requires several essential steps. First, it is necessary to identify the purpose and goals of the database and clarify the specific problems or requirements it needs to address. The next step is gathering requirements by interviewing stakeholders and subject matter experts to comprehensively understand the required data elements, relationships, and constraints. Entity analysis and definition follow, which involves identifying the key objects or concepts to be represented in the database and defining their attributes and relationships.

We begin with a light normalization as we design the initial sketches for the appearance of the database. This ensures integrity between the identified entities and relationships and minimizes redundancy by organizing entities and attributes around semantic structures that are conceptually related. Identifying keys, including primary and foreign keys, is critical to maintaining uniqueness and establishing relationships among tables.

These database designs are often created through diagrams, textual descriptions, or other methods that capture and effectively convey the design and concepts of the database. One of the most commonly used tools to visually represent database concepts is the entity-relationship diagram (ERD). The visual models created using an ERD serve as a diagrammatic representation that effectively describes the entities to be modeled, their relationships, and the cardinality of those relationships. By employing the ERD model, we can visually describe the database structure, including the entities as the main components, the connections or associations among entities, and the quantity or extent of the relationships.

Let's do a very simple conceptual design of a database. Imagine O'Reilly aims to track books and authors previously published, along with launch dates for new books yet to be published. We engage in a series of interviews with the publisher's managers and start to understand exactly what data needs to be stored in the database. The main goal is to identify the entities involved, their relationships, and the attributes of each entity. Keep in mind this exercise is illustrative and is simplified on purpose. We identify three distinct entities in this sub-universe of book management:

Book
> This entity represents a book published by O'Reilly. Attributes may include `book_id`, `title`, `publication_date`, `ISBN`, `price`, and a particular category. The interviewers said that one book may have only one category in this model.

Author
> This entity represents an author who has written books for O'Reilly. Attributes may include `author_id`, `author_name`, `email`, and `bio`.

Category
> This entity represents the book category and can contain attributes such as `category_id` as the unique identifier and `category_name`.

The next step would be to identify relationships among entities. In database design, a few types of relationships can exist among entities, and the type of relationship can be called the relationship's *cardinality*. For example, in a one-to-one relationship, we could have a Book entity connected to an Author entity, where each book is associated with a single author, and vice versa. In a one-to-many relationship, consider a Category entity linked to a Book entity, where each book can belong to only one category, but each category can have multiple books. Contrarily, in a many-to-one relationship, think of a Publisher entity connected to a Book entity, where the same publisher publishes multiple books. Finally, in a many-to-many relationship, we could have a Book entity associated with a Reader entity, indicating that multiple readers can have multiple books in their possession. Continuing our exercise, we also identified two clear relationships:

Book-Category relationship
Establishes the connection between books and categories. A book can have one category, and a category can have multiple books. This relationship is represented as a one-to-many relationship.

Book-Author relationship
Establishes the connection between books and authors. A book can have multiple authors, and an author can write multiple books. This relationship is represented as a many-to-many relationship. It's in this relationship that a specific book's publication happens.

When identifying relationships, using relationship names that represent the real interaction between entities is common. For example, instead of calling it Book-Category, we could say *Classifies* because the category classifies the book, or instead of Book-Author, we might say *Publishes* because the author has books published.

Now that we have an idea of entities, attributes, and relationships, we have what is needed to design our database with an ERD. By doing so, we can visually represent the entities, relationships, and cardinality, as shown in Figure 2-1.

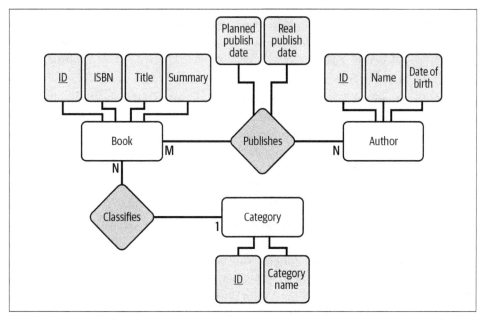

Figure 2-1. ERD example for the books database

As we can observe, entities are represented as while rectangular boxes and represent real-world objects or concepts, such as Book or Author. Relationships are represented as diamonds and illustrate how entities are related.

Attributes are represented as shaded boxes and describe properties or characteristics of an entity. An example could be Name or Publish date. In addition, attributes can be classified as key attributes (underlined shaded boxes) that uniquely identify an entity or as nonkey attributes (nonunderlined shaded boxes) that provide additional information about an entity. More types of attributes exist when designing such diagrams, but we will stick with the basics.

Other components in an ERD include cardinality and participation constraints. Cardinality defines the number of instances in a relationship, usually represented with symbols such as 1, M, or N to indicate a one-to-one or one-to-many relationship, respectively. (N indicates that there is an undetermined number of relationships.)

The Logical Phase of Modeling

In the *logical phase* of modeling, the focus is on normalizing the data to eliminate redundancies, improve data integrity, and optimize query performance. The result is a normalized logical model that accurately reflects the relationships and dependencies among entities.

This phase can be divided into two steps. First, the restructuring of the Entity-Relationship schema focuses on optimizing the schema based on specific criteria. This step is not tied to any particular logical model. The second step translates the optimized ERD into a specific logical model.

Assuming we have decided to map the ERD to a relational database model (which will be our case)—as opposed to a document or graph database—each entity from the conceptual ERD exercise is represented as a table. The attributes of each entity become the columns of the respective table. The primary-key constraint is indicated for the primary-key columns of each table. Additionally, the many-to-many relationships are represented by separate junction tables that hold the foreign keys referencing the corresponding entities.

By translating the conceptual ERD exercise into a logical schema using the relational model, we establish a structured representation of the entities, their attributes, and their relationships. This logical schema can be a foundation for implementing the database in a specific database management system (DBMS) while remaining independent of any particular system. To achieve this translation effectively, all the normalization steps apply, but we would like to share an effective algorithm:

- Entity E is converted to table T.
- The name of E becomes the name of T.

- The primary key of *E* becomes the primary key of *T*.

- Simple attributes of *E* become simple attributes of *T*.

When it comes to relationships, we can also share a few steps:

N:1 relationships
> A foreign key is defined in table T1 that references the primary key of table T2. This establishes the connection between the two tables, indicating the N:1 relationship. The attributes (Attrs) associated with the relationship are mapped and included in table T1.

N:N relationships
> A specific *cross-reference table* is created to represent the relationship REL. The primary key of REL is defined as the combination of the primary keys of both tables T1 and T2, which act as foreign keys in the cross-reference table. The attributes (Attrs) associated with the relationship are mapped and included in the cross-reference table.

Now let's apply these rules to our previous conceptual model; see Figure 2-2.

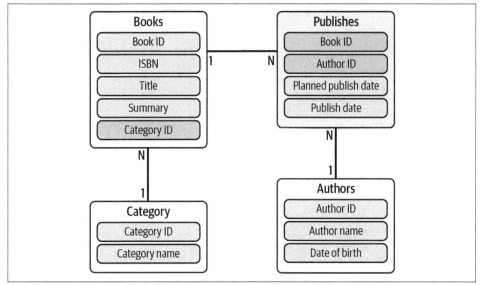

Figure 2-2. Logical ERD example for the books database

In our example, we have a few entities that, as our algorithm suggests, are directly mapped to tables. Such is the case of Authors, Books, and Category.

We identified a 1:N relationship between Books and Category where one book has one category, but one category has multiple books. To map this relationship, we create a foreign key in the books table to reference the corresponding category.

We also have an N:N relationship. In this case, we must create a new table (cross-reference table) that stores the relationship. In our case, we create the Publishes tables for which the primary key becomes a composite between the related entities (Book ID and Author ID). At the same time, the attributes of the relationship become attributes of this cross-reference table.

The Physical Phase of Modeling

We are now ready to convert the normalized logical model into a physical database design in a step called the *physical phase*, or *physical model creation*. This step defines storage structures, indexing strategies, and data types to ensure efficient data storage and retrieval. While the logical model focuses on the conceptual representation, the physical model deals with the implementation details required for smooth data management.

In our case, let's continue from the previous logical model and assume we would be working with a MySQL database engine. Example 2-1 shows the physical model of the books database.

Example 2-1. The books database in a physical model

```
CREATE TABLE category (
  category_id INT PRIMARY KEY,
  category_name VARCHAR(255)
);

CREATE TABLE books (
  book_id INT PRIMARY KEY,
  ISBN VARCHAR(13),
  title VARCHAR(50),
  summary VARCHAR(255)
  FOREIGN KEY (category_id) REFERENCES category(category_id),
);

CREATE TABLE authors (
  author_id INT PRIMARY KEY,
  author_name VARCHAR(255),
  date_birth DATETIME
);

CREATE TABLE publishes (
  book_id INT,
  author_id INT,
  publish_date DATE,
  planned_publish_date DATE
  FOREIGN KEY (book_id) REFERENCES books(book_id),
  FOREIGN KEY (author_id) REFERENCES author(author_id)
);
```

In Example 2-1, we've created four tables: category, books, authors, and publishes. The physical design aspect fine-tunes the table structures, data types, and constraints to align with the MySQL database system.

For example, in the category table, we could specify the data type for the category _id column as INT, ensuring that it is suitable for storing integer values while defining it as a primary key, given that it identifies unique records on the table. Similarly, the category_name column could be defined as VARCHAR(255) to accommodate variable-length category names.

In the books table, appropriate data types and lengths can be assigned to columns such as book_id (INT), ISBN (VARCHAR(13)), title (VARCHAR(50)), and summary (VARCHAR(255)). Additionally, the category_id column can be configured as a foreign key referencing the category_id column in the category table. Note that each ISBN code is composed of 13-character-length strings. Thus, we don't need bigger strings than that.

Similarly, in the authors table, data types can be defined for columns such as author_id (INT), author_name (VARCHAR(255)), and date_birth (DATETIME), all respecting the expected domain of values.

In the publishes table, we highlight that we defined foreign-key constraints to establish the relationships between the book_id column in the books table and the author_id column in the authors table. At the same time, the foreign key is composed of the primary keys of the two tables it's relating.

After all these steps, we've successfully moved from requirements to concept to a logical relational model and finished with a practical implementation of the model in MySQL, thus building our database.

The Data Normalization Process

The data normalization technique consists of several steps, each aimed at organizing data into logical and efficient structures. Example 2-2 illustrates the books table containing a few relevant attributes.

Example 2-2. books table to be normalized

```
CREATE TABLE books (
    book_id INT PRIMARY KEY,
    title VARCHAR(100),
    author VARCHAR(100),
    publication_year INT,
    genre VARCHAR(50)
);
```

The first step in normalization, known as the *first normal form* (1NF), requires eliminating repeating groups by breaking the data into smaller atomic units. We'll create a table called `authors` that includes the author ID and author's name. The books table now references the author ID instead of storing the full name repeatedly, as shown in Example 2-3.

Example 2-3. books table in 1NF

```
-- Table Authors
CREATE TABLE authors (
    author_id INT PRIMARY KEY,
    author_name VARCHAR(100)
);

-- Table Books
CREATE TABLE books (
    book_id INT PRIMARY KEY,
    title VARCHAR(100),
    publication_year INT,
    genre VARCHAR(50),
    author_id INT,
    FOREIGN KEY (author_id) REFERENCES authors(author_id)
);
```

Moving to the *second normal form* (2NF), we examine dependencies within the data. We observe that the publication year functionally depends on the book ID, while the genre depends on the author ID. To adhere to 2NF, we split the books table into three tables:

- books, containing book ID and title

- authors, with author ID and name

- bookDetails, storing book ID, publication year, and genre

This ensures that each column depends solely on the primary key, as shown in Example 2-4.

Example 2-4. books table in 2NF

```
-- Table Authors
CREATE TABLE authors (
    author_id INT PRIMARY KEY,
    author_name VARCHAR(100)
);

-- Table Books
CREATE TABLE books (
```

```
    book_id INT PRIMARY KEY,
    title VARCHAR(100),
);

-- Table book details
CREATE TABLE bookDetails (
    book_id INT PRIMARY KEY,
    author_id INT,
    genre VARCHAR(50),
    publication_year INT,
    FOREIGN KEY (author_id) REFERENCES authors(author_id)
);
```

The *third normal form* (3NF) focuses on eliminating transitive dependencies. We realize that the genre can be derived from the book ID through the bookDetails table. To resolve this, we create a new table called genres with genre ID and genre name, and the bookDetails table now references the genre ID instead of storing the genre name directly (Example 2-5).

Example 2-5. books table in 3NF

```
CREATE TABLE authors (
    author_id INT PRIMARY KEY,
    author_name VARCHAR(100)
);

CREATE TABLE books (
    book_id INT PRIMARY KEY,
    title VARCHAR(100),
);

CREATE TABLE genres (
    genre_id INT PRIMARY KEY,
    genre_name VARCHAR(50)
);

CREATE TABLE bookDetails (
    book_id INT PRIMARY KEY,
    author_id INT,
    genre_id INT,
    publication_year INT,
    FOREIGN KEY (author_id) REFERENCES authors(author_id),
    FOREIGN KEY (genre_id) REFERENCES genres(genre_id)
);
```

These resulting normalized structures (3NF) are often used in operational systems, also known as *online transaction processing systems* (OLTP), that are designed to efficiently process and store transactions and retrieve transaction data, such as customer orders, bank transactions, or even payroll. It's important to highlight that we can apply further normalization steps if necessary, such as the fourth normal form (4NF) and fifth normal form (5NF), to address complex data dependencies and ensure even higher levels of data integrity.

Data normalization is crucial to achieve efficient processing and storage of individual transactions in an OLTP system. In this process, the data is divided into smaller, less redundant parts to achieve this goal, bringing several advantages to OLTP systems. Data normalization is known for its emphasis on reducing data redundancy and improving data integrity because data is organized into multiple tables, each serving a specific purpose. These tables are linked by primary and foreign keys to establish their relationships, ensuring that records in each table are unique and that the same field is not replicated in multiple tables, except for key fields or in-system fields such as ID or creation timestamps.

Another reason data normalization is relevant is that it enhances and maximizes performance. These normalized databases are designed to efficiently handle fast reads and writes by minimizing data redundancy and establishing well-defined relationships among tables so that the database can handle a large number of transactions with lightning-fast performance. This is important for transactional systems in which the timely execution of operations is critical.

Last but not least, a normalized database focuses on storing only current data so that the database represents the most current information available. In a table that stores customer information, each record always reflects the customer's up-to-date details, such as first name, phone number, and other relevant data, ensuring that the database accurately represents the current state of affairs.

However, the paradigm is somewhat different when it comes to an analytics project or system. Often, users want to be able to retrieve the data they need without having to do a lot of linking, which is a natural consequence of a normalization process. While an OLTP system is optimized for write operations to avoid increased latency in live systems like a web application, users of analytics systems want read optimization to get their analytics data as quickly as possible. Unlike normalized transactional databases that store live data, analytics databases are expected to contain both real-time and non-real-time data and act as a historical archive for past data. And often, an analytics database is expected to contain data from multiple OLTP systems to provide an integrated view of business processes.

These differences are indeed critical to grasp as they underpin distinct requirements for data organization, retention, and utilization. However, it's important to clarify that what we've just explored pertains primarily to the realm of normalization for performance optimization and adhering to best practices in OLTP database design. While this foundation is valuable, it represents just one facet of the broader landscape of analytics engineering.

To provide a clearer roadmap, let's establish that our journey begins with an exploration of this foundational type of data modeling, which forms the basis for OLTP systems. Following this, we will pivot toward a discussion of data modeling approaches optimized for OLAP environments. By making this distinction, we aim to provide a comprehensive understanding of both aspects of data modeling, setting the stage for a deeper dive into analytics engineering methodologies and their application in the subsequent sections.

Dimensional Data Modeling

Data modeling is a fundamental aspect of designing and organizing databases to store and manage data efficiently. As we previously discussed, it involves defining the structure, relationships, and attributes of the data entities within a system.

One popular approach to data modeling is *dimensional modeling*, which focuses on modeling data to support analytics and reporting requirements. Dimensional modeling is particularly well suited for data warehousing and BI applications. It emphasizes the creation of dimensional models that consist of fact tables representing measurable data and dimension tables providing descriptive context. By using dimensional modeling techniques, such as star schemas and snowflake schemas, data can be organized in a way that simplifies complex queries and enables efficient data analysis.

The relationship between data modeling and dimensional modeling lies in their complementary nature. Data modeling provides the foundation for capturing and structuring data, whereas dimensional modeling offers a specialized technique for modeling data to support analytical and reporting needs. Jointly, these approaches enable organizations to design robust and flexible databases that facilitate transactional processing and in-depth data analysis.

To understand dimensional modeling, we should first pay our respect to two individuals considered to be the fathers of data warehousing and dimensional modeling: Bill Inmon and Ralph Kimball, respectively. They are recognized as pioneers in the field of enterprise-wide information gathering, management, and analytics for decision support.

They have contributed to a significant debate on the topic of data warehousing, each advocating for different philosophies and approaches. Inmon proposes the creation of a centralized data warehouse that encompasses the entire enterprise, aiming to generate a comprehensive BI system. On the other hand, Kimball suggests creating multiple smaller data marts focused on specific departments, enabling department-level analysis and reporting. Their divergent viewpoints result in contrasting design techniques and implementation strategies for data warehousing.

In addition to their differing approaches, Inmon and Kimball propose distinct methods for structuring data in the context of data warehousing. Inmon advocates for using the relational (ERD) model, specifically the third normal form (3NF), in the enterprise data warehouse. On the contrary, Kimball's approach employs a multidimensional model in the dimensional data warehouse, utilizing star schemas and snowflakes.

Inmon argues that structuring data in a relational model ensures enterprise-wide consistency. This consistency facilitates the creation of data marts in the dimensional model with relative ease. On the other hand, Kimball contends that organizing data in a dimensional model facilitates the information bus, allowing users to comprehend, analyze, aggregate, and explore data inconsistencies more effectively. Moreover, Kimball's approach enables direct access to data from analytics systems. In contrast, Inmon's approach restricts analytics systems from accessing data solely from the enterprise data warehouse, necessitating interaction with data marts for retrieval.

A *data mart* is a specific part of a data warehouse that is meant to fulfill the unique demands of a particular department or business unit.

In the following sections, we will delve deep into three modeling techniques: star schema, snowflake modeling, and the emerging Data Vault. Data Vault, introduced by Dan Linstedt in 2000, has been gaining momentum in recent years. It follows a more normalized structure, which is not entirely aligned with Inmon's approach but is similar.

Modeling with the Star Schema

The *star schema* is a widely used modeling approach in relational data warehouses, especially for analysis and reporting purposes. It involves classifying tables as either dimension tables or fact tables to effectively organize and represent business units and related observations or events.

Dimension tables are used to describe the business entities to be modeled. These entities can include various aspects such as products, people, places, and concepts, including time. In a star schema, you will typically find a date dimension table that provides a comprehensive set of dates for analysis. A dimension table usually consists of one or more key columns that serve as unique identifiers for each entity, as well as additional descriptive columns that provide further information about the entities.

Fact tables, on the other hand, store observations or events that occur in the business. These include sales orders, inventory levels, exchange rates, temperatures, and other measurable data. A fact table contains dimension key columns, which refer to the dimension tables, and numeric measurement columns. The dimension key columns determine the dimensionality of the fact table and specify which dimensions are included in the analysis. For example, a fact table that stores sales targets may contain dimension key columns for Date and ProductKey, indicating that the analysis includes dimensions related to time and products.

The granularity of a fact table is determined by the values in its dimension key columns. If the Date column in a sales target fact tables stores values representing the first day of each month, for example, then the granularity of the table is at the Month/Product level. This means that the fact table captures sales target data at the monthly level, specific to each product.

By structuring data in a star schema with dimension tables representing business units and fact tables capturing observations or events, companies can efficiently perform complex analysis and gain meaningful insights. The star schema provides a clear and intuitive structure for querying and aggregating data, making it easier to analyze and understand the relationships among dimensions and facts within the dataset.

Returning to our books table, we will follow the modeling steps to develop a simple star schema model. The first step would be to identify the dimension tables. But first, let's remember our base table in Example 2-6.

Example 2-6. Base table for our star schema

```
-- This is our base table
CREATE TABLE books (
    book_id INT PRIMARY KEY,
    title VARCHAR(100),
    author VARCHAR(100),
    publication_year INT,
    genre VARCHAR(50)
);
```

We should identify all the individual dimensions (attributes related to a particular business entity) in the books table and create separate dimension tables for each. In our example, and just as in the normalization steps, we identify three entities: books, authors, and genres. Let's see the physical model with Example 2-7.

Example 2-7. Dimension tables for our star schema

```
-- Create the dimension tables
CREATE TABLE dimBooks (
    book_id INT PRIMARY KEY,
    title VARCHAR(100)
);

CREATE TABLE dimAuthors (
    author_id INT PRIMARY KEY,
```

```
    author VARCHAR(100)
);

CREATE TABLE dimGenres (
    genre_id INT PRIMARY KEY,
    genre VARCHAR(50)
);
```

When it comes to naming dimension tables, it is recommended to use descriptive and intuitive names that reflect the entities they represent. For example, if we have a dimension table representing books, we could name it dimBook or simply books. Similarly, relevant and self-explanatory names like dimAuthor or dimGenre can be used for dimension tables representing authors, genres, or other entities.

For the fact tables, it is advisable to use names that indicate the measurements or events being captured. For instance, if we have a fact table recording book sales, we could name it factBookSales or salesFact. These names indicate that the table contains data related to book sales.

We can now create a fact table called factBookPublish, as shown in Example 2-8, to capture publication data.

Example 2-8. Fact table for our star schema

```
-- Create the fact table
CREATE TABLE factBookPublish (
    book_id INT,
    author_id INT,
    genre_id INT,
    publication_year INT,
    FOREIGN KEY (book_id) REFERENCES dimBooks (book_id),
    FOREIGN KEY (author_id) REFERENCES dimAuthors (author_id),
    FOREIGN KEY (genre_id) REFERENCES dimGenres (genre_id)
);
```

This code creates a new fact table factBookPublish with columns representing the measurements or events related to the dimensions. In this case, it's only the publication year. The foreign-key constraints establish the relationships between the fact table and the dimension tables.

With the star schema model representing the books dataset, we now have a strong foundation for conducting various analytical operations and extracting valuable insights. The dimensional structure of the star schema allows for efficient and intuitive querying, enabling us to explore the data from different perspectives. Once we finish the modeling process, we should end up with a model similar to Figure 2-3 that resembles a star, thus its name, star schema.

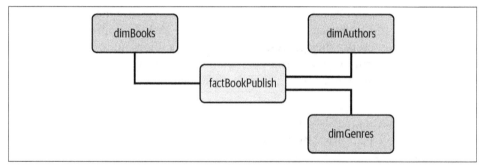

Figure 2-3. Star schema model

Using this model, we can now easily analyze book publications by applying filters such as genre, author, or publication year. For instance, we could quickly retrieve the total publications for a specific genre. By joining the dimension tables with the fact table, as represented in Example 2-9, we can effortlessly gain insights into the relationships among books, authors, genres, and sales.

Example 2-9. Retrieving data from a star schema

```
-- Example for retrieving the total publications for a specific genre.
SELECT COALESCE(dg.genre, 'Not Available'), -- Or '-1'
            COUNT(*) AS total_publications
FROM factBookPublish bp
LEFT JOIN dimGenres dg ON dg.genre_id = bp.genre_id
GROUP BY g.genre;
```

As you can see, we used a LEFT JOIN when joining a fact table with a dimension table. This is quite common. It ensures that all the records from the fact table are included in the result, regardless of whether there is a matching record in the dimension table. This consideration is important because it acknowledges that not every fact record may necessarily have a corresponding entry in every dimension.

By using a LEFT JOIN, you retain all the data from the fact table while enriching it with the relevant attributes from the dimension table. This allows you to perform analysis and aggregations based on various dimensions and explore the data from different perspectives. However, we must handle any missing correspondence. Thus we use the COALESCE operator, which is often used to set a default value like -1 or Not available.

A LEFT JOIN also allows for incremental dimension updates. If new records are added to the dimension table, the LEFT JOIN will still include the existing fact records, associating them with the available dimension data. This flexibility ensures that your analysis and reporting remain consistent even as your dimension data evolves over time.

Overall, the star schema's simplicity and denormalized structure make it conducive to aggregations and summarizations. You can generate various reports, such as sales trends over time, best-selling genres, or revenue by author. Additionally, the star schema facilitates drill-down and roll-up operations, allowing you to drill into more detailed information or roll up to higher levels of aggregation for a comprehensive view of the data.

This modeling technique also aligns seamlessly with integration into data visualization tools and BI platforms. By connecting your model to tools such as Tableau, Power BI, or Looker, you can craft visually captivating dashboards and interactive reports. These resources empower stakeholders to swiftly grasp insights and make data-driven decisions at a glance.

However, it's worth noting that the preceding example doesn't fully highlight the denormalization aspect championed by star schemas. For instance, if your dataset strictly adheres to a one-genre-per-book scenario, you have the opportunity to further streamline your model by consolidating the genre information directly within a unified dimBooks table, promoting denormalization and simplifying data access.

Modeling with the Snowflake Schema

In a *snowflake schema*, the data model is more normalized than in a star schema. It contains additional levels of normalization by splitting dimension tables into multiple contiguous tables. This allows for better data integrity and reduces data redundancy. For example, consider a snowflake schema for an ecommerce database. We have a dimension table customers that contains customer information such as ID, name, and address. In a snowflake schema, we could split this table into several contiguous tables.

The customers table could be split into a customers table and a separate addresses table. The customers table would contain customer-specific attributes such as ID and the customer's name. In contrast, the addresses table would contain address-related information such as ID and the customer's street, city, and zip code. If several customers have the same address, we need to store the address information only once in the addresses table and link it to the respective customers.

To retrieve data from a snowflake schema, we usually need to perform multiple joins over the associated tables to get the desired information. For example, if we want to query the customer name and address, we must join the customers table with the addresses table on the ID page. While a snowflake schema provides better data integrity, it also requires more complex queries because of the additional links. However, this schema can be beneficial for large datasets and complex relationships because it provides better normalization and flexibility in data management.

Both the star schema and snowflake schema are two common data warehouse schema designs. In a star schema, dimension tables are denormalized, meaning they contain redundant data. The star schema offers advantages such as more accessible design and implementation and more efficient querying due to fewer JOIN operations. However, it may require more storage space because of denormalized data and can be more challenging to update and troubleshoot.

This is one of the reasons we often see hybrid models, in which companies model star schemas and often normalize a few dimensions for different optimization strategies. The choice depends heavily on your unique needs and requirements. A star schema could be the ideal choice if you prioritize simplicity and efficiency in a data warehouse solution. This schema offers easy implementation and efficient querying, making it suitable for straightforward data analysis tasks. However, a snowflake schema might be better if you anticipate frequent changes in your data requirements and require more flexibility since it allows easier adaptation to evolving data structures.

Imagine we have a dimension that represents the location of specific customers across the globe. One way to model it in a star schema would be to create a single dimension table with all the location hierarchies denormalized. Example 2-10 shows the dimLocation under a star schema paradigm.

Example 2-10. Star schema location dimension

```
CREATE TABLE dimLocation (
  locationID INT PRIMARY KEY,
  country VARCHAR(50),
  city VARCHAR(50),
  State VARCHAR(50)
);
```

Example 2-11 models the location dimension following a snowflake schema.

Example 2-11. Snowflake schema location dimension

```
CREATE TABLE dimLocation (
  locationID INT PRIMARY KEY,
  locationName VARCHAR(50),
  cityID INT
);

CREATE TABLE dimCity (
  cityID INT PRIMARY KEY,
  city VARCHAR(50),
  stateID INT
);

CREATE TABLE dimState (
```

```
  stateID INT PRIMARY KEY,
  state VARCHAR(50),
  countryID INT
);

CREATE TABLE dimCountry (
  countryID INT PRIMARY KEY,
  country VARCHAR(50),
);
```

In the snowflake schema example, the location dimension is split into four tables: dimLocation, dimCity, dimState, and dimCountry. The tables are connected using primary and foreign keys to establish relationships among them.

One important topic is that although we have four tables to represent the location dimension, only the table with the highest hierarchy connects to the fact table (or fact tables) via its primary key. All the other hierarchy levels follow the lineage from highest to lowest granularity. Figure 2-4 illustrates this case.

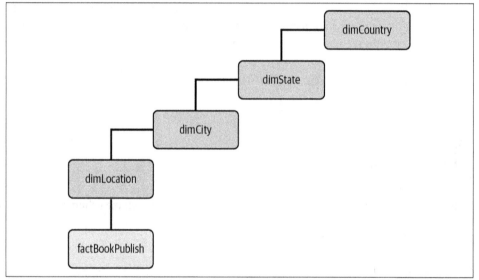

Figure 2-4. Snowflake schema model

Modeling with Data Vault

Data Vault 2.0 is a modeling approach that does not fall under dimensional modeling but is still worth mentioning. Its approach combines 3NF elements and dimensional modeling to create a logical enterprise data warehouse. It is designed to handle various data types, including structured, semi-structured, and unstructured data, by providing flexible and scalable patterns. One of its most highlighted characteristics is that it focuses on building a modular and incremental Data Vault model that integrates raw data based on business keys. This approach ensures that the data warehouse can accommodate changing business requirements and evolving datasets.

Going deeper, this modeling technique provides a scalable and flexible data warehousing and analytics solution. It is designed to handle large data volumes, changing business requirements, and evolving data sources. Data Vault's model consists of three main components: hubs, links, and satellites.

Hubs represent business entities and serve as a central point for storing unique identifiers called *business keys*. Each hub corresponds to a specific entity, such as customers, products, or locations. The hub table contains the business-key column along with any descriptive attributes related to the entity. By separating the business key from the descriptive attributes, Data Vault enables easy tracking of changes to the descriptive information without compromising the integrity of the business key.

Links capture the relationships among business entities. They are created to represent many-to-many relationships or complex associations. The link table contains foreign keys from the participating hubs that form a bridge between the linked entities. This approach allows for modeling complicated relationships without duplicating data or creating unnecessary complexity.

Satellites store the context-specific attributes related to the hubs and links. They contain additional descriptive information that is not part of the business key but provides valuable context about the entities. Satellites are associated with the corresponding hubs or links via foreign keys, which allows for the storage of time-varying data and the preservation of historical records. Multiple satellites can be associated with a hub or link, each capturing specific attributes for different points in time or different perspectives.

Data Vault architecture promotes traceability, scalability, and auditability while providing a solid foundation for data integration, analytics, and data governance. Using hubs, links, and satellites, organizations can build a Data Vault that supports their analytical needs, adapt to changing business requirements, and maintain a reliable historical record of data changes.

Returning to our books table, let's follow the three modeling steps to develop a simple Data Vault model. The first step is identifying the business keys and creating the corresponding hub and satellite tables. In this case, we have only one business entity, so links won't be used. Example 2-12 shows the Data Vault modeling of the books table.

Example 2-12. Modeling the books table with Data Vault 2.0

```
-- This is our base table
CREATE TABLE books (
    book_id INT PRIMARY KEY,
    title VARCHAR(100),
    author VARCHAR(100),
    publication_year INT,
    genre VARCHAR(50)
);
```

In Data Vault modeling, we begin to identify the business keys, which are unique identifiers for each entity. In this case, the primary key of the books table, book_id, serves as the business key.

Now it's time to model and create our first table: the hub table, which stores the unique business keys and their corresponding hash keys for stability. Example 2-13 creates the hub table.

Example 2-13. Hub creation

```
CREATE TABLE hubBooks (
    bookKey INT PRIMARY KEY,
    bookHashKey VARCHAR(50),
    Title VARCHAR(100)
);
```

In the hub table, we store the unique identifier for each book as the primary key (bookKey) and a hash key (bookHashKey) for stability. The Title column contains descriptive information about the book.

Next comes our satellite table, shown in Example 2-14, which captures additional book details and maintains the historical changes.

Example 2-14. Satellite creation

```
CREATE TABLE satBooks (
    bookKey INT,
    loadDate DATETIME,
    author VARCHAR(100),
    publicationYear INT,
    genre VARCHAR(50),
    PRIMARY KEY (bookKey, loaddate),
    FOREIGN KEY (bookKey) REFERENCES hubBooks(bookKey)
);
```

By separating the core book information into the hub table and storing the historical details in the satellite table, we ensure that changes to attributes like the author, publication year, or genre can be captured over time without modifying existing records.

In a Data Vault model, we may have additional tables, such as link tables to represent relationships among entities or other satellite tables to capture historical changes in specific attributes.

Monolith Data Modeling

Until recently, the prevailing approach to data modeling revolved around the creation of extensive SQL scripts. In this conventional method, a single SQL file, often stretching over thousands of lines, encapsulated the entirety of the data modeling process. For a more sophisticated workflow, practitioners might have divided the file into multiple SQL scripts or stored procedures, which were then executed sequentially via Python scripts. To make the workflow more complex, these scripts typically remained largely unknown within the organization. Consequently, even if another individual wished to undertake data modeling in a similar fashion, they would invariably start from scratch, eschewing the opportunity to leverage preexisting work.

This approach can aptly be described as a *monolithic* or traditional approach to data modeling, where each data consumer independently reconstructed their data transformations from the raw source data. Within this paradigm, several notable challenges persisted, including the absence of version control for scripts, the daunting task of managing dependencies between views, and the common practice of crafting new views or tables from raw data sources to the final reporting stage, damaging reusability. Moreover, the concept of idempotency was not uniformly applied to large tables, sometimes resulting in redundancy, and backfills—which, while common, often proved to be intricate and labor-intensive affairs.

In today's rapidly evolving world of data engineering, monolithic data models, particularly in the context of SQL transformations, pose a significant challenge that engineers grapple with. Consider the following scenario: you discover that something in your production system is broken, only to find that what initially appears to be a simple change has set off a chain reaction of errors that propagates throughout the entire infrastructure. This nightmarish scenario, characterized by highly interconnected systems and a minor alteration that acts as the catalyst for a cascading domino effect, is a hauntingly familiar problem for many data professionals.

The risks associated with monolithic data models are precisely what we seek to avoid when designing a data model. The last thing you want is tightly coupled data models that make debugging and implementing changes a daunting task, as each change can potentially disrupt the entire data pipeline. The lack of modularity hinders the flexibility, scalability, and maintainability that are critical in today's data-driven landscape.

In a monolithic data model, all components are tightly interconnected, rendering the identification and isolation of problems a challenging endeavor. In essence, this traditional approach to designing data systems tends to unify the entire system into a single, although not always cohesive, unit.

This interconnectedness of the model means that seemingly unrelated changes can have unintended consequences that impact the entire system. This complexity not only makes troubleshooting more difficult but also increases the risk of introducing errors or overlooking critical dependencies. All data and functionality are so tightly integrated and interdependent that it becomes tough to modify or update any one part of the system without affecting the entire system.

In addition, the lack of modularity in data models hinders the ability to adapt to changing business requirements. In a dynamic environment of data needs with sources constantly changing, a monolithic model becomes a bottleneck to progress. Incorporating new data sources, scaling infrastructure, or integrating new technologies and frameworks becomes increasingly challenging.

Also, maintenance and updates to a monolithic data model become time-consuming and resource-intensive undertakings. Each change carries more risk due to the complicated dependencies within the system. The fear of inadvertently breaking critical components leads to an overly cautious approach that slows development cycles and inhibits innovation.

The challenges posed by monolithic data models in today's data engineering landscape are significant. The risks of interdependencies, lack of flexibility, and difficulties with maintenance and scalability necessitate a shift to modular data models. By adopting modularity, data engineers can achieve greater flexibility, robustness, and adaptability in their data infrastructure to manage the complexity of a rapidly evolving data ecosystem. By moving away from monolithic structures, organizations can realize the full potential of their data, drive innovation, and gain a competitive advantage in the data-driven world we live in.

dbt has been instrumental in taking a modular approach and overcoming the challenges of monolithic models. It allows us to improve maintainability, flexibility, and scalability by breaking the singular data model into individual modules, each with its own SQL code and dependencies. This modular structure allows us to work on individual modules independently, making it easier to develop, test, and debug specific parts of the data model. This eliminates the risk of unintended changes affecting the entire system, which makes introducing changes and updates safer.

This topic of modularity in the dbt will receive more attention in the coming subsections, and Chapter 4 will dive into a comprehensive exploration of dbt.

Building Modular Data Models

The previous example highlights how much dbt and data model modularization, in general, can contribute to a better data development process. However, why isn't this a given for data engineers and scientists? The truth is that in the software development world, over the last few decades, engineers and architects have chosen new ways to employ modularization as a means to simplify their coding process. Instead of tackling one large piece of code at a time, modularization breaks the coding process into various steps. This method offers several advantages over alternative strategies.

One major advantage of modularization is its ability to enhance manageability. When developing a large software program, it can be challenging to stay focused on a single piece of coding. However, the job becomes more manageable by breaking it into individual tasks. This helps developers stay on track and prevents them from feeling overwhelmed by the project's magnitude.

Another advantage of modularization is its support for team programming. Instead of assigning a large job to a single programmer, it can be divided among a team. Each programmer is assigned specific tasks as part of the overall program. In the end, the work from all the programmers is combined to create the final program. This approach accelerates the development process and allows for specialization within the team.

Modularization also contributes to improving code quality. Breaking the code into small parts and assigning responsibility to individual programmers enhances the quality of each section. When a programmer focuses on their assigned section without worrying about the entire program, they can ensure the flawlessness of their code. Consequently, the overall program is less likely to contain errors when all the parts are integrated.

Additionally, modularization enables the reuse of code modules that have already been proven to work effectively. By dividing the program into modules, the fundamental aspects are broken down. If a particular piece of code functions well for a specific task, there is no need to reinvent it. Instead, the same code can be reused, saving programmers time and effort. This can be repeated throughout the program whenever similar features are required, further streamlining development.

Furthermore, modular code is highly organized, which enhances its readability. By organizing code based on tasks, programmers can easily find and reference specific sections based on their organization scheme. This improves collaboration among multiple developers, as they can follow the same organizational scheme and understand the code more efficiently.

All the advantages of modularization ultimately lead to improved reliability. Code that is easier to read, debug, maintain, and share operates with fewer errors. This becomes crucial when working on large projects with numerous developers who need to share code or interface with one another's code in the future. Modularization enables the creation of complex software in a reliable manner.

Although modularization is a must and a given in the software engineering world, in the data space, it has been left behind and picked up only in the last few years. The reason behind this is the need for more clarity between data architecture and software engineering. Yet, recently the industry has evolved into a blend of both worlds as the advantages mentioned before also apply to data analytics and engineering.

Just as modularization simplifies the coding process, it can also streamline the design and development of data models. By breaking complex data structures into modular components, data engineers can better manage and manipulate data at various levels of granularity. This modular approach enables efficient data integration, scalability, and flexibility, allowing for easier updates, maintenance, and enhancements to the overall data architecture.

At the same time, modularization facilitates the reuse of data modules, ensuring consistency and accuracy across data models and reducing redundancy. Overall, modularization principles provide a solid foundation for effective data modeling and engineering, enhancing the organization, accessibility, and reliability of data systems.

Thus, modular data modeling is a powerful technique for designing efficient and scalable data systems. Developers can build more robust and maintainable systems by breaking complex data structures into smaller reusable components. This is a powerful technique for designing efficient and scalable data systems, and both dbt and SQL provide efficient tools to help us implement this technique.

In summary, the core principles of modular data modeling can be defined as follows:

Decomposition
  Breaking the data model into smaller, more manageable components

Abstraction
  Hiding the implementation details of the data model behind interfaces

Reusability
  Creating components that can be reused across multiple parts of the system

This kind of data modeling can be achieved using normalization, data warehousing, and data virtualization techniques. For example, using the normalization technique, the data is separated into tables based on its characteristics and relationships, leading to a modular data model.

Another option is to leverage dbt because it helps to automate the process of creating a modular data model, providing several features that support the principles of modular data modeling. For example, dbt allows us to tackle decomposition by allowing us to split our data model into smaller reusable components, which provides a way to create reusable macros and modular model files. It also gives us a way to abstract the implementation details of the data model by providing a simple, consistent interface for working with data sources.

Furthermore, dbt encourages reusability by providing a way to define and reuse common code across various models. Additionally, dbt helps improve maintainability by providing a way to test and document your data models. Finally, dbt allows you to optimize performance by defining and testing different materialization strategies for your models, which, in the end, allows you to fine-tune the performance of individual components of your data model.

However, it's important to acknowledge that modularity also comes with potential drawbacks and risks. Integrated systems can often be better optimized than modular systems, whether it's because of the minimization of data movement and memory usage or the ability for the database optimizer to improve SQL behind the scenes. Creating views to then create tables can sometimes result in suboptimal models. However, this trade-off is often worth it for the benefits of modularity. Modularity creates more files, which can mean more objects to own, govern, and potentially deprecate. Without a mature data governance strategy, this can lead to a proliferation of modular but unowned tables, which can be challenging to manage when issues arise.

Enabling Modular Data Models with dbt

As we previously highlighted, building modular data models is an essential aspect of developing a robust and maintainable data infrastructure. However, the process of managing and orchestrating these models can become complex as the project grows in size and complexity.

This is where a robust data transformation tool like dbt comes in. By combining the principles of modular data modeling with the features of dbt, we can easily unlock a whole new level of efficiency and scalability in our data infrastructure.

With the adoption of this modular approach, every data producer or consumer within an organization gains the ability to build upon the foundational data modeling work accomplished by others, eliminating the need to start from scratch with the source data on every occasion.

Upon integrating dbt into the data modeling framework, a shift in perspective occurs, transforming the concept of data models from a monolithic entity into a distinct component. Every individual contributor to a model starts identifying transformations that could be shared across various data models. These shared transformations are extracted and organized into foundational models, allowing for their efficient referencing in multiple contexts.

As illustrated by Figure 2-5, using basic data models across multiple instances, rather than starting from scratch each time, simplifies the visualization of the DAG in data modeling. This modularized multilevel structure clarifies how the layers of data modeling logic build on one another and shows dependencies. However, it is essential to note that simply adopting a data modeling framework like dbt does not automatically ensure modular data models and an easy-to-understand DAG.

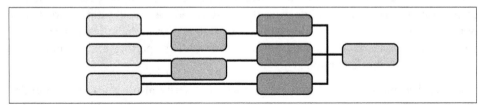

Figure 2-5. dbt modularity

The structure of your DAG depends on your team's data modeling ideas and thought processes, as well as the consistency with which they are expressed. To achieve modular data modeling, consider principles such as naming conventions, readability, and ease of debugging and optimization. These principles can be applied to various models in dbt, including staging models, intermediate models, and mart models, to improve modularity and maintain a well-structured DAG.

Let's start this journey toward leveraging dbt for modular data models by understanding how dbt enables model reusability via the Jinja syntax through the usage of referencing data models: {{ ref() }}.

Referencing data models

By adopting dbt's features, such as model referencing and Jinja syntax, data engineers and analysts can establish clear dependencies among models, enhance code reusability, and ensure the consistency and accuracy of their data pipelines. *Jinja*, in this context, is a templating language that allows dynamic and programmatic transformations within SQL code, offering a powerful tool for customizing and automating data transformations. This powerful combination of modularity and dbt's capabilities empowers teams to build flexible and maintainable data models, accelerating the development process and enabling seamless collaboration among stakeholders.

To leverage the full capabilities of dbt and ensure accurate model building, it is crucial to employ model referencing using the {{ ref() }} syntax. By referencing models this way, dbt can automatically detect and establish dependencies among models based on upstream tables. This enables a smooth and reliable execution of the data transformation pipeline.

On the other hand, the {{ source() }} Jinja syntax should be used sparingly, typically limited to the initial selection of raw data from the database. It is important to avoid direct references to non-dbt-created tables because they can hinder the flexibility and modularity of the dbt workflow. Instead, the focus should be on establishing relationships among models by using the {{ ref() }} Jinja syntax, ensuring that changes in upstream tables are correctly propagated downstream, and maintaining a clear and coherent data transformation process. By sticking to these best practices, dbt enables efficient model management and promotes scalability and maintainability in the analytics workflow.

For example, suppose we have two models: orders and customers, where the orders table contains information about customer orders and the customers table stores customer details. We want to perform a join between these two tables to enrich the orders data with customer information (Example 2-15).

Example 2-15. Referencing model

```
-- In the orders.sql file
SELECT
  o.order_id,
  o.order_date,
  o.order_amount,
  c.customer_name,
  c.customer_email
FROM
  {{ ref('orders') }} AS o
JOIN
  {{ ref('customers') }} AS c
ON
  o.customer_id = c.customer_id

-- In the customers.sql file
-- customers.sql
SELECT
  customer_id,
  customer_name,
  customer_email
FROM
  raw_customers
```

This example demonstrates referencing models in a SQL query by using the ref() function. The scenario involves two model files: *orders.sql* and *customers.sql*.

In the *orders.sql* file, a SELECT statement is written to retrieve order information from the orders model. The {{ ref('orders') }} expression references the orders model, allowing the query to use the data defined in that model. The query joins the orders model with the customers model by using a customer_id column, retrieving additional customer information such as name and email.

In the *customers.sql* file, a SELECT statement is written to extract customer information from the raw_customers table. This model represents the raw customer data before any transformations.

This referencing mechanism in dbt enables the creation of modular and interconnected models that build upon one another to generate meaningful insights and reports. To illustrate the need for it, let's consider a practical example: imagine you're dealing with a complex dataset, such as weekly product orders. Without a structured approach, managing this data can quickly become chaotic. You might end up with a tangled web of SQL queries, making it challenging to track dependencies, maintain code, and ensure data accuracy.

By organizing your data transformation process into distinct layers, from source to mart tables, you gain several benefits. This simplifies the data pipeline, making it more understandable and manageable. It also allows for incremental improvements, as each layer focuses on a specific transformation task. This structured approach enhances collaboration among data engineers and analysts, reduces errors, and ultimately leads to more reliable and insightful reports.

Staging data models

The staging layer plays a crucial role in data modeling, as it serves as the basis for the modular construction of more complex data models. Each *staging model* corresponds to a source table with a 1:1 relationship to the original data source. Keeping staging models simple and minimizing transformations within this layer is important. Acceptable transformations include type conversion, column renaming, basic calculations (such as unit conversion), and categorization using conditional statements such as CASE WHEN.

Staging models usually materialize as views to preserve data timeliness and optimize storage costs. This approach allows intermediate or mart models that reference the staging layer to access up-to-date data while saving space and cost. It is advisable to avoid joins in the staging layer to prevent redundant or duplicate computations. Join operations are better suited for subsequent layers where more complex relationships are established.

Also, aggregations in the staging layer should be avoided because they can group and potentially limit access to valuable source data. The primary purpose of the staging layer is to create the basic building blocks for subsequent data models, providing flexibility and scalability in downstream transformations. Following these guidelines, the staging layer becomes a reliable and efficient starting point for building robust data models in a modular data architecture.

Utilizing staging models in dbt allows us to adopt the Don't Repeat Yourself (DRY) principle in our code. By following dbt's modular and reusable structure, we aim to push any transformations that are consistently required for a specific component model as far upstream as possible. This approach helps us avoid duplicating code, which reduces complexity and computational overhead.

For example, suppose we consistently need to convert monetary values from integers in cents to floats in dollars. In that case, performing the division and type casting early in the staging model is more efficient. This way, we can reference the transformed values downstream without repeating the same transformation multiple times. By leveraging staging models, we optimize code reuse and streamline the data transformation process in a scalable and efficient manner.

Let's say we have a source table called `raw_books` that contains the raw books data. We now want to create a staging model called `stg_books` to transform and prepare the data before further processing. In our dbt project, we can create a new dbt model file named *stg_books.sql* and define the logic to generate the staging model, as shown in Example 2-16.

Example 2-16. Staging model

```
/* This should be file stg_books.sql, and it queries the raw table to create
the new model */

SELECT
  book_id,
  title,
  author,
  publication_year,
  genre
FROM
  raw_books
```

A staging model, like `stg_books` in this example, selects relevant columns from the `raw_books` table. It can include basic transformations such as renaming columns or converting data types. By creating a staging model, you separate the initial data transformation from the downstream processing. This ensures data quality, consistency, and compliance with standards before further use. Staging models serve as the foundation for more complex data models in your data pipeline's intermediate and mart layers. They streamline transformations, maintain data integrity, and improve the reusability and modularity of your dbt project.

Base data models

In dbt, the *base models* often serve as staging models, but they can also encompass additional transformation steps depending on your project's specific needs. These models are typically designed to directly reference the raw data entered into your data warehouse, and they play a crucial role in the data transformation process. Once you have created your staging or base models, other models in your dbt project can reference them.

The change from "base" to "staging" models in the dbt documentation reflects a desire not to be restrained by the name "base," which implies the first step in building a data model. The new terminology allows more flexibility in describing the role and purpose of these models within the dbt framework.

Intermediate data models

The intermediate layer plays a crucial role in data modeling by combining the atomic building blocks from the staging layer to create more complex and meaningful models. These *intermediate models* represent constructs that hold significance for the business but are typically not directly exposed to end users through dashboards or applications.

To maintain separation and optimize performance, it is advisable to store intermediate models as ephemeral models. *Ephemeral models* are not created directly on the database or dataset, but rather their code is interpolated into the models that reference them as common table expressions (CTEs). However, sometimes materializing them as views is more suitable. Ephemeral models cannot be selected directly, which makes troubleshooting challenging. Additionally, macros invoked through run-operation cannot reference ephemeral models. Therefore, whether to materialize a particular intermediate model as ephemeral or as a view depends on the specific use case, but starting with ephemeral materialization is recommended.

If you choose to materialize intermediate models as views, it may be beneficial to place them in a custom schema outside the main schema defined in your dbt profile. This helps in organizing the models and managing permissions effectively.

The primary purpose of the intermediate layer is to bring together different entities and absorb complexity from the final mart models. These models facilitate readability and flexibility in the overall data model structure. It is important to consider the frequency of referencing an intermediate model in other models. Multiple models referencing the same intermediate model may indicate a design issue. In such cases, transforming the intermediate model into a macro could be a suitable solution to enhance modularity and maintain a cleaner design.

By effectively leveraging the intermediate layer, data models can be made more modular and manageable, ensuring the absorption of complexity while maintaining the readability and flexibility of the components.

Let's say we have two staging models, stg_books and stg_authors, representing the book and author data, respectively. Now we want to create an intermediate model called int_book_authors that combines the relevant information from both staging models. In our dbt project, we can create a new dbt model file named *int_book_authors.sql*, as shown in Example 2-17, and define the logic to generate the intermediate model.

Example 2-17. Intermediate model

```
-- This should be file int_book_authors.sql

-- Reference the staging models
WITH
  books AS (
    SELECT *
    FROM {{ ref('stg_books') }}
  ),
  authors AS (
    SELECT *
    FROM {{ ref('stg_authors') }}
  )

-- Combine the relevant information
SELECT
  b.book_id,
  b.title,
  a.author_id,
  a.author_name
FROM
  books b
JOIN
  authors a ON b.author_id = a.author_id
```

In Example 2-17, the `int_book_authors` model references the staging models, `stg_books` and `stg_authors`, using the `{{ ref() }}` Jinja syntax. This ensures that dbt can infer the model dependencies correctly and build the intermediate model based on the upstream tables.

Mart models

The top layer of the data pipeline consists of *mart models*, which are responsible for integrating and presenting business-defined entities to end users via dashboards or applications. These models combine all relevant data from multiple sources and transform it into a cohesive view.

To ensure optimal performance, mart models are typically materialized as tables. Materializing the models enables faster execution of queries and better responsiveness in delivering results to end users. If the creation time or cost of materializing a table is an issue, configuration as an incremental model can be considered, allowing for efficient updates as new data is included.

Simplicity is key to mart models, and excessive joins should be avoided. If you need multiple joins in a mart model, rethink the design and consider restructuring the intermediate layer. By keeping mart models relatively simple, you can ensure efficient query execution and maintain the overall performance of your data pipeline.

Let's consider the example of a data mart for book publication analysis. We have an intermediate model called int_book_authors that contains the raw books data, including information about the authors of each book (Example 2-18).

Example 2-18. Mart model

```
-- This should be file mart_book_authors.sql

{{
  config(
    materialized='table',
    unique_key='author_id',
    sort='author_id'
  )
}}

WITH book_counts AS (
  SELECT
    author_id,
    COUNT(*) AS total_books
  FROM {{ ref('int_book_authors') }}
  GROUP BY author_id
)
SELECT
  author_id,
  total_books
FROM book_counts
```

We start by setting the configuration for the model, specifying that it should be materialized as a table. The unique key is set to author_id to ensure uniqueness, and the sorting is done based on author_id as well.

Next, we use a CTE called book_counts to aggregate the book data. We select the author_id column and count the number of books associated with each author from the stg_books staging model. Finally, the SELECT statement retrieves the aggregated data from the book_counts CTE, returning the author_id and the corresponding count of books for each author. Given that it's a materialized table, this model can be refreshed whenever needed to reflect any changes in the original data.

Testing Your Data Models

Testing in dbt is a vital aspect of ensuring the accuracy and reliability of your data models and data sources. dbt provides a comprehensive testing framework that allows you to define and execute tests by using SQL queries. These tests are designed to identify rows or records that do not meet the specified assertion criteria rather than check specific conditions' correctness.

dbt has two main types of tests: singular and generic. *Singular tests* are specific and targeted tests written as SQL statements and stored in separate SQL files. They allow you to test specific aspects of your data, such as checking for the absence of NULL values in a fact table or validating certain data transformations. With singular tests, we can leverage the power of Jinja to dynamically define assertions based on our data and business requirements. Let's look at a singular test in dbt by analyzing Example 2-19.

Example 2-19. Singular test example in dbt

```
version: 2

models:
  - name: my_model
    tests:
      - not_null_columns:
          columns:
            - column1
            - column2
```

In this example, we define a single test called not_null_columns for the dbt model my_model. This test checks whether specific columns in the model contain NULL values. The columns parameter specifies the columns to check for NULL values. In this case, column1 and column2 are specified. If any of these columns contain NULL values, the test fails.

Generic tests, on the other hand, are more versatile and can be applied to multiple models or data sources. They are defined in dbt project files by using a special syntax. These tests allow us to define more comprehensive criteria for validating our data, such as checking data consistency among tables or ensuring the integrity of specific columns. Also, they provide a flexible and reusable way to define assertions that can be applied across dbt models. These tests are written and stored in YAML (*.yml*) files, which allows us to parameterize the queries and easily reuse them in various contexts. The parameterization of queries in generic tests enables you to adapt the tests to multiple scenarios quickly. For example, you can specify different column names or condition parameters when applying the generic test to different models or datasets.

Let's look at one of these generic tests in Example 2-20.

Example 2-20. Generic test example in dbt

```
version: 2

tests:
  - name: non_negative_values
    severity: warn
    description: Check for non-negative values in specific columns
    columns:
      - column_name: amount
        assert_non_negative: {}
      - column_name: quantity
        assert_non_negative: {}
```

In this example, the generic test is defined with the name non_negative_values. Here, we can observe the columns to be tested and the assertion criteria for each column. The test checks whether the values in the amount and quantity columns are nonnegative. Generic tests allow you to write reusable test logic that can be applied to multiple models in your dbt project.

To reuse the generic test in multiple models, we can reference it in the tests section of each individual model's YAML file, as presented in Example 2-21.

Example 2-21. Reusing a generic test

```
version: 2

models:
  - name: my_model
    columns:
      - column_name: amount
        tests: ["my_project.non_negative_values"]
      - column_name: quantity
        tests: ["my_project.non_negative_values"]
```

In this example, the model my_model is defined, and the amount and quantity columns are specified with the corresponding tests. The tests refer to the generic test non_negative_values from the namespace my_project (assuming my_project is the name of your dbt project).

By specifying the generic test in the tests section of each model, you can reuse the same test logic in multiple models. This approach ensures consistency of data validation and allows you to easily apply the generic test to specific columns in different models without duplicating the test logic.

Note that you must ensure that the YAML file for the generic test is in the correct directory within your dbt project structure, and you may need to modify the test reference to match your project's namespace and folder structure.

Generating Data Documentation

Another integral component of proper data modeling is *documentation*. Specifically, ensuring that everyone in your organization, including business users, can easily understand and access metrics such as ARR (annual recurring revenue), NPS (net promoter score), or even MAU (monthly active users) is crucial for enabling data-driven decision making.

By leveraging dbt's features, we can document how metrics like these are defined and the specific source data they rely on. This documentation becomes a valuable resource anyone can access, fostering transparency and enabling self-service data exploration.

As we remove these semantics barriers and provide accessible documentation, dbt enables users at all levels of technical expertise to navigate and explore datasets, ensuring that valuable insights are available to a broader audience.

Let's assume we have a dbt project with a model called *nps_metrics.sql*, which calculates the net promoter score. We can easily document this metric by using comments within the SQL file, enhanced with Markdown syntax, as shown in Example 2-22.

Example 2-22. Documentation

```
/* nps_metrics.sql

-- This model calculates the Net Promoter Score (NPS)
for our product based on customer feedback.

Dependencies:
- This model relies on the "customer_feedback"
table in the "feedback" schema, which stores customer feedback data.
 - It also depends on the "customer" table in the "users"
schema, containing customer information.

Calculation:
-- The NPS is calculated by categorizing customer
feedback from Promoters, Passives, and Detractors
based on their ratings.
-- Promoters: Customers with ratings of 9 or 10.
-- Passives: Customers with ratings of 7 or 8.
-- Detractors: Customers with ratings of 0 to 6.
-- The NPS is then derived by subtracting the percentage
of Detractors from the percentage of Promoters.
*/

-- SQL Query:
WITH feedback_summary AS (
  SELECT
    CASE
```

```
      WHEN feedback_rating >= 9 THEN 'Promoter'
      WHEN feedback_rating >= 7 THEN 'Passive'
      ELSE 'Detractor'
    END AS feedback_category
  FROM
    feedback.customer_feedback
  JOIN
    users.customer
    ON customer_feedback.customer_id = customer.customer_id
)
SELECT
  (COUNT(*) FILTER (WHERE feedback_category = 'Promoter')
  - COUNT(*) FILTER (WHERE feedback_category = 'Detractor')) AS nps
FROM
  feedback_summary;
```

In this example, the comments provide essential details about the NPS metric. They specify the dependencies of the `nps_metrics` model, explain the calculation process, and mention the relevant tables involved in the query.

After documenting the model, we can generate the documentation for our dbt project by using the dbt command-line interface (CLI) to run the following command (Example 2-23).

Example 2-23. Running documentation generation

```
dbt docs generate
```

Running the command generates HTML documentation for your entire dbt project, including the documented NPS metric. The generated documentation can be hosted and made accessible to users in your organization, enabling them to find and understand the NPS metric easily.

Debugging and Optimizing Data Models

A valuable optimization suggestion for improving the performance of dbt is to analyze and optimize the queries themselves carefully. One approach is to leverage the capabilities of the query planner, such as the PostgreSQL (Postgres) query planner. Understanding the query planner will help you identify potential bottlenecks and inefficiencies in query execution.

Another effective optimization technique is deconstructing complex queries by breaking them into smaller components, such as CTEs. Depending on the complexity and nature of the operations involved, these CTEs can then be transformed into either views or tables. Simple queries involving light computations can be materialized as views, whereas more complex and computationally intensive queries can be materialized as tables. The dbt config block can be used to specify the desired materialization approach for each query.

Significant performance improvements can be achieved by selectively using an appropriate materialization technique. This can result in faster query execution times, reduce processing delays, and improve overall data modeling efficiency. In particular, the use of table materialization has shown impressive performance gains that can dramatically improve the speed, depending on the scenario.

Implementing these optimization recommendations will enable a leaner and more efficient dbt workflow. By optimizing queries and using appropriate materialization strategies, you can optimize the performance of your dbt models, resulting in better data processing and more efficient data transformations.

Let's look at the complex query in Example 2-24.

Example 2-24. Complex query 1

```
SELECT column1, column2, SUM(column3) AS total_sum
  FROM table1
  INNER JOIN table2 ON table1.id = table2.id
  WHERE column4 = 'some_value'
  GROUP BY column1, column2
  HAVING total_sum > 1000
```

This query involves joining tables, applying filters, and performing aggregations. Let's deconstruct it into multiple CTEs before creating our final model (Example 2-25).

Example 2-25. Deconstructing complex query 1

```
-- Deconstructing a complex query using CTEs for optimization

-- CTE 1: Joining required data
WITH join_query AS (
  SELECT table1.column1, table1.column2, table2.column3
  FROM table1
  INNER JOIN table2 ON table1.id = table2.id
)
-- CTE 2: Filtering rows
, filter_query AS (
  SELECT column1, column2, column3
  FROM join_query
  WHERE column4 = 'some_value'
)

-- CTE 3: Aggregating and filtering results
, aggregate_query AS (
  SELECT column1, column2, SUM(column3) AS total_sum
  FROM filter_query
```

```
  GROUP BY column1, column2
  HAVING total_sum > 1000
)

-- Final query to retrieve the optimized results, and this will be our model
SELECT *
FROM aggregate_query;
```

The `join_query` CTE focuses on joining the required tables, while the `filter_query` CTE applies the filter condition to narrow down the rows. The `aggregate_query` CTE then performs the aggregation and applies the final filter condition.

By splitting the complex query into individual CTEs, you can simplify and organize the logic to optimize execution. This approach allows for better readability, maintainability, and potential performance improvements because the database engine can optimize the execution plan for each CTE. The final query retrieves the optimized results by selecting columns from the `aggregate_query` CTE.

Let's now explore the process of debugging materialized models in dbt. This can be a difficult task at first, as it requires thorough validation. One important aspect is ensuring that the data model appears as expected and the values match the non-materialized version.

To facilitate debugging and validation, it may be necessary to fully refresh the entire table and treat it as if it were not incremental. This can be accomplished with the `dbt run --full-refresh` command, which updates the table and runs the model as if it were being executed for the first time.

In some cases, it may be helpful to perform a full update of the model and the incremental model in parallel during the first few days. This comparative approach allows validation of consistency between the two versions and minimizes the risk of future data discrepancies. This technique is particularly effective when working with a well-established, reliable data model in production, as it builds confidence in the changes that have been made. By comparing the updated and incremental models, we can ensure the accuracy of the changes and mitigate potential data-related issues.

Consider an example scenario with a materialized dbt model that calculates monthly revenue based on transactional data. We want to debug and validate this model to ensure its accuracy. We start with the suspicion that the values generated by the materialized model may not match the expected results. To troubleshoot, we decide to fully refresh the table as if it were not incremental. Using the `dbt full-refresh` command, we trigger the process that updates the entire table and runs the model from scratch.

In the first few days, we also run a parallel process to update the materialized and incremental models. This allows us to compare the results between the two versions and ensure they match. By checking the consistency of the updated model and the incremental model, we gain confidence in the accuracy of the changes made.

For example, if we have a well-established revenue model that has been in production for a while and is considered reliable, comparing the updated and incremental models is even more meaningful. In this way, we can confirm that the changes made to the model have not caused any unintended discrepancies in the calculated revenue figures. Additionally, comprehensive testing is essential to ensure the accuracy and reliability of your data models. Implementing tests throughout your workflow can help identify issues early and provide valuable insights into the performance of your SQL queries.

All these dbt functionalities, from building dbt models to testing and documentation, will be discussed and reinforced in Chapters 4 and 5.

Medallion Architecture Pattern

Data warehouses have a rich history in decision support and BI, but they have limitations when it comes to handling unstructured, semi-structured, and high-variety data. At the same time, data lakes emerged as repositories for storing diverse data formats, but they lack critical features such as transaction support, data quality enforcement, and consistency.

This has inhibited their ability to deliver on their promises and led to the loss of benefits associated with data warehouses. To meet the evolving needs of companies, a flexible and high-performance system is required to support diverse data applications like SQL analytics, real-time monitoring, data science, and machine learning. However, some recent advancements in AI focus on processing a wide range of data types, including semi-structured and unstructured data, which traditional data warehouses are not optimized for.

Consequently, organizations often use multiple systems, including data lakes, data warehouses, and specialized databases, which introduces complexity and delays due to data movement and copying between systems. As a natural consequence of the need to combine all these traditional systems into something that answers all the new market requirements, a new type of system is emerging: the data lakehouse.

The *data lakehouse* combines the strengths of both data lakes and data warehouses, implementing data structures and management features similar to warehouses directly on cost-effective cloud storage in open formats such as Apache Delta Lake, Iceberg, or Apache Hudi. These formats offer various advantages over traditional file formats like CSV and JSON. While CSV lacks typing for columns, JSON provides more flexible structures but inconsistent typing. Parquet, Apache Avro, and the ORC (optimized row columnar) file format improve on these by being column-oriented and more strongly typed but not ACID (atomicity, consistency, isolation, durability) compliant (except for ORC, in some cases). In contrast, Delta Lake, Iceberg, and Hudi enhance data storage by adding ACID compliance and the ability to serve as two-way data stores, enabling high throughput of modifications while supporting high volumes of analytical queries. These formats are particularly well suited for modern cloud-based data systems, unlike traditional formats like Parquet, which were initially designed for on-premises Hadoop-based systems.

Lakehouses offer key features such as transaction support for concurrent data reading and writing, schema enforcement and governance, direct BI tool support, decoupling of storage and computing for scalability, openness with standardized storage formats and APIs for efficient data access, support for diverse data types, and compatibility with various workloads including data science, machine learning, and SQL analytics. They also often provide end-to-end streaming capabilities, eliminating the need for separate systems for real-time data applications. Enterprise-grade lakehouse systems include features like security, access control, data governance, data discovery tools, and compliance with privacy regulations. Implementing a lakehouse enables organizations to consolidate these essential features into a single system shared by data engineers, analytics engineers, scientists, analysts, and even machine learning engineers, who can then collaborate to develop new data products.

It is in the context of lakehouses and the new open formats that the *medallion architecture* emerges. In simple terms, this is a data modeling paradigm employed to strategically structure data within a lakehouse environment, aiming to iteratively enhance data quality as data transits different levels of iteration. This architectural framework often comprises three discernible tiers, the bronze, silver, and gold layers, each symbolizing ascending degrees of data refinement:

Bronze layer
> This serves as the initial destination for data from external source systems. The tables in this layer mirror the structures of the source system tables as they are, including any extra metadata columns to capture information like load date/time and process ID. This layer prioritizes efficient change data capture (CDC), maintaining a historical archive of the source data, ensuring data lineage, facilitating audits, and enabling reprocessing without rereading data from the source system.

Silver layer
> Within the lakehouse architecture, this layer plays an essential function in consolidating and refining data sourced from the bronze layer. The silver layer creates a holistic view that encompasses key business entities, concepts, and transactions through processes such as matching, merging, conforming, and cleansing. This includes master customers, stores, nonduplicated transactions,

and cross-reference tables. The silver layer serves as a comprehensive source for self-service analytics, empowering users with ad hoc reporting, advanced analytics, and machine learning capabilities. It is often observed that the silver layer can take the form of a 3NF data model, a star schema, a Data Vault, or even a snowflake. Similar to a traditional data warehouse, this is a valuable resource for anyone who leverages data to undertake projects and analyses aimed at solving business problems.

Gold layer

This layer delivers valuable insights that address business questions. It aggregates data from the silver layer and serves it to BI ad hoc reporting tools and machine learning applications. This layer ensures reliability, improved performance, and ACID transactions for data lakes, while also unifying streaming and batch transactions on top of cloud data stores.

Figure 2-6 represents the medallion architecture in the context of a lakehouse and shows where dbt can support the creation of such systems.

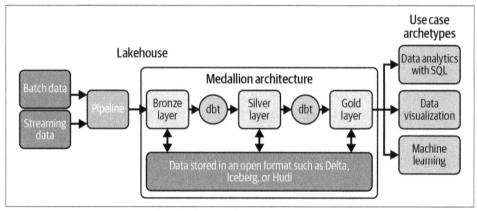

Figure 2-6. Representation of medallion architecture and how it relates to dbt

Through the progression from the bronze to gold layers, data undergoes several steps, such as ingestion, cleansing, enhancement, and aggregation processes, delivering incalculable business insights. This approach represents a significant advancement over conventional data architectures, such as a data warehouse with a staging and dimensional model layer or even a sole data lake, often involving more file organization rather than creating proper semantic layers.

The medallion architecture doesn't replace other dimensional modeling techniques. The structure of schemas and tables in each layer can vary based on the frequency and type of data updates, as well as the intended uses of the data. Instead, it guides how the data should be organized across three layers to enable a more modular data modeling approach.

It's valuable for analytics engineers to understand the foundations of the medallion architecture and the concepts behind the lakehouse, because in some scenarios, this is where they may spend a significant amount of their time. This involvement could include modeling structures to be deployed in one of the layers of the medallion, leveraging an interface provided by open formats, or building transformation scripts (using tools like dbt, for example) to enable data progression across the layers of the architecture.

However, it's important to note that the significance of open formats and lakehouses can vary depending on the specific data architecture in use. For example, in architectures like Snowflake, data may primarily be ingested into native tables rather than open formats like Iceberg, making the understanding of lakehouses more of a nice-to-have rather than an essential requirement for analytics engineering.

Summary

Data modeling has evolved significantly in the field of analysis to suit diverse business insights and reporting requirements. The star schema provides a simple query method by having a central fact table surrounded by dimension tables. The snowflake schema allows deeper granularity by breaking down these dimensions further. In contrast, the Data Vault approach prioritizes flexibility to deal with environments where data sources change rapidly. The new medallion design combines all these models, forming a complete plan for various analytical needs.

All the modeling advancements have been designed to tackle particular analytical issues. The central goal is to efficiently provide insights that can be acted upon, whether in the performance improvements of star and snowflake schemas or the versatility of the Data Vault. As the requirements for analytics become more complex, it is crucial to choose the correct modeling approach to not only make data available but also ensure it is meaningful and provides insights.

Analytics engineers use modeling structures such as star, snowflake, Data Vault, or medallion to create and maintain robust, scalable, and efficient data structures. Their work ensures the optimal organization of data, making it easily accessible and helpful to data analysts and scientists. Analytics engineers lay the foundation for accurate insights and informed decision making by creating coherent datasets from massive data streams through understanding and applying these models.

## CHAPTER 3

SQL for Analytics

In the vast landscape of data and analytics, it is critical to choose the right tools and technologies to efficiently process and manipulate data. One such tool that has stood the test of time and remains at the forefront is *Structured Query Language* (SQL). It offers a powerful and versatile approach to working with data, making it an excellent first choice for any analytical development task. SQL is a standardized programming language for managing and manipulating relational databases that enables data professionals to efficiently retrieve, store, modify, and analyze data stored in databases. Thanks to its intuitive syntax and wide acceptance in the community, SQL has become the standard language of data specialists, who use it to interact with databases and gain valuable insights from complex datasets.

SQL serves as the spine for data consumption and analysis in today's data-driven world. Businesses rely heavily on it in performing their data analytics operations to gain a competitive advantage. SQL's versatility and rich functionality make it an essential tool for analytics professionals, empowering them to retrieve specific subsets of data, perform complex aggregations, and join multiple tables to find hidden patterns and relationships within the data.

One of SQL's key strengths is its ability to retrieve and manipulate data quickly, which provides a wide range of query capabilities. This allows data specialists to filter, sort, and group data based on specific criteria, retrieving only the necessary data, and thus minimizing resource usage and improving performance. Furthermore, SQL enables data manipulation operations, such as inserting, updating, and deleting records, facilitating data cleaning and preparation tasks before analysis.

Another relevant benefit of using SQL is its seamless integration with various analytics tools and ecosystems, such as Python or BI platforms, making it a preferred language for data professionals and allowing them to combine the power of SQL with advanced statistical analysis, machine learning algorithms, and interactive visualizations. Additionally, the rise of cloud-based databases and data warehouses has further enhanced the relevance of SQL in analytics consumption, with platforms like Google BigQuery, Amazon Redshift, and Snowflake supporting SQL as their primary querying language.

In this chapter, we'll discuss the resiliency of the SQL language as one of the most commonly used analytics languages. Then we will explore the fundamentals of databases, introducing SQL as the standard language for interacting with them. We also examine the creation and usage of views, which provide a powerful mechanism for simplifying complex queries and abstracting data structures.

As we dig deeper into SQL, we will review the window functions that empower you to perform advanced calculations and aggregations. Furthermore, we'll dive into CTEs, which provide a means to create temporary result sets and simplify complex queries. Finally, we will also provide a glimpse into SQL for distributed data processing, ending with a bonus section presenting SQL in action for training machine learning models.

The Resiliency of SQL

Over time, we have seen that data engineering pipelines developed in SQL often endure for many years and that queries and stored procedures are still the core of several critical systems supporting financial institutions, retail companies, and even scientific activities. What is amazing, however, is that SQL has been widely used and continuously evolved to meet the demands of modern data processing with new features. Also, it is fascinating that technologies such as dbt, DuckDB, and even the new data manipulation library Polars provide their functionalities through a SQL interface. But what is the main reason for this popularity? We believe that a few factors can be highlighted.

First and foremost is the readability of the code. This is a crucial aspect of data engineering. SQL's syntax, while versatile, allows for both imperative and declarative usage, depending on the context and specific requirements. Many queries involve imperative tasks, such as retrieving specific data for a user or calculating results for a given date range. However, SQL's declarative nature shines when specifying what data you want rather than dictating how to retrieve it. This flexibility enables a wide range of users, including BI developers, business analysts, data engineers, and data scientists, to understand and interpret the code. Unlike some other strictly imperative data processing languages, SQL allows authors to focus on describing desired results. This self-documenting feature makes SQL code more readable and understandable, promoting effective collaboration in cross-functional teams.

Another exciting factor is that although SQL as an interface has survived over time, the reality is that the engines behind it have evolved dramatically over the last few years. Traditional SQL engines have improved, while distributed tools like Spark and Presto have enabled SQL to process massive datasets. In recent times, DuckDB has emerged as a game-changer, empowering SQL with extremely fast parallelized analytics queries on a single machine. With its functionality rivaling other high-performance alternatives, DuckDB opens new possibilities for data engineering tasks of all sizes.

However, it's important to note that not all SQL-powered systems are the same. While SQL Server, for example, was commonly used for warehousing, it is designed for OLTP. On the other hand, platforms like Snowflake and Redshift are specialized OLAP data warehouses. They excel in handling large-scale analytical workloads and are optimized for complex queries and reporting. These distinctions highlight the versatility of SQL, which can be adapted to various database architectures and purposes. SQL remains a unifying language that bridges the gap between OLAP and OLTP systems, facilitating data access and analytics across database types and technologies.

Data typing is another notable strength of SQL, particularly in data engineering. Seasoned data engineers understand the challenges of managing data types across various programming languages and SQL engines, a process that can be laborious and error-prone. However, SQL engines excel in enforcing strong data typing, guaranteeing consistent handling of data types throughout the data pipeline. Moreover, the SQL ecosystem offers valuable tools like Apache Arrow that tackle the compatibility issues arising from diverse tools and databases. Arrow facilitates robust and consistent data type handling across environments, including R, Python, and various databases. Selecting SQL engines compatible with Arrow can effectively mitigate many data typing challenges, simplifying maintenance efforts and reducing the burdens of dependency management, thus allowing data engineers to focus more on the core aspects of their data engineering work.

SQL's compatibility with software engineering best practices is a significant advantage in the field of data engineering. Data engineers often deal with complex SQL scripts that are important components of their organization's data pipelines. In the past, maintaining and modifying such scripts was a major challenge and often resulted in code that was difficult to understand and modify. However, the development of SQL tools has addressed these challenges and made it easier to adapt SQL code to good technical practices. One notable advance is the advent of DuckDB, a specialized SQL engine designed for analytical queries. DuckDB's unique features, such as the absence of dependencies and optimization for analytical workloads, enable data engineers to perform unit tests and facilitate rapid iteration of SQL code. This ensures that SQL code conforms to established technical principles, increasing its reliability and maintainability.

Another helpful tool in the SQL ecosystem is CTEs, which can be used to break large queries into smaller, more manageable, and testable pieces. By breaking complex queries into semantically meaningful components, data engineers can easily validate and verify each part independently, promoting a more modular and robust development process.

Other improvements are also helping push SQL to the forefront of analytics engineering. Lambda functions allow data engineers to write arbitrary functions directly into SQL statements. This capability improves the flexibility and agility of SQL code and enables dynamic calculations and transformations during data processing.

Window functions have also long been recognized as a valuable tool in SQL because they provide enhanced analytical capabilities by dividing data into manageable segments. With window functions, data engineers can perform complex aggregations, rankings, and statistical calculations over defined subsets of data, opening up new possibilities for analysis and reporting.

Last but not least, modern SQL engines have incorporated features such as full-text search, geodata functions, and user-defined functions, further expanding SQL's capabilities. These additions target specific use cases and domain-specific requirements and enable data engineers to perform specialized operations within the SQL environment.

All these and many more have contributed to the resiliency of SQL over time and encouraged many people to invest in learning and applying it in their day-to-day analytics activities. Now let's step back and revisit the core concepts of SQL.

Database Fundamentals

A strong understanding of database fundamentals is crucial for analytics and data engineers. Databases serve as the backbone for storing, organizing, and retrieving vast amounts of data. Over time, the evolution of databases has paved the way for the emergence and refinement of SQL as a powerful and widely adopted language for working with relational databases. However, before we explore the specificities of databases, it's essential to understand the broader context of data, information, and knowledge, as they all either live in or are derived from databases.

At the foundation of this context, we have the *DIKW pyramid*, shown in Figure 3-1. This conceptual model describes the hierarchical relationships among data, information, knowledge, and wisdom. Through a series of iterative processes, the DIKW pyramid provides a framework for understanding how to transform raw data into actionable wisdom.

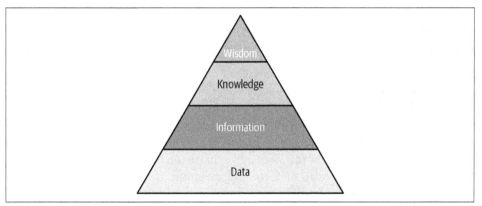

Figure 3-1. DIKW pyramid

To better understand the DIKW pyramid, let's decompose each layer:

Data
Raw facts and figures that lack context and meaning. Data can be considered as the building blocks of information. Examples of data: 1989, teacher, green.

Information
Organized and structured representation of data that provides context and answers specific questions. Examples of information:

- My math teacher was born in 1989.
- The traffic light at the intersection of Albany Ave and Avenue J is green.

Knowledge
Emerges when we combine information with experience, expertise, and understanding. It represents the insights gained from analyzing and interpreting information, which enable individuals and organizations to make informed decisions and take appropriate actions. Examples of knowledge:

- Since my math teacher was born in 1989, he is an adult.
- The traffic light that I am driving toward is turning green.

Wisdom
A level of deep understanding that exceeds knowledge. Wisdom occurs when individuals and organizations can apply their knowledge and make sound judgments, leading to positive effects and transformative insights. Examples of wisdom:

- It might be time for my math teacher to start thinking about a retirement savings plan.
- With the traffic light turning green, I can move ahead.

Databases play a vital role in the DIKW pyramid, serving as the basis for storing, managing, and organizing data. This enables the conversion of data into meaningful insights, which ultimately allows businesses to gain the necessary knowledge to make educated decisions.

Types of Databases

Databases are a core component of modern data management systems, delivering structured approaches to storing, organizing, and retrieving data. To better understand how a database achieves this, let's first explore the two main categories of databases: relational and non-relational. By understanding the features and differences between these two types, you will be more capable of selecting a database solution for your specific data needs.

Figure 3-2 shows the two primary categories of databases, mapping in each the most common types of databases.

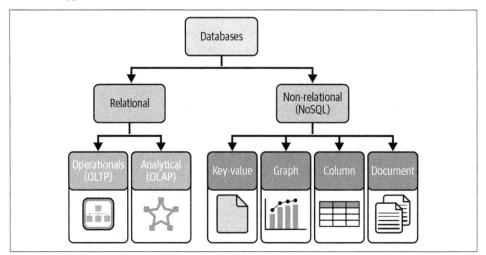

Figure 3-2. Database categories and their types

Relational databases
   In this most common and widely adopted database category, the data is organized into tables of rows and columns. Key are used to enforce relationships between tables, and SQL is used for querying and manipulating data. Relational databases provide strong data integrity, transactional reliability, and support for ACID properties, ensuring that database transactions are reliable, maintain data integrity, and can recover from failures.

Non-relational databases

Also known as *NoSQL* (not only SQL) databases, non-relational databases have emerged as an alternative for managing large volumes of unstructured and semi-structured data with scalability and flexibility. Compared to relational databases, non-relational databases do not rely on fixed schemas. They can store data in various formats, such as key-value pairs, documents, wide-column stores, or graphs. Non-relational databases prioritize high performance, horizontal scalability, and schema flexibility. They are well suited for scenarios like real-time analytics, applications dealing with unstructured data, and IoT data, among others.

In the following sections, we will primarily focus on relational databases as a consequence of the overall goal of this chapter, namely, to present the fundamentals of SQL.

We can imagine a database as a subset of a universe of data—built, designed, and fed with data that has a purpose specific to your organization. Databases are an essential component of society. Some activities, such as the ones listed, are widely distributed across society in general, with a database in the center to store the data:

- Book a hotel
- Book an airplane ticket
- Buy a phone in a well-known marketplace
- Enter your favorite social network
- Go to the doctor

But what does this look like in practice? Funneling into the relational databases, we organize the data into tables with rows and columns. Tables represent an entity of our universe, like a student in a university or a book in a library. A column describes an attribute of the entity. For example, a student has a name or address. A book has a title or an ISBN (International Standard Book Number). Finally, a row is the data itself. A student's name can be Peter Sousa or Emma Rock. For the book title, a row can be "Analytics Engineering with SQL and dbt." Figure 3-3 presents an example of a table with its respective columns and rows.

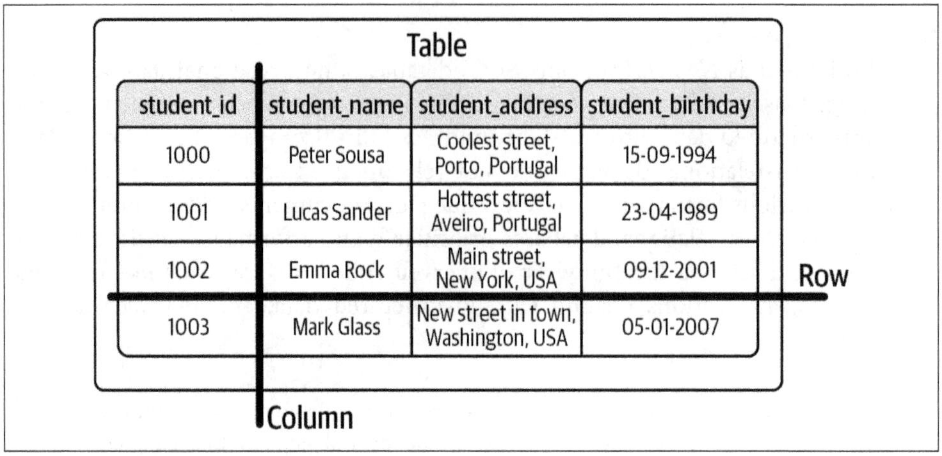

Figure 3-3. Sample of a table with its rows and columns

Another topic to consider is how we establish relationships with the data and grant consistency. This is an essential factor to highlight in relational databases, where we can enforce connections between tables by using keys. Enforcing these relationships and connections in a relational database involves implementing mechanisms to maintain the integrity and consistency of the data across related tables. These mechanisms maintain the relationships among tables, preventing inconsistencies or data anomalies.

One way to enforce relationships is by using primary and foreign keys. We will get there, but for now, Figure 3-4 presents an interrelationship between tables. The use case is a university in which one or more students can enroll in one or more classes.

Understanding these types of databases sets the stage for our next topic: database management systems (DBMSs). In the next section, we will dive deeper into the functionalities and importance of DBMSs, which serve as the software tools that enable efficient data storage, retrieval, and management in various types of databases.

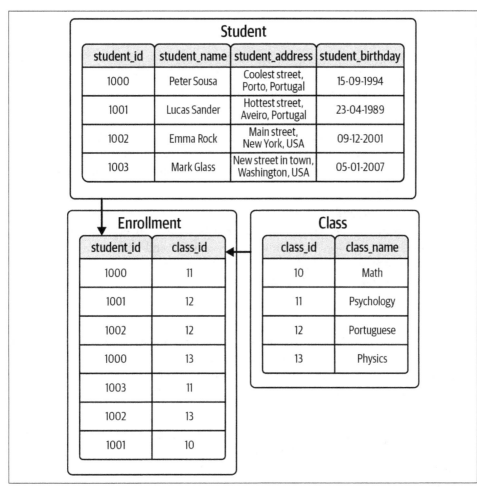

Figure 3-4. Tables interrelationship

Database Management System

A *DBMS* is a software system that enables database creation, organization, management, and manipulation. It provides an interface and set of tools for users and applications to interact with databases, allowing for efficient data storage, retrieval, modification, and deletion.

A DBMS acts as an intermediary between users or applications and the underlying database. It abstracts the complexities of interacting with the database, providing a convenient and standardized way to work with data. It acts as a software layer that handles the storage, retrieval, and management of data while also ensuring data integrity, security, and concurrency control.

The primary functions of a DBMS include the following:

Data definition
> A DBMS allows users to define the structure and organization of the data by creating and modifying database schemas. It enables the definition of tables, columns, relationships, and constraints that govern the data stored in the database.

Data manipulation
> Users can perform operations on the data stored in the database by using a query language, typically SQL. A DBMS provides mechanisms to insert, retrieve, update, and delete data, allowing for efficient and controlled manipulation of the database content.

Data security and integrity
> A DBMS provides mechanisms to ensure data security by enforcing access control policies. It enables the definition of user roles and permissions, restricting access to sensitive data. Additionally, a DBMS enforces data integrity by implementing constraints and validations to maintain the consistency and accuracy of the data.

Data concurrency and transaction management
> A DBMS handles the concurrent access to the database by multiple users or applications, ensuring that data remains consistent and protected from conflicts. It provides transaction management capabilities to ensure that groups of operations are executed reliably and consistently, following the ACID properties.

Data recovery and backup
> A DBMS incorporates features to ensure data durability and recoverability. It provides data backup and restore mechanisms, allowing for data recovery in case of system failures or disasters.

Some of the most common DBMSs for both relational and non-relational databases can be found in Table 3-1.

Table 3-1. Common DBMSs

Relational databases	Non-relational databases
Microsoft Access	MongoDB
Microsoft SQL Server	Apache Cassandra
Postgres	Apache CouchDB
MySQL	Redis
SQLite	Elasticsearch

"Speaking" with a Database

From an external point of view, interacting with a database through a DBMS provides four types of language:

Data definition language (DDL)
    To handle schemas, like table creation

Data manipulation language (DML)
    To work with the data

Data control language (DCL)
    To manage permissions to the database

Transaction control language (TCL)
    To address the transactions that occur in the database

Figure 3-5 shows the main languages used while interacting with a database and their primary commands.

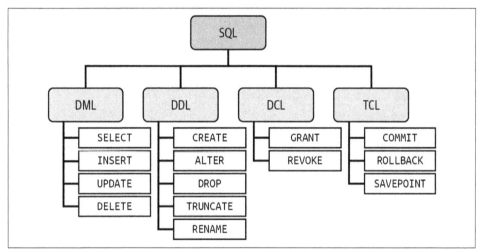

Figure 3-5. Main SQL commands

For this book, our primary focus will be providing solid foundations on SQL by learning how to query, manipulate, and define database structures, and so we will discuss DDL and DML. The activities related to administration tasks, like the ones performed with DCL and TCL, will not be covered.

Creating and Managing Your Data Structures with DDL

DDL, a subset of SQL, is a standardized language used to create and modify the structure of objects in a database. It includes commands and syntax for defining tables, indexes, sequences, aliases, etc.

The most common DDL commands are the following:

CREATE

Creates new database objects such as tables, views, indexes, or constraints. It specifies the name of the object and its structure, including columns, data types, and any additional properties.

DROP

Removes or deletes existing database objects. It permanently deletes the specified object and all associated data.

ALTER

Modifies the structure of an existing database object. You can use it to add, modify, or delete a table's columns, constraints, or other properties. It provides flexibility to adapt the database schema to changing requirements.

RENAME

Renames an existing database object, such as a table or a column. It provides a way to change the name of an object without altering its structure or data.

TRUNCATE

Quickly removes all data from a table, while keeping the table structure. It is faster than using the DELETE command to remove all rows since it deallocates the data pages without logging individual row deletions.

CONSTRAINT

Defines constraints on table columns, ensuring the integrity and validity of the data by specifying rules or conditions that the data must meet.

INDEX

Creates an index on one or multiple columns of a table. Usually, an index improves the performance of data retrieval operations by creating a sorted structure that allows faster data searching and sorting.

Before jumping into a hands-on use case, there are some topics we need to discuss in detail and one additional topic we need to introduce. The truth is that the majority of the DDL commands are, in a sense, self-explanatory, and as long as we see them in the code later, they will be easy to understand. Nonetheless, the discussion of the CONSTRAINT command should be slightly more detailed to introduce its particularities.

As mentioned earlier, constraints are rules or conditions the data must meet to grant their integrity. Typically, these constraints are applied to a column or a table. The most common constraints are as follows:

Primary key

A primary-key constraint ensures that a column or a combination of columns uniquely identifies each row in a table, preventing duplicate and null values. It is essential for data integrity and often used as a reference for foreign-key constraints in related tables.

Foreign key

A foreign-key constraint specifies a relationship between two tables. It ensures that values in a column or a combination of columns in one table match the primary-key values in another table, helping maintain referential integrity and enforcing data consistency across related tables.

Unique

A unique constraint ensures that the values in a column or a combination of columns are unique, and does not allow duplicates. Unlike a primary key, a unique constraint can allow null values, but only one null value is allowed if a column has a unique constraint.

Check

A check constraint imposes a condition on the values allowed in a column. These constraints are typically used to enforce business rules, domain-specific requirements, or any other custom conditions on the data.

Not null

A not-null constraint guarantees that a column does not contain null values, and so a specific column with this constraint must have a value for every row inserted or updated. This helps enforce data completeness and avoids unexpected null values.

Finally, there is one last point to discuss: the data types that categorize the data that can be stored in a column or variable. These fields can vary from database engine to engine. In our case, we will keep it simple and use the MySQL data types as reference:

Integer

A whole number without a fractional part. The most common are INT, SMALLINT, BIGINT, TINYINT. Examples of possible values: 1, 156, 2012412, 2.

Decimal

A number with a fractional part. Some of the most common are DECIMAL, NUMERIC, FLOAT, DOUBLE. Examples of possible values: 3.14, 94.5482, 5161.17620.

Boolean

> A binary value. Traditionally written as `BOOLEAN`, `BOOL`, `BIT`, `TINYINT`. Used for storing true/false or 0/1 values.

Date

> Mostly self-explanatory, but it can vary in format. Declared as `DATE`, and a standard format used is 2023-07-06.

Time

> You can decide the format of the time data type as well. Written as `TIME` in the database, one common format is 18:34:59.

Timestamp

> The date and the time together. Usually, we use `TIMESTAMP` or `DATETIME`. Example: 2017-12-31 18:34:59.

Text

> The most general data type. But it can only be alphabetical letters or a mix of letters, numbers, or any other characters. Normally declared as `CHAR`, `VARCHAR`, `NVARCHAR`, `TEXT`. Note that choosing the correct text data type is relevant since each one has a maximum specified length. Examples of text: "hello world," "porto1987," "Hélder," "13,487*5487+588".

 We will use MySQL because of its broad adoption. You can download the MySQL Workbench through the MySQL website (*https://oreil.ly/Mzrdt*).

Now that you have a better idea of the DDL commands and the most common database data types, let's create a database for managing O'Reilly books. This aligns with the example in Chapter 2, when we introduced a database for O'Reilly to track books, but now let's start with the physical model creation.

As a note, for data engineers, proficiency in all types of SQL commands is crucial as they are responsible for both database design (DDL) and data manipulation (DML). Analysts primarily focus on DML SQL commands, often limited to `SELECT` queries for data analysis. On the other hand, analytics engineers typically work with a combination of DML and some DDL SQL commands, although they often abstract DDL operations through tools like dbt.

First, let's create the database itself. In your MySQL client, execute the command in Example 3-1.

Example 3-1. Create the database

```
-- Create the OReillyBooks database statement
CREATE DATABASE OReillyBooks;
```

Now, with the database created, execute the code in Example 3-2.

Example 3-2. Create the database, part 2

```
-- Use the database
USE OReillyBooks;

-- Create the tables

-- Table: Authors
CREATE TABLE authors (
  author_id INT PRIMARY KEY,
  author_name VARCHAR(100)
);

-- Table: Books
CREATE TABLE books (
  book_id INT PRIMARY KEY,
  book_title VARCHAR(100),
  author_id INT,
  rating DECIMAL(10,2),
  FOREIGN KEY (author_id) REFERENCES Authors(author_id)
);

-- Table: Category
CREATE TABLE category (
  category_id INT PRIMARY KEY,
  category_name VARCHAR(50)
);

-- Table: bookCategory
CREATE TABLE book_category (
  book_id INT,
  category_id INT,
  FOREIGN KEY (book_id) REFERENCES books(book_id),
  FOREIGN KEY (category_id) REFERENCES category(category_id)
);
```

In summary, these two examples have created a database called OReillyBooks and
defined four tables: authors, books, category, and book_category (which represents
the many-to-many relationship between books and categories). Each table has its own
set of columns and constraints, such as primary keys and foreign keys.

Finally, and to also test other DDL commands, imagine that a new requirement arises, and now we also need to store the publication_year, which refers to the year a particular book was published. The syntax to do so is shown in Example 3-3.

Example 3-3. ALTER TABLE syntax

```
-- Add a new column
ALTER TABLE table_name
ADD column_name datatype [column_constraint];

-- Modify a datatype of an existing column
ALTER TABLE table_name
ALTER COLUMN column_name [new_datatype];

-- Rename a column
ALTER TABLE table_name
RENAME COLUMN old_column_name TO new_column_name;

-- Add a new constraint to a column
ALTER TABLE table_name
ADD CONSTRAINT constraint_name constraint_type (column_name);

-- Modify an existing constraint
ALTER TABLE table_name
ALTER CONSTRAINT constraint_name [new_constraint];

-- Remove an existing column
ALTER TABLE table_name
DROP COLUMN column_name;
```

As per the syntax shown in Example 3-3, the modification that fits our needs is adding a new column. Let's now add the publication_year by executing the code snippet in Example 3-4.

Example 3-4. Add the publication year

```
-- Add publication_year to the books table
ALTER TABLE books
ADD publication_year INT;
```

Manipulating Data with DML

DML serves as an essential component in database management. This language enables data selection, insertion, deletion, and updating within a database system. Its primary purpose is to retrieve and manipulate data residing in a relational database while encompassing several key commands.

Inserting Data with INSERT

The INSERT command facilitates the addition of new data into a table. With this command, users can seamlessly insert one or multiple records into a specific table within the database. By utilizing INSERT, it becomes possible to expand the content of a table by including additional entries. This command is instrumental in adding records to an initially empty table but also allows for continuously augmenting existing data within the database. Example 3-5 shows the standard syntax of this command.

Example 3-5. Syntax of an INSERT statement

```
INSERT INTO table_name (column1, column2, ...)
VALUES (value1, value2, ...);
```

The INSERT INTO statement specifies the table where the data will be inserted, where *table_name* represents the name of the table itself. The component (__column1__, __column2__, ...) is optional and allows for the specification of the columns into which the data will be inserted. If the columns are omitted, it is assumed that values will be provided for all columns in the table. The VALUES keyword indicates the start of the list of values to be inserted into the specified columns. Within the VALUES clause, (__value1__, __value2__, ...), we have the actual values to be inserted into the respective columns. It is crucial to ensure that the number of values provided matches the number of columns specified. This is the only way to ensure the values are correctly mapped to the corresponding columns during the insertion process. Most database engines raise an error if this is not respected.

Let's now extend our use case, which we started with "Manipulating Data with DML" on page 82, and insert data into the previously created tables. For that, execute the command in Example 3-6.

Example 3-6. Create dummy data

```
-- Inserting data into the authors table
INSERT INTO authors (author_id, author_name) VALUES
(1, 'Stephanie Mitchell'),
(2, 'Paul Turner'),
(3, 'Julia Martinez'),
(4, 'Rui Machado'),
(5, 'Thomas Brown');

-- Inserting data into the books table
INSERT INTO books (book_id, book_title,
            author_id, publication_year,
            rating)
VALUES
(1, 'Python Crash Course', 1, 2012, 4.5),
```

```
(2, 'Learning React', 2, 2014, 3.7),
(3, 'Hands-On Machine Learning with Scikit-Learn, Keras, and TensorFlow',
  3, 2017, 4.9),
(4, 'JavaScript: The Good Parts', 4, 2015, 2.8),
(5, 'Data Science for Business', 5, 2019, 4.2);

-- Inserting data into the category table
INSERT INTO category (category_id, category_name) VALUES
(1, 'Programming'),
(2, 'Machine Learning'),
(3, 'Data Science'),
(4, 'Software Engineering'),
(5, 'Algorithms'),
(6, 'Computer Science');

-- Inserting data into the book_category table
INSERT INTO book_category (book_id, category_id) VALUES
(1, 1),
(2, 1),
(3, 2),
(4, 1),
(5, 3);
```

This code creates several INSERT statements, each targeting a specific table. We start by inserting data into the authors table. Each row represents an author, with author_id and author_name columns indicating the author's unique identifier and name, respectively.

Then, we inserted data into the books table. Each row represents a book, with book_id, book_title, and author_id columns indicating the unique identifier, title, and author identifier of the book, respectively. The author_id column is linked to the author_id column in the authors table to establish the relationship between books and authors. Note that we cannot insert a book referencing a nonexistent author because of referential integrity.

We also created a category table to correctly classify the book based on its content type. Each row represents a category, with category_id and category_name columns indicating the unique identifier and name of the category, respectively.

Finally, our intermediate table, book_category, stores the relationship between books and their corresponding categories. Each row represents one occurrence of this relationship, with book_id and category_id columns indicating the book and category identifiers, respectively. These columns establish the many-to-many relationship between books and categories.

Let's have a look at the data we've inserted. Execute the code in Example 3-7, line by line. We will cover the SELECT statement in detail in the next section, but for now, it is enough to check the data in each table.

Example 3-7. A SELECT statement querying the authors, book_category, books, and category tables

```
select * from authors;
select * from book_category;
select * from books;
select * from category;
```

Selecting Data with SELECT

SELECT is one of the most fundamental DML commands in SQL. This command allows you to extract specific data from a database. When this statement is executed, it retrieves the desired information and organizes it into a structured result table, commonly referred to as the *result set*. This result set contains data that meets the specified criteria, allowing users to access and analyze the selected information easily. In Example 3-8, we can analyze the (simplest) syntax of this command.

 If you are already proficient with SQL and SELECT commands and seeking more advanced SQL statements, we recommend referring to "Window Functions" on page 105. If you already want to jump into the dbt world, you can find it in Chapter 4.

Example 3-8. Syntax of a SELECT statement

```
SELECT column1, column2, ...
FROM table_name;
```

The SELECT part of this structure indicates the specific columns or expressions that are retrieved from the table. The FROM component specifies the table from which the data will be retrieved. We have much more to elaborate on about this command, from data filtering and respective operators to data grouping or joins. In the next sections, we will discuss each property.

Filtering data with WHERE

The optional WHERE clause allows users to define conditions the retrieved data must meet, effectively filtering rows based on specified criteria. It is a fundamental part of SQL queries, allowing you to filter and retrieve specific subsets of data from tables. Example 3-9 shows the syntax of the WHERE statement.

Example 3-9. Syntax of a SELECT statement with a WHERE clause

```
SELECT column1, column2, ...
FROM table_name
WHERE condition ;
```

To correctly understand how to write *conditions* in SQL and adequately filter the data, we must first become familiarized with the SQL operators with single or multiple conditions.

SQL operators. SQL operators are frequently used in the WHERE clause to establish conditions for filtering data. These operators allow you to compare values and expressions in SQL that meet the defined conditions. Table 3-2 summarizes the most common operators.

Table 3-2. SQL operators

Operator	Operator type	Meaning
=	Comparison	Equal to
<> or !=	Comparison	Not equal to
<	Comparison	Less than
>	Comparison	Greater than
< =	Comparison	Less than or equal to
> =	Comparison	Greater than or equal to
LIKE '%expression%'	Comparison	Contains "expression"
IN ("exp1", "exp2")	Comparison	Contains any of "exp1" or "exp2"
BETWEEN	Logical	Selects values within a given range
AND	Logical	Combines two or more conditions and returns true only if all the conditions are true
OR	Logical	Combines two or more conditions and returns true if at least one of the conditions is true
NOT	Logical	Negates a condition, returning true if the condition is false, and vice versa
UNION	Set	Combines the result of two SELECT statements, removing the duplicated rows
UNION ALL	Set	Combines all records from two SELECT statements, yet with UNION ALL, duplicated rows aren't eliminated

To better understand their applications, let's explore examples for comparison operators and logical operators. To simplify things, since we didn't dig into other elements of SQL, such as joins, let's use the books table as the source of our use cases.

As an initial example of conditional and logical operators, let's try to find books published earlier than 2015. Then, let's find only the books published in 2017 and, last, the books with "Python" in the title. Example 3-10 has the three code snippets to help you solve this challenge.

Example 3-10. Select data with conditional operators

```
-- Books published earlier than 2015
SELECT
  book_title,
  publication_year
FROM books
WHERE publication_year < 2015;

-- Books published in 2017
SELECT
  book_title,
  publication_year
FROM books
WHERE publication_year = 2017;

-- Books with "Python" in the title
SELECT
  book_title,
  publication_year
FROM books
WHERE book_title LIKE '%Python%';
```

Example 3-10 shows three examples of working with conditional operators. Feel free to play with the code and test the others introduced previously.

Finally, to be familiarized with a logical operator, let's search for books published in 2012 or after 2015. Example 3-11 will help with this.

Example 3-11. Select data with a logical operator

```
-- Books published in 2012 or after 2015
SELECT
  book_title,
  publication_year
FROM books
WHERE publication_year = 2012 OR publication_year > 2015;
```

It is also essential to note that these operators are not exclusive to the WHERE clause. They can also be used along with other filtering techniques, such as the HAVING clause, that we will introduce in the next section.

Aggregating data with GROUP BY

The GROUP BY clause is an optional feature in SQL utilized to group the result set by one or more columns. Often used with aggregate functions, GROUP BY calculates subsets of rows that share a common value in the specified column or columns. In other words, when using the GROUP BY clause, the result set is divided into groups, where each group represents a unique combination of values from the given aggregated column or columns. As stated, GROUP BY is typically used with aggregate functions for these groups, providing valuable insights into the data. Some of the most common aggregate functions are shown in Table 3-3.

Table 3-3. Aggregate functions

Aggregate function	Meaning
COUNT()	Calculates the number of rows or non-null values in a column.
SUM()	Calculates the sum of numeric values in a column.
AVG()	Calculates the average (mean) value of a column.
MAX()	Retrieves the maximum value from a column.
MIN()	Retrieves the minimum value from a column.
DISTINCT	Although not an aggregate function in the rigorous sense, the DISTINCT keyword is often used with an aggregate function, inside the SELECT statement, to calculate distinct values.

GROUP BY is typically used in trend analysis and summary reports, like monthly sales reports and quarterly user accesses, among others. The generic syntax of the GROUP BY clause is presented in Example 3-12.

Example 3-12. Syntax of a SELECT statement with a GROUP BY clause

```
SELECT column1, column2, ...
FROM table_name
GROUP BY column1, column2, ...
```

Let's now apply those functions in a straightforward use case. Using the table book_category, let's analyze the average number of books per category. To help you with this challenge, let's look at Example 3-13.

Example 3-13. Select and aggregate data

```
SELECT
  category_id,
  COUNT(book_id) AS book_count
FROM bookCategory
GROUP BY category_id;
```

We're using the COUNT() aggregate function, but others could be used, depending on the desired use case. Finally, this is a simple example since we see only category_id, but it could be better if we had the category name instead; however, this field is visible only in the category table. To include it, we need to know how to use joins. We will discuss this further in "Joining data with INNER, LEFT, RIGHT, FULL, and CROSS JOIN" on page 90.

At last, we come to the HAVING filter. An optional clause closely related to GROUP BY, the HAVING filter applies conditions to the grouped data. Compared with the WHERE clause, HAVING filters the rows after the aggregation, while in the WHERE clause, the filtering occurs before the grouping operation. Yet the same operators, such as "equal" and "greater than," among others, are applied as in the WHERE statement.

The SQL syntax for a HAVING filter is displayed in Example 3-14.

Example 3-14. Syntax of a SELECT statement with a GROUP BY clause and HAVING filter

```
SELECT column1, column2, ...
FROM table_name
GROUP BY column1, column2, ...
HAVING condition
```

Let's see the HAVING filter in action. Referring to Example 3-13, we now want only the categories with at least two books published. Example 3-15 helps you with that.

Example 3-15. Select and aggregate data, applying the HAVING filter

```
SELECT
  category_id,
  COUNT(book_id) AS book_count
FROM bookCategory
GROUP BY category_id
HAVING COUNT(book_id) >= 2;
```

By leveraging the GROUP BY clause and the HAVING filter, you can effectively organize and summarize data to perform calculations on aggregated datasets, enabling you to uncover patterns, trends, and relationships within the data; facilitate data analysis; and support the decision-making processes.

Sorting data with ORDER BY

The ORDER BY clause is a sorting statement within SQL generally used to organize the query results in a specific sequence, making it simpler to analyze and interpret the data. It sorts the result set of a query based on one or more columns, allowing you to specify the sorting order for each column, namely, by ascending (the default) and descending order.

The basic syntax of the ORDER BY clause is shown in Example 3-16.

Example 3-16. Syntax of a SELECT statement with an ORDER BY clause

```
SELECT column1, column2, ...
FROM table_name
ORDER BY column1 [ASC|DESC], column2 [ASC|DESC], ...
```

In the previous use cases, one that stands out is the books published yearly. Looking at the table, it is difficult to determine which are the newest and the oldest books. The ORDER BY clause substantially simplifies this analysis. To test this clause, execute the code snippet in Example 3-17 and check the results with and without ORDER BY. As a note, if the order ASC/DESC is not explicitly declared, SQL will use ASC by default.

Example 3-17. SELECT statement with an ORDER BY clause

```
SELECT
  book_title,
  publication_year
FROM books
ORDER BY publication_year DESC;
```

In conclusion, the ORDER BY clause allows you to arrange your result set in a desired sequence that best suits your data exploration and analysis, simplifying the capture of meaningful data.

Joining data with INNER, LEFT, RIGHT, FULL, and CROSS JOIN

Joins are a mechanism in SQL that combine data from multiple tables. Understanding and working with joins can largely improve your capacity to pull valuable insights and make more informed decisions from complex datasets. This section will guide you through the types of joins available in SQL, their syntax, and their usage.

SQL has several types of joins. Each allows you to combine data from multiple tables based on specified conditions. Before seeing the joins in action, let's increment our dataset with a new author. This author will not have any books. To do this, execute the statement in Example 3-18.

Example 3-18. Insert an author without books

```
INSERT INTO authors (author_id, author_name) VALUES
(6, 'John Doe')
```

The reason we created an author without any books is to explore the several joins we will introduce. Following are the most common types of SQL joins.

INNER JOIN. The `INNER JOIN` returns only the matching rows from both tables based on the specified join condition. If we think of a Venn diagram with circle A and circle B representing each dataset, in an `INNER JOIN` we would see only the overlapping area that contains the matching values of both tables. Let's look at Figure 3-6 to better visualize the Venn diagram.

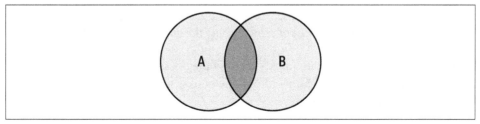

Figure 3-6. Venn diagram illustrating an INNER JOIN

The code syntax for the `INNER JOIN` is shown in Example 3-19.

Example 3-19. Syntax of an INNER JOIN

```
SELECT
  columns
FROM Table_A
INNER JOIN Table_B ON join_condition;
```

To see the `INNER JOIN` in action, let's gather only authors with books. Example 3-20 shows the required code.

Example 3-20. Gather only authors with books

```
SELECT
  authors.author_id,
  authors.author_name,
  books.book_title
FROM authors
INNER JOIN books ON Authors.author_id = Books.author_id
```

Figure 3-7 shows the query output.

author_id	author_name	book_title
1	Stephanie Mitchell	Python Crash Course
2	Paul Turner	Learning React Fundamentals
3	Julia Martinez	Hands-On Machine Learning with Scikit-Learn, Keras, and TensorFlow
4	Rui Machado	JavaScript: The Good Parts
5	Thomas Brown	Data Science for Business

Figure 3-7. INNER JOIN query output showing only the authors who have books

By analyzing the results, we can quickly identify the missing author John Doe. As you may remember, we've created him without any books, so when using an INNER JOIN, he was expected to be omitted.

LEFT JOIN (or LEFT OUTER JOIN). Returns all rows from the left table and the matching rows from the right table. If there is no match, null values are included for the columns from the right table. Similar to the previous exercise, a Venn diagram with a circle A on the left and a circle B on the right represents each dataset. In a LEFT JOIN, the left circle includes all rows from the left table, and the overlapping region represents the matching rows based on the join condition. The right circle includes the nonmatching rows from the right table, represented by null values in the result set. Have a look at Figure 3-8 to better visualize the Venn diagram.

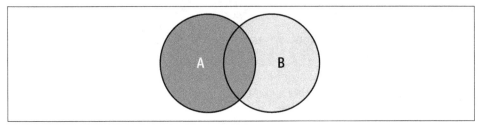

Figure 3-8. Venn diagram illustrating a LEFT JOIN

The code syntax for the LEFT JOIN is in Example 3-21.

Example 3-21. Syntax of a LEFT JOIN

```
SELECT
  columns
FROM Table_A
LEFT JOIN Table_B ON join_condition;
```

To test the LEFT JOIN, let's keep the same use case of relating the authors with their books, but now we want to list all authors and their respective books, and we must also include the authors with any book. Execute the code snippet in Example 3-22.

Example 3-22. Gather authors and their books

```
SELECT
  authors.author_id,
  authors.author_name,
  books.book_title
FROM authors
LEFT JOIN books ON authors.author_id = books.author_id
```

The query output is shown in Figure 3-9.

author_id	author_name	book_title
1	Stephanie Mitchell	Python Crash Course
2	Paul Turner	Learning React Fundamentals
3	Julia Martinez	Hands-On Machine Learning with Scikit-Learn, Keras, and TensorFlow
4	Rui Machado	JavaScript: The Good Parts
5	Thomas Brown	Data Science for Business
6	John Doe	NULL

Figure 3-9. LEFT JOIN query output displaying the authors and their respective books

When compared with the INNER JOIN, the LEFT JOIN enables us to see the author John Doe. This is because on a LEFT JOIN, the left table, authors, is fully shown, while the right table, books, shows only the intersected result with authors.

RIGHT JOIN (or RIGHT OUTER JOIN). A right join returns all rows from the right table and the matching rows from the left table. If there is no match, null values are included for the columns from the left table. Continue thinking of a Venn diagram with circle A (left) and circle B (right) representing each dataset. In a RIGHT JOIN, the right circle includes all rows from the right table, and the overlapping region represents the matching rows based on the join condition. The left circle includes the nonmatching rows from the left table, represented by null values in the result set. Finally, have a look at Figure 3-10 to better visualize the Venn diagram.

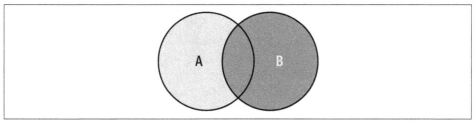

Figure 3-10. Venn diagram illustrating a RIGHT JOIN

The code syntax for the RIGHT JOIN is shown in Example 3-23.

Example 3-23. Syntax of a RIGHT JOIN

```
SELECT
  columns
FROM Table_A
RIGHT JOIN Table_B ON join_condition;
```

Let's first contextualize our training to see the `RIGHT JOIN` in action. In this case, we want to see all the books and their authors, so execute the code in Example 3-24.

Example 3-24. Gather books and their authors

```
SELECT
  authors.author_id,
  authors.author_name,
  books.book_title
FROM authors
RIGHT JOIN books ON authors.author_id = books.author_id
```

The query output is shown in Figure 3-11.

author_id	author_name	book_title
1	Stephanie Mitchell	Python Crash Course
2	Paul Turner	Learning React Fundamentals
3	Julia Martinez	Hands-On Machine Learning with Scikit-Learn, Keras, and TensorFlow
4	Rui Machado	JavaScript: The Good Parts
5	Thomas Brown	Data Science for Business

Figure 3-11. RIGHT JOIN query output displaying the books and their respective authors

By analyzing the query output, we see all books and their respective authors. Since we don't have any books without an author, we cannot see any intersection between books and `authors` where a book exists without an author.

FULL JOIN (or FULL OUTER JOIN). In this join, all rows are returned from both tables. It combines the result of the `LEFT JOIN` and the `RIGHT JOIN`. If there is no match, null values are included for the columns from the nonmatching table. In a Venn diagram with circle A (left) and circle B (right) representing each dataset, the diagram for a `FULL JOIN` will show the overlapping region representing the matching rows based on the join condition, while the nonoverlapping portions of each circle include the non-matching rows from their respective tables. In the end, the result set generated includes all rows from both tables, with null values for nonmatching rows. Let's see Figure 3-12 to visualize it better.

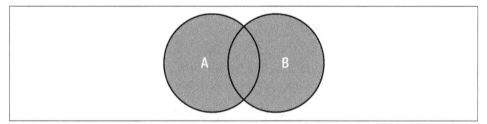

Figure 3-12. Venn diagram illustrating a FULL JOIN

The code syntax for the FULL JOIN is shown in Example 3-25.

Example 3-25. Syntax of a FULL JOIN

```
SELECT
  columns
FROM Table_A
FULL JOIN Table_B ON join_condition;
```

 MySQL doesn't support the FULL JOIN natively. We must do a UNION between a LEFT JOIN and a RIGHT JOIN statement to achieve it. This effectively combines the data from both directions, replicating the behavior of a FULL JOIN.

CROSS JOIN. The CROSS JOIN (or Cartesian join) returns the Cartesian product of both tables, combining every row from the first table with every row from the second table. It does not require a join condition. In a Venn diagram of a CROSS JOIN, we don't have overlapping circles since it combines each row from circle A, left, and circle B, right. The result set includes all possible combinations of rows from both tables, as shown in Figure 3-13.

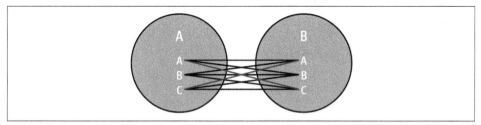

Figure 3-13. Venn diagram illustrating a CROSS JOIN

The code syntax for the CROSS JOIN is in Example 3-26.

Example 3-26. Syntax of a CROSS JOIN

```
SELECT
  columns
FROM Table_A
CROSS JOIN Table_B;
```

A CROSS JOIN of the authors table and books table is shown in Example 3-27.

Example 3-27. CROSS JOIN of authors and books tables

```
SELECT
*
FROM authors
CROSS JOIN books;
```

In summary, SQL joins provide flexibility in combining data from multiple tables based on conditions. Understanding their usage and syntax allows you to extract the desired information and establish relationships for related data across tables. Visualizing the joins through a Venn diagram helps explain how the tables' data overlaps and combines based on the join conditions by highlighting the matched and unmatched rows in the result set, and providing a clear representation of the relationship between tables during the join operation.

Updating Data with UPDATE

The UPDATE command allows us to modify records within an existing table in a database. By executing this command, users can effectively update and alter the data stored in specific records. UPDATE enables changes to be made to one or more records within a table, ensuring that the data accurately reflects the latest information. By utilizing this command, users can seamlessly modify the content of a table, allowing for data refinement, corrections, or updates as needed. Example 3-28 shows the syntax of this command.

Example 3-28. Syntax of an UPDATE statement

```
UPDATE table_name
SET column1 = value1, column2 = value2, ...
WHERE condition;
```

The UPDATE keyword is used to specify the table that will be updated, and *table_name* represents the name of the table to be modified. The SET keyword indicates that columns will be updated and assigns new values to them. Within the SET clause, *column1 = value1, column2 = value2...* specifies the columns to be updated and their corresponding new values. Finally, the WHERE clause, which is optional, allows for the specification of conditions that the rows must satisfy to be updated. It filters the rows based on the specified conditions.

To test the UPDATE statement in reality, let's assume that we have a typo in a book title: instead of "Learning React," we want "Learning React Fundamentals." Looking at the books table, we can see that Learning React has book_id = 2. You can refer to the code in Example 3-29 for guidance on how to achieve this update.

Example 3-29. Update the books table

```
UPDATE books
SET book_title = 'Learning React Fundamentals'
WHERE book_id = 2;
```

And that's it. If you look at the books table data again, you can see the new name (Figure 3-14).

book_id	book_title	author_id
1	Python Crash Course	1
2	Learning React Fundamentals	2
3	Hands-On Machine Learning with Scikit-Learn, Keras, and TensorFlow	3
4	JavaScript: The Good Parts	4
5	Data Science for Business	5
NULL	NULL	NULL

Figure 3-14. Updating the books table

Deleting Data with DELETE

The DELETE command provides the ability to selectively delete certain records based on specified criteria or delete all records within a table. DELETE plays a vital role in data maintenance, allowing users to effectively manage and clean up the contents of a table by removing unnecessary or outdated records. This command ensures data integrity and helps optimize the database by eliminating redundant or irrelevant information. Example 3-30 shows the syntax of this command.

Example 3-30. Syntax of a DELETE statement

```
DELETE FROM table_name
WHERE condition;
```

The DELETE FROM portion indicates the specific table from which data will be deleted, and *table_name* indicates the table's name. The optional WHERE clause plays an essential function by allowing users to define conditions that must be met for rows to be deleted. By utilizing this clause, rows can be filtered based on specific criteria. If we don't use the WHERE clause, all rows within the table will be deleted. Finally, *condition* refers to the specific conditions that rows must satisfy to be eligible for deletion.

To practically apply this command, let's imagine that we will not publish any book from the Computer Science category. By looking into the category_id, we can see it's the number 6. Let's now execute Example 3-31 and see what happens.

Example 3-31. Delete a category from the category table

```
DELETE FROM Category
WHERE category_id = 6
```

If everything went well, you should be able to select the category table and see we no longer have the Computer Science category, as shown in Figure 3-15.

category_id	category_name
1	Programming
2	Machine Learning
3	Data Science
4	Software Engineering
5	Algorithms
NULL	NULL

Figure 3-15. Deleted category from the category table

Finally, you can also use another data management technique, named *soft delete*, to "delete" the data. This technique, instead of permanently erasing a record, sets a flag or attribute in the database to indicate that the record should be considered deleted. This preserves historical data, ensures easy recovery when needed, and supports compliance by maintaining an audit trail of changes.

Storing Queries as Views

A *view* is a virtual table in a database defined by a query. It is similar to a regular table, consisting of named columns and rows of data. However, unlike a table, a view does not physically store data values in the database. Instead, it retrieves data dynamically from the tables referenced in its query when the view is accessed.

In Example 3-32, we see the generic syntax for creating a view.

Example 3-32. VIEW syntax

```
CREATE VIEW view_name AS
SELECT column1, column2, ...
FROM table_name
WHERE condition;
```

Using our `OReillyBooks` database, Example 3-33 creates a view for analyzing the number of books each author has created.

Example 3-33. A view for the books database

```
CREATE VIEW author_book_count AS
SELECT authors.author_id,
       authors.author_name,
       COUNT(books.book_id) AS book_count
FROM authors
LEFT JOIN books ON authors.author_id = books.author_id
GROUP BY authors.author_id, authors.author_name;
```

We can then query the `author_book_count` view to analyze the number of books each author has created; see Example 3-34.

Example 3-34. Query a view in the books database

```
SELECT * FROM author_book_count;
```

One of the primary purposes of a view is to act as a filter on the underlying tables. The query to define a view can involve one or more tables or other views from the same or different databases. In fact, views can be created to consolidate data from multiple heterogeneous sources, allowing you to combine similar data from different servers across your organization, each storing data for a specific region.

Views are commonly used to simplify and customize each user's perception of the database. By defining views, you can present a focused and tailored view of the data to different users, hiding unnecessary details and providing a more intuitive interface. Additionally, a view can serve as a security mechanism by allowing users to access data through the view without granting them direct access to the underlying base tables. This provides an additional layer of control and ensures that users see only the data they are authorized to view.

In Example 3-35, we create the `renamed_books` view based on the books table. We use column aliases within the `SELECT` statement to rename the columns to something more familiar to a particular user without changing the table structure. We can even have different views on top of the same data with different naming conventions depending on the audience.

Example 3-35. A view for renaming columns

```
CREATE VIEW renamed_books AS
SELECT
    id AS BookID,
    title AS BookTitle,
    rating AS BookRating
FROM books;
```

Furthermore, views are helpful when the schema of a table has changed. Instead of modifying existing queries and applications, you can create a view that emulates the old table structure, providing a backward-compatible interface for accessing the data. This way, you can maintain compatibility while changing the underlying data model.

Although views offer numerous advantages, they also have certain limitations and potential dangers. One limitation is the dependence on the underlying table structure, which we previously highlighted as a benefit; however, it's also a curse. If the base table structure changes, the view definition must be updated accordingly, which can lead to increased maintenance overhead. In addition, views can affect query performance, especially for complex views that involve multiple tables or extensive calculations.

To avoid unnecessary overhead, it is essential to continuously optimize view queries and learn to use execution plans effectively to stop inefficiencies. Another danger is the possibility of creating overly complex or inefficient views, leading to poor performance and difficulty maintaining or modifying views over time. In addition, views can provide an illusion of data security by restricting access to specific columns or rows. However, they do not provide foolproof security, and unauthorized users can still access the underlying data if they gain access to the view. To ensure data protection, we must implement appropriate database-level security measures. Finally, views can lead to potential data integrity issues if not properly maintained, as they may not enforce constraints or referential integrity like physical tables. Overall, while views provide valuable functionality, we should understand and minimize their limitations and potential risks to ensure their effective and secure use.

In Example 3-36, we demonstrate that because of the extensive number of joins and the inclusion of various columns from different tables, the complexity of the view increases, making it challenging to read and comprehend at a glance. An interesting way to fix this would be through the use of CTEs, which we describe in the next section.

Example 3-36. Complex views

```
CREATE VIEW complex_books_view AS
SELECT
    b.book_id,
```

```
        b.book_title,
        b.author_id,
        b.rating,
        b.publication_year,
        a.author_id,
        a.author_name,
        c.category_id,
        c.category_name
FROM books b
INNER JOIN authors a ON a.author_id = b.author_id
LEFT JOIN bookCategory bc ON bc.book_id = b.book_id
LEFT JOIN category c ON c.category_id = bc.category_id;
```

Common Table Expressions

Many data analysts and developers have faced the challenge of understanding complex SQL queries. It's not uncommon to struggle with knowing the purpose and dependencies of specific query components, especially when dealing with complicated business logic and multiple upstream dependencies. Add to this the frustration of unexpected query results that leave the analyst uncertain about which section of the query is causing the discrepancy. Common table expressions (CTEs) provide a valuable solution in such scenarios.

CTEs offer a powerful tool for simplifying complex queries and improving query maintainability. Acting as a temporary result set, CTEs enhance the readability of SQL code by breaking complex queries into manageable blocks.

Example 3-37 shows the generic syntax to create a CTE in SQL. Even though it looks complex, it follows simple patterns.

Example 3-37. CTE syntax

```
WITH cte_name (column1, column2, ..., columnN) AS (     ❶
    -- Query definition goes here                       ❷
)
SELECT column1, column2, ..., columnN                   ❸
FROM cte_name                                           ❸
-- Additional query operations go here                  ❹
```

❶ Declare the CTE by using the WITH keyword and give the expression a name. You can also specify the columns if needed, or use the * character.

❷ Define the CTE query after the AS keyword by writing the query that defines the CTE. This query can be as simple or complex as needed, including filtering, joining, aggregating, or any other SQL operations.

❸ Use the CTE in a subsequent query, referencing the CTE by its name as if it were an actual table. You can select columns from the CTE or perform additional operations on the CTE's data.

❹ Add more query operations—pipelining CTEs along your query. This step is optional. We can include additional query operations like filtering, sorting, grouping, or joining to further manipulate the data retrieved from the CTE.

Example 3-38 creates a CTE using the books table as a reference.

Example 3-38. A simple CTE

```
WITH popular_books AS (
    SELECT title,
           author,
           rating
    FROM books
    WHERE rating >= 4.5
)
SELECT title,
       author
FROM popular_books
ORDER BY rating DESC;
```

Similar to derived tables and database views, CTEs provide several advantages that make query writing and maintenance easier. By breaking complex queries into smaller reusable blocks, CTEs enhance code readability and simplify the overall query structure. Let's examine the difference between using a CTE and using only a subquery. For this exercise, we used a fictitious sales table with all book sales, as shown in Example 3-39. This table is connected with the books table by the book_id primary key.

Example 3-39. A query without a CTE

```
SELECT pb.book_id,
       pb.title,
       pb.author,
       s.total_sales
FROM (
    SELECT book_id,
           title,
           author
    FROM books
    WHERE rating >= 4.6
) AS pb
JOIN sales s ON pb.book_id = s.book_id
WHERE s.year = 2022
```

```
ORDER BY s.total_sales DESC
LIMIT 5;
```

This code uses subqueries instead of CTEs to get the top five best-selling books in 2022. Now, let's use CTEs and see how readability improves in Example 3-40.

Example 3-40. A query with a CTE

```
WITH popular_books AS (
    SELECT book_id,
           title,
           author
    FROM books
    WHERE rating >= 4.6
),
best_sellers AS (
    SELECT pb.book_id,
           pb.title,
           pb.author,
           s.total_sales
    FROM popular_books pb
    JOIN sales s ON pb.book_id = s.book_id
    WHERE s.year = 2022
    ORDER BY s.total_sales DESC
    LIMIT 5
)
SELECT *
FROM best_sellers;
```

We have created two levels of CTEs. popular_books is the first CTE, and it selects the book_id, title, and author columns from the books table, filtering for books with a rating of 4.6 or higher. Note that this CTE focuses on a clear responsibility: get only the top-reviewed books.

Then we have best_sellers, the second CTE that builds upon the first CTE. It selects the book_id, title, author, and total_sales columns from popular_books and joins them with the sales table based on the book_id column. Additionally, it filters for sales that occurred in the year 2022, orders the results by total sales in descending order, and limits the output to the top five best-selling books. Again, this CTE focuses on another clear responsibility: getting the top five best sellers based on sales, but only for the books preselected with a rating = 4.6.

Finally, the main query selects all columns from best_sellers and retrieves the combined results. We could apply additional aggregations or filters on this main query. Still, it's a best practice to keep the code simple and focused only on selecting the attributes needed for the final analysis.

One common use case for CTEs is referencing a derived table multiple times within a single query. CTEs eliminate the need for redundant code by allowing the derived table to be defined once and referenced multiple times. This improves query clarity and reduces the chance of errors due to code duplication. To see it in action, let's have a look at Example 3-41, where we will keep using our fictional `sales` table.

Example 3-41. Query with CTE, derived tables

```
WITH high_ratings AS (
    SELECT book_id,
           title,
           rating
    FROM books
    WHERE rating >= 4.5
),
high_sales AS (
    SELECT book_id,
           count(book_id) AS nbr_sales
    FROM sales
    GROUP BY book_id
)
SELECT hr.title,
       hr.rating,
       hs.sales
FROM high_ratings hr
JOIN high_sales hs ON hr.book_id = hs.book_id;
```

As we can see, by using CTEs in this scenario, we eliminate the need for redundant code by defining the derived tables (`high_ratings` and `high_sales`) once. With this strategy, we could reference these tables multiple times within the main query or any subsequent CTE.

Another scenario in which CTEs shine is as an alternative to creating a permanent database view. Sometimes creating a view might not be necessary or feasible. A CTE can be used as a temporary and dynamic substitute in such cases, providing flexibility and simplicity by allowing you to define and reference the result set within the scope of a single query. We can see in Example 3-42 that by using a CTE in this scenario, we avoid the need to create a permanent database view.

Example 3-42. Query with a CTE to avoid permanent creation of a view

```
WITH filtered_books AS (
    SELECT title,
           author
    FROM books
    WHERE rating > 4.0
)
```

```
SELECT *
FROM filtered_books;
```

CTEs are also helpful when the same calculation must be performed across query components. Instead of duplicating the calculation in multiple places, a CTE allows the calculation to be defined once and reused as needed. This promotes code reusability, reduces maintenance efforts, and enhances query performance. Let's start with Example 3-43.

Example 3-43. Query with a CTE to promote code reusability

```
WITH total_sales AS (
    SELECT customer_id,
           SUM(sales_amount) AS total_amount
    FROM sales
    GROUP BY customer_id
)
SELECT ts.customer_id,
       ts.total_amount,
       avg(total_amount) AS avg_amount
FROM total_sales ts;
```

We can see that by using the `total_sales` CTE, the calculation for total sales is defined once in the CTE and reused in the main query for calculating an average, showing the reusability of the first aggregation for another aggregation.

In conclusion, CTEs allow us to tackle complex problems by breaking them into smaller, more manageable pieces. By utilizing CTEs, we can organize and structure our queries more modularly and readably. They offer a solution for unpacking complex problems by allowing us to define intermediate result sets and reference them multiple times within a single query. This eliminates the need for redundant code and promotes code reusability, reducing maintenance efforts and the chance of errors due to code duplication.

Window Functions

Window functions are a helpful tool that improves efficiency and reduces query complexity when analyzing partitions or windows of a dataset. They provide an alternative approach to more complicated SQL concepts, such as derived queries, making it easier to perform advanced analysis operations.

A common use case for window functions is ranking results within a given window, which allows ranking per group or creating relative rankings based on specific criteria. In addition, window functions allow access to data from another row within the same window, which is useful for tasks such as generating reports over a period of time or comparing data between adjacent rows.

At the same time, window functions facilitate aggregation within a given window, simplifying calculations such as running or cumulative totals. Using window functions makes queries more efficient, streamlined, and meaningful, allowing analysts and data scientists to perform sophisticated analyses of data partitions without having to use complicated subqueries or procedural logic. Ultimately, window functions enhance SQL's analytical capabilities and provide a versatile tool for data analysis.

A more practical way of seeing a window function is as a calculation performed on a set of table rows related to the current row. It is similar to an aggregate function but doesn't group rows into a single output row. Instead, each row retains its separate identity. Window functions can access more than just the current row in the query result.

The syntax for window functions, as seen in Example 3-44, includes several components. First, we use the SELECT statement to specify the columns we want to include in the result set. These columns can be any combination of the available columns in the table. Next, we choose the window function we want to use. Standard window functions include SUM(), COUNT(), ROW_NUMBER(), RANK(), LEAD(), LAG(), and many more. We can use these functions to perform calculations or apply aggregate operations to a specific column or set of columns.

Example 3-44. Window function syntax

```
SELECT column1,
       column2,
       ...,
       window_function() OVER (PARTITION BY column1,
               column2,
               ... ORDER BY column3, column4, ...)
FROM table_name;
```

To define the window frame over which the window function is calculated, use the OVER clause. Inside the OVER clause, we have two main components: PARTITION BY and ORDER BY.

The PARTITION BY clause divides the rows into partitions based on one or more columns. The window function is then applied separately to each partition. This is useful when we want to perform calculations on different data groups within the table.

The ORDER BY clause allows you to specify one or more columns to determine the order within each partition. The window function is applied based on this order. It helps define the logical sequence or order of the data that the window function will work with. Combining the PARTITION BY and ORDER BY clauses within the OVER clause lets us control precisely how the window function acts on the data, allowing us to perform calculations or apply aggregate functions to a specific window or subset of rows in the table without changing the entire result set.

One practical example of using window functions is the calculation of a running total. In the given query, the `running_count` column displays the sequential count of books based on their publication year. The window function `ROW_NUMBER() OVER (ORDER BY publication_year)` assigns a row number to each book, ordered by the publication year. This code can be seen in Example 3-45, and the query output is shown in Figure 3-16.

Example 3-45. Window function example

```
SELECT book_id,
       book_title,
       publication_year,
       ROW_NUMBER() OVER (ORDER BY publication_year) AS running_count
FROM books;
```

book_id	book_title	publication_ye...	running_count
1	Python Crash Course	2012	1
2	Learning React Fundamentals	2014	2
4	JavaScript: The Good Parts	2015	3
3	Hands-On Machine Learning with Scikit-Learn, Keras, and TensorFlow	2017	4
5	Data Science for Business	2019	5

Figure 3-16. Running count

With window functions, you can also use aggregate functions like `COUNT()` and `AVG()`, which are introduced in "Aggregating data with GROUP BY" on page 87. These functions can be used similarly to regular aggregations, but they operate on the specified window.

Window functions provide additional functionalities such as `ROW_NUMBER()`, `RANK()`, and `DENSE_RANK()` for numbering and ranking rows, `NTILE()` for determining percentiles or quartiles, and `LAG()` and `LEAD()` for accessing values from previous or subsequent rows.

Table 3-4 summarizes the multiple types of window functions.

Table 3-4. Window functions

Type	Function	Example
Aggregate functions	Aggregate within each window and return a single value for each row	MAX( ), MIN( ), AVG( ), SUM( ), COUNT( )
Ranking functions	Assign a rank or position to each row within the window based on a specified criterion	ROW_NUMBER( ), RANK( ), DENSE_RANK( ), NTILE( ), PER CENT_RANK( ), CUME_DIST( )
Analytics functions	Compute values based on the data in the window without modifying the number of rows	LEAD( ), LAG( ), FIRST_VALUE( ), LAST_VALUE( )

To gain insight into each type of function, we'll utilize the publication_year column as a foundation and experiment with a range of functions.

In the first example, we want to rank the newest to the oldest book by ascending order. Let's have a look at the snippet in Example 3-46.

Example 3-46. Window function—RANK( )

```
SELECT book_id,
       book_title,
       publication_year,
       RANK() OVER (ORDER BY publication_year) AS rank
FROM books;
```

While using the RANK( ) function, one important consideration is that it assigns a unique rank to each row within the window based on the specified criteria, yet, if multiple rows share the same value and are assigned the same rank, the subsequent ranks are skipped. For example, if two books have the same publication_year, the next rank will be incremented by the number of rows with the same rank. If you don't want repeated ranks, where distinct rows share the same rank, you might want to use the ROW_NUMBER( ) instead.

In Example 3-47, we want to bucket our data by the publication_year.

Example 3-47. Window function—NTILE( )

```
SELECT book_id,
       book_title,
       publication_year,
       NTILE(3) OVER (ORDER BY publication_year) AS running_ntile
FROM books;
```

NTILE( ) is commonly used when you want to distribute rows into a specified number of groups evenly or when you need to divide data for further analysis or processing.

This helps with tasks such as data segmentation, percentile calculations, or creating equal-sized samples.

Finally, we want to know the `publication_year` of the previously published book. For that, we use the `LAG()` function, as presented in Example 3-48.

Example 3-48. Window function—LAG()

```
SELECT book_id,
       book_title,
       publication_year,
       LAG(publication_year) OVER (ORDER BY publication_year) AS previous_year
FROM books;
```

The `LAG()` function in SQL allows you to access data from a previous row within the window frame. It retrieves the value of a specified column from a preceding row based on the ordering specified in the `OVER` clause.

SQL for Distributed Data Processing

As enterprises make their way to the cloud, they encounter a common challenge. Their existing relational databases, which are the foundation for critical applications, cannot fully realize the potential of the cloud and are difficult to scale effectively. It is becoming clear that the database itself is emerging as a bottleneck, hindering the speed and efficiency of the transition. As a result, organizations are looking for a solution that combines the reliability of proven relational data stores such as Oracle, SQL Server, Postgres, and MySQL with the scalability and global reach of the cloud.

In an attempt to meet these needs, some companies have turned to NoSQL databases. While these alternatives often meet scalability requirements, they tend to be unsuitable as transactional databases. The reason for this limitation lies in their design, as they were not originally designed to provide true consistency from the ground up. Although specific NoSQL solutions have recently introduced advances to handle certain types of challenges, they are subject to a variety of caveats and ultimately do not provide the necessary isolation levels for critical workloads such as banks or hospitals.

Recognizing the shortcomings of both legacy relational databases and NoSQL storage, companies have turned to a promising solution known as *distributed SQL*. This innovative approach deploys a single logical database across multiple physical nodes, either in a single data center or distributed across multiple data centers as needed. By leveraging the power of a distributed architecture, distributed SQL combines elastic scalability with unwavering resilience.

One of the key benefits of distributed SQL is its ability to scale seamlessly to meet the evolving needs of modern cloud environments. As data volumes grow and user demands increase, organizations can effortlessly add additional nodes to the distributed deployment, allowing the database to expand horizontally. This elastic scaling ensures that performance remains optimal even under heavy workloads and eliminates the limitations often faced by traditional relational databases.

At the same time, distributed SQL provides unparalleled resilience. Because data is distributed across multiple nodes, it is inherently fault-tolerant. If one node fails or becomes unavailable, the system can automatically forward queries to the remaining healthy nodes, ensuring uninterrupted access to critical data. This robust resilience significantly reduces the risk of downtime and data loss and increases the overall reliability of the database. Its distributed nature also enables global coverage and data availability. Organizations can deploy nodes in different geographic regions to strategically place them closer to end users and reduce latency. This geographically distributed approach ensures that data can be accessed quickly from anywhere worldwide, facilitating efficient data delivery and enabling organizations to serve a global user base.

The focus of this book is not on the actual distributed processing engines nor on how they work; rather, we touch upon only the interfaces they expose for us, to interact with. Most of them end up exposing either an API or SDK. However, a few that are more focused on data analytics use SQL as an interface language. In reality, distributed processing and SQL have emerged as a powerful combination, with SQL serving as a convenient and familiar interface for leveraging distributed computing capabilities.

Distributed processing frameworks like Spark, Hadoop, and Dask provide the infrastructure for processing large-scale data across multiple machines or clusters. These frameworks distribute the workload and parallelize computations, enabling faster and more efficient data processing. On the other hand, SQL offers a declarative and intuitive way to express data operations. Users can leverage their SQL skills to harness the power of distributed computing frameworks by integrating SQL as an interface for distributed processing. This approach allows for seamless scalability, efficient data processing, and the ability to handle complex analytics tasks on vast datasets, all while using the familiar SQL syntax.

This combination empowers users to perform advanced data analytics and processing tasks in a straightforward and efficient manner. Examples of this powerful combination are DuckDB, dbt itself, and even FugueSQL. These interfaces act as a layer on top of distributed computing engines, allowing users to write SQL queries and leverage their familiarity with SQL syntax and semantics. DuckDB specifically aims to enable efficient and scalable execution of SQL queries while leveraging the power of distributed computing. It allows users to formulate their analysis and data processing workflows using SQL, while the underlying distributed processing engine handles parallel execution on multiple clusters of machines.

However, despite the existence of these SQL interfaces, they are frequently utilized in conjunction with Python code. Even in the Spark documentation, Python code is still required for various tasks, such as data transformations, DataFrame loading, and post processing after executing the SQL query. This reliance on Python code stems from standard SQL lacking the grammatical constructs to express many of the operations typically performed by users in distributed computing environments. Consequently, SQL alone is often insufficient for expressing comprehensive end-to-end workflows.

Let's dive deeper with an example. Say we need to create a SQL query to understand all the units sold by O'Reilly authors since its inception. This would be a straightforward consultation, as shown in Example 3-49.

Example 3-49. A basic SQL query

```
-- Retrieve top-selling O'Reilly books
SELECT Title,
       UnitsSold
FROM Sales
WHERE Publisher = 'O''Reilly'
ORDER BY UnitsSold DESC
LIMIT 5
```

At this point, the SQL query provides us with the desired aggregated results. However, if we want to perform additional data manipulations or integrate the results with external systems, we usually need to resort to Python or other programming languages.

For instance, we could join the aggregated results with customer demographic data stored in a separate dataset to gain deeper insights. This operation typically requires writing Python code to perform the data merge and post-processing steps. Additionally, if we intend to visualize the results or export them to another format, Python code is again necessary to accomplish these tasks.

A common use case is actually exposing data as an API, which SQL doesn't provide capabilities for. Example 3-50 shows how combining SQL with Python can enable an end-to-end flow.

Example 3-50. A basic FastAPI

```
from fastapi import FastAPI
import duckdb

app = FastAPI()
```

```
@app.get("/top_books")
def get_top_books():
    # Establish a connection to the DuckDB database
    conn = duckdb.connect()

    # Execute the SQL query
    query = '''
        SELECT Title, UnitsSold
        FROM sales
        WHERE Publisher = "O'Reilly"
        ORDER BY UnitsSold DESC
        LIMIT 5
    '''
    result = conn.execute(query)

    # Convert the query result to a list of dictionaries
    books = []
    for row in result:
        book = {
            "title": row[0],
            "units_sold": row[1]
        }
        books.append(book)

    # Return the result as JSON
    return {"top_books": books}
```

We have developed a FastAPI application and set up a single endpoint GET that is accessible via the /top_books route. In simpler terms, an *endpoint* is a specific web address (URL) that we can use to retrieve information from our application. When someone accesses this URL in their web browser or through an application, it triggers the execution of a specific function that we have defined, get_top_books. This function contains the instructions on what to do when someone retrieves information from the /top_books endpoint. Essentially, it's as if we had a specific button that, when pressed, causes our application to perform a specific action, such as providing a list of the top-selling books.

Inside the function, we establish a connection to the DuckDB database by using duckdb.connect(). Then the SQL query is executed using the execute() method on the connection object. The query selects the titles and units sold from the sales table, filtered by the publisher O'Reilly. The result is ordered by units sold in descending order and limited to the top five books.

The query result is then transformed into a list of dictionaries; each dictionary represents a book with its title and units sold. Finally, the result is returned as JSON by wrapping it in a dictionary with the key top_books.

By leveraging both languages, we can create and manipulate data via our friendly interface SQL and expose it as an API via the excellent FastAPI framework. In the following section, we will explore three well-known Python frameworks that abstract access to distributed data processing with a SQL-like interface: DuckDB, FugueSQL, and Polars.

Data Manipulation with DuckDB

When it comes to data processing libraries, most data scientists are very familiar with pandas, the predominant data processing library in Python. Pandas is known for its simplicity, versatility, and ability to manage multiple data formats and sizes. It provides an intuitive user interface for data manipulation. Those who are familiar with SQL appreciate the powerful features that allow users to perform complicated data transformations using a concise syntax. However, in some cases a trade-off must be made between the speed of execution and the ease of use or expressiveness of the tools. This dilemma becomes especially difficult when dealing with large datasets that exceed memory limits or require complex data processing operations.

In such cases, using SQL instead of pandas may be a better solution. This is where DuckDB comes into play. DuckDB combines the strengths of pandas and SQL by providing a fast and efficient SQL query execution engine capable of processing complex queries on large datasets. It integrates seamlessly with pandas DataFrames and allows queries to be executed directly on the DataFrames without the need for frequent data transfers. With DuckDB, data scientists can harness the power of SQL while working with pandas, balancing performance with ease of use.

In addition, we are seeing the trend of some companies deciding to replace Spark as a data processing engine with dbt in combination with DuckDB. Of course, this has to be judged on a case-by-case basis, but it definitely opens the door for analysts to support more complex data transformations that can run ad hoc or automated in a data pipeline.

Installing DuckDB

DuckDB is a remarkably lightweight database engine that works within the host process without external dependencies. Installation is straightforward and requires only a few simple steps.

To install DuckDB, we have several options, depending on the operating system and the type of installation we want to do. For now, let's look at how to install DuckDB by using the pip package manager, as shown in Example 3-51.

Example 3-51. Installing DuckDB

```
pip install duckdb
```

And that's it. We can now use DuckDB in Python just like any other library. Example 3-52 shows how easy it is to load a pandas DataFrame into DuckDB, manipulate the data, and store the result back as a DataFrame.

Example 3-52. Using DuckDB

```
import pandas as pd
import duckdb

mydf = pd.DataFrame({'a' : [1, 2, 3]})
result = duckdb.query("SELECT SUM(a) FROM mydf").to_df()
```

As we can observe, the code imports both the pandas library as pd and the DuckDB library. This allows the code to access the functionalities provided by these libraries. Next, a pandas DataFrame named mydf is created, which consists of a single column a with three rows containing the values [1, 2, 3]. The subsequent line of code executes a SQL query using the DuckDB interface. The query is SELECT SUM(a) FROM mydf, which calculates the sum of values in the a column of the mydf DataFrame. The result of the SQL query is stored in the result variable. By using the to_df() method on the DuckDB query result, the data is converted into a pandas DataFrame. This allows further data manipulation or analysis using the rich set of functions and methods in pandas.

Running SQL queries with DuckDB

Now that we have seen a simple example, let's take a closer look at some of the core features of DuckDB. Unlike traditional systems, DuckDB works directly within the application, eliminating the need for external processes or client/server architectures. This paradigm is closely aligned with SQLite's in-process model and ensures seamless integration and efficient execution of SQL queries.

The importance of this approach also extends to the area of OLAP, a technology that enables sophisticated analysis of large enterprise databases while minimizing the impact on transactional systems. Just like other OLAP-oriented database management systems, DuckDB handles complex analytical workloads by leveraging its innovative vectorized query execution engine. Its column-oriented approach improves performance and scalability, making it an optimal choice for processing analytical queries.

A notable advantage of DuckDB is its self-contained design. Unlike traditional databases, DuckDB doesn't require you to install, update, or maintain any external dependencies or server software. This streamlined, self-contained architecture simplifies deployment and enables rapid data transfer between the application and the database. The result is an exceptionally responsive and efficient system.

Another interesting feature of DuckDB is that it owes its technical capabilities to the hardworking and capable developers who have ensured its stability and maturity. Rigorous testing with millions of queries from leading systems confirms DuckDB's performance and reliability. It adheres to the ACID property principles, supports secondary indexes, and provides robust SQL capabilities, proving its versatility and suitability for demanding analytical workloads.

DuckDB integrates with popular data analysis frameworks such as Python and R, enabling seamless and efficient interactive data analysis. Moreover, it not only supports Python and R, but also provides APIs for C, C++, and Java, which allows it to be used in a variety of programming languages and environments. It is known for its exceptional performance and flexibility, making it well suited for efficiently processing and querying large amounts of data. Running SQL queries with DuckDB is a valuable skill for analysts. Analysts can leverage the power of DuckDB to effortlessly execute complex SQL queries and gain valuable insights from the data.

Now that we've learned more about DuckDB, let's do a step-by-step exercise to illustrate some of the benefits. We'll use the same book analysis query we used earlier. First, import the libraries we need, pandas and DuckDB, as shown in Example 3-53.

Example 3-53. Importing libs in DuckDB

```
import duckdb
import pandas as pd
```

The next step is connecting to DuckDB's in-memory database (Example 3-54).

Example 3-54. Connecting to DuckDB

```
con = duckdb.connect()
```

Let's start by creating a fictitious pandas DataFrame to play with using DuckDB. Execute the code in Example 3-55.

Example 3-55. Loading the data file

```
import pandas as pd

data = [
    {
        'Title': 'Python for Data Analysis',
        'Author': 'Wes McKinney',
        'Publisher': "O'Reilly",
        'Price': 39.99,
        'UnitsSold': 1000
    },
    {
```

```
        'Title': 'Hands-On Machine Learning',
        'Author': 'Aurélien Géron',
        'Publisher': "O'Reilly",
        'Price': 49.99,
        'UnitsSold': 800
    },
    {
        'Title': 'Deep Learning',
        'Author': 'Ian Goodfellow',
        'Publisher': "O'Reilly",
        'Price': 59.99,
        'UnitsSold': 1200
    },
    {
        'Title': 'Data Science from Scratch',
        'Author': 'Joel Grus',
        'Publisher': "O'Reilly",
        'Price': 29.99,
        'UnitsSold': 600
    }
]

df = pd.DataFrame(data)
```

Now this is where we introduce DuckDB to our code. Specifically, we create a DuckDB table from the DataFrame. This is done by registering the DataFrame by using the connection and giving it a name (in this case, sales), as shown in Example 3-56. This allows us to use SQL to query and manipulate the data.

Example 3-56. Creating a DuckDB table

```
con.register('sales', df)
```

With our table available to be queried, we can now perform whatever analytics tasks are needed. For example, we could calculate total revenue for the O'Reilly books, as seen in Example 3-57.

Example 3-57. Applying an analytics query

```
query_total_revenue = """
    SELECT SUM(Price * UnitsSold) AS total_revenue
    FROM sales
    WHERE Publisher = "O'Reilly"
"""
total_revenue = con.execute(query_total_revenue).fetchall()[0][0]
```

In case we are not interested in fetching the results but instead storing the result of the execution as a DataFrame, we can easily call the duckdb df() function right after the execution. Example 3-58 creates the DataFrame df_total_revenue that we can continue manipulating in pandas. This shows how smooth it is to transition between DuckDB's SQL interface and pandas.

Example 3-58. Calling the df() function

```
query_total_revenue = """
    SELECT SUM(price * unitsSold) AS total_revenue
    FROM sales
    WHERE publisher = "O'Reilly"
"""
df_total_revenue = con.execute(query_total_revenue).df()
```

Last but not least, we plot the results by using any available data visualization library in Python, as shown in Example 3-59.

Example 3-59. Data visualization

```
# Create a bar plot
plt.bar("O'Reilly", total_revenue)

# Set the plot title and axis labels
plt.title("Total Revenue for O'Reilly Books")
plt.xlabel("Publisher")
plt.ylabel("Total Revenue")
```

Going back to pandas, it does provide a `pandas.read_sql` command, which allows SQL queries to be executed over an existing database connection and then loaded into pandas DataFrames. While this approach is suitable for lightweight operations, it is not optimized for intensive data processing tasks. Traditional relational database management systems (such as Postgres and MySQL), process rows sequentially, which results in long execution times and significant CPU overhead. DuckDB, on the other hand, was designed specifically for online analytical processing and uses a column vectorized approach. This decision allows DuckDB to effectively parallelize both disk I/O and query execution, resulting in significant performance gains.

Internally, DuckDB uses the Postgres SQL parser and provides full compatibility with SQL functions with Postgres. This uses the SQL functions you are familiar with while taking advantage of DuckDB's efficient column processing. With its focus on performance and efficiency, DuckDB is a compelling solution for running SQL queries and resource-intensive data processing tasks, especially when compared to traditional RDBMSs.

Data Manipulation with Polars

Like DuckDB, Polars also focuses on overcoming the low performance and inefficiency of pandas when dealing with large datasets. Polars is a high-performance

DataFrame library written entirely in Rust, and one of the key advantages is that it does not use an index for the DataFrame. Unlike pandas, which relies on an index that can often be redundant, Polars eliminates the need for an index, simplifying DataFrame operations and making them more intuitive and efficient.

In addition, Polars utilizes Apache Arrow arrays for internal data representation. This is in contrast to pandas, which uses NumPy arrays (pandas 2.0 might fix that). The use of Arrow arrays provides significant benefits in terms of load time, memory usage, and computation. Polars leverages this efficient data representation to handle large datasets effortlessly and perform computations more efficiently.

Another advantage of Polars is its support for parallel operations. Written in Rust, a language known for its focus on performance and concurrency, Polars can leverage multithreading and run multiple operations in parallel. This enhanced parallelization capability allows for faster and more scalable data processing tasks. Finally, it also introduced a powerful optimization technique called *lazy evaluation*. When executing a query in Polars, the library examines and optimizes the query and looks for opportunities to accelerate execution or reduce memory usage. This optimization process improves the overall performance of queries and enhances the efficiency of data processing. In contrast, pandas supports only eager evaluation, where expressions are immediately evaluated as soon as they are encountered.

Data manipulation with Polars is of great value to analytics engineers because of its unique capabilities. Polars was designed with a strong focus on performance and scalability, making it well suited for efficiently processing large amounts of data. Analytics engineers working with large datasets can benefit from its memory-efficient operations and parallel processing support, resulting in faster data transformations. The integration of Polars with the Rust ecosystem also makes it a valuable tool for analysts working with Rust-based data pipelines, providing compatibility and ease of use. The query optimization capabilities, advanced data manipulation features, and support for multiple data sources make Polars a valuable addition to our toolkits, allowing them to tackle complex data tasks with efficiency and flexibility.

Installing Polars

To install Polars, we have several options depending on our operating system and the type of installation we want to do, but let's look at Example 3-60, which presents a simple example of how to install Polars by using the pip package manager.

Example 3-60. Installing Polars

```
pip install polars
```

This will immediately make the Polar library available for us to use within our Python context. Let's test it by executing the code snippet in Example 3-61.

Example 3-61. Polars DataFrame

```
import polars as pl

df = pl.DataFrame(
    {
        'Title': ['Python Crash Course', 'Hands-On Machine Learning',
                  'Data Science for Business', 'Learning SQL',
                  'JavaScript: The Good Parts', 'Clean Code'],
        'UnitsSold': [250, 180, 320, 150, 200, 280],
        'Publisher': ["O'Reilly", "O'Reilly", "O'Reilly", "O'Reilly",
                      "O'Reilly", "O'Reilly"],
    }
)
df
```

We have a DataFrame with three columns: `Title`, `UnitsSold`, and `Publisher`. The `Title` column represents the titles of various O'Reilly books. The `UnitsSold` column indicates the number of units sold for each book, and the `Publisher` column specifies that O'Reilly publishes all the books.

Running SQL queries with Polars

Using Polars, we can perform various operations on this DataFrame to gain insights into O'Reilly's book sales. Whether it's calculating total revenue, analyzing sales by book title or author, or identifying the top-selling books, as shown in Example 3-62, Polars provides a versatile and efficient platform for data analysis.

Example 3-62. Polars DataFrame—top-selling books

```
# Sort the DataFrame by UnitsSold column in descending order
top_selling_books = df.sort(by="UnitsSold", reverse=True)

# Get the top-selling books' title and units sold
top_books_data = top_selling_books.select(["Title",
  "UnitsSold"]).limit(5).to_pandas()

print("Top-selling O'Reilly Books:")
print(top_books_data)
```

As you can see, we sort the DataFrame `df` based on the `UnitsSold` column in descending order by using the `sort` method. Then, we select the top five books using the `limit` method. Finally, we convert the resulting DataFrame to a pandas DataFrame by using `to_pandas()` for easier printing and display.

Although this is interesting and shows the similarity to pandas in terms of syntax, we did mention the capability of Polars to expose its functionalities as SQL. In reality, Polars offers multiple approaches for utilizing SQL capabilities within its framework.

Just like pandas, Polars seamlessly integrates with external libraries such as DuckDB, allowing you to leverage their SQL functionalities. You can import data into Polars from DuckDB or pandas, perform SQL queries on the imported data, and seamlessly combine SQL operations with Polars DataFrame operations. This integration provides a comprehensive data analysis and manipulation ecosystem, offering the best of both SQL and Polars.

In Example 3-63, we create a DuckDB connection by using `duckdb.connect()`. Then, we create a Polars DataFrame `df` with columns for `Title`, `Author`, `Publisher`, `Price`, and `UnitsSold`, representing the O'Reilly books data. We register this DataFrame as a table named `books` in DuckDB by using `con.register()`. Next, we execute a SQL query on the `books` table by using `con.execute()`, selecting the `Title` and `UnitsSold` columns and filtering by `Publisher = "O'Reilly"`. The result is returned as a list of tuples. We convert the result to a Polars DataFrame `result_df` with specified column names.

Example 3-63. Polars DataFrame with DuckDB

```
import polars as pl
import duckdb

# Create a DuckDB connection
con = duckdb.connect()

# Create a Polars DataFrame with O'Reilly books data
df = pl.DataFrame({
    'Title': ['Python for Data Analysis'
            , 'Hands-On Machine Learning'
            , 'Deep Learning'
            , 'Data Science from Scratch'],
    'Author': ['Wes McKinney'
            , 'Aurélien Géron'
            , 'Ian Goodfellow'
            , 'Joel Grus'],
    'Publisher': ["O'Reilly"
            , "O'Reilly"
            , "O'Reilly"
            , "O'Reilly"],
    'Price': [39.99, 49.99, 59.99, 29.99],
    'UnitsSold': [1000, 800, 1200, 600]
})

# Register the DataFrame as a table in DuckDB
con.register('books', df)

# Execute a SQL query on the DuckDB table using Polars
result = con.execute("SELECT Title, UnitsSold FROM books WHERE Publisher =
  'O''Reilly'")
```

```
# Convert the result to a Polars DataFrame
result_df = pl.DataFrame(result, columns=['Title', 'UnitsSold'])

# Print the result
print(result_df)

# Close the DuckDB connection
con.close()
```

Polars also provides native support for executing SQL queries without relying on external libraries. With Polars, you can write SQL queries directly within your code, leveraging the SQL syntax to perform data transformations, aggregations, and filtering operations. This allows you to harness the power of SQL within the Polars framework, thus providing a convenient and efficient approach to working with structured data.

Using SQL in Polars is a simple and straightforward process. You can follow these steps to perform SQL operations on a Polars DataFrame. First, create a SQL context that sets up the environment for executing SQL queries. This context enables you to work with SQL seamlessly within the Polars framework, as shown in Example 3-64.

Example 3-64. Create a SQL context

```
# Create a Polars DataFrame with O'Reilly books data
df = pl.DataFrame({
    'Title': ['Python for Data Analysis'
             , 'Hands-On Machine Learning'
             , 'Deep Learning'
             , 'Data Science from Scratch'],
    'Author': ['Wes McKinney'
              , 'Aurélien Géron'
              , 'Ian Goodfellow'
              , 'Joel Grus'],
    'Publisher': ["O'Reilly"
                 , "O'Reilly"
                 , "O'Reilly"
                 , "O'Reilly"],
    'Price': [39.99, 49.99, 59.99, 29.99],
    'UnitsSold': [1000, 800, 1200, 600]
})

# Create the SQL Context
sql = pl.SQLContext()
```

Example 3-65 demonstrates the next step: registering the DataFrame you want to query.

Example 3-65. Register the DataFrame

```
# Register the DataFrame in the context
sql.register('df', df)
```

By providing a name for the DataFrame, you establish a reference point for your SQL queries. This registration step ensures that the DataFrame is associated with a recognizable identifier.

Once the DataFrame is registered, you can execute SQL queries on it by using the `query()` function provided by Polars. This function takes the SQL query as input and returns a Polars DataFrame as the result. This DataFrame contains the data that matches the criteria specified in the SQL query. Let's take a look at Example 3-66.

Example 3-66. Run analytics queries

```
# Run your SQL query
result_df = sql.execute(
    """
    select
      *
    from df
    where Title = 'Python for Data Analysis'
    """
).collect()
```

By integrating SQL with Polars, data professionals with deep SQL knowledge can easily leverage the power and efficiency of Polars. They can leverage their existing SQL skills and apply them directly to their data analysis and manipulation tasks within the Polars framework. This seamless integration allows users to take advantage of the library's optimized query execution engine while using the familiar SQL syntax they are used to.

Data Manipulation with FugueSQL

Fugue is a powerful unified interface for distributed computing that allows users to seamlessly run Python, pandas, and SQL code on popular distributed frameworks like Spark, Dask, and Ray. With Fugue, users can realize the full potential of these distributed systems with minimal code changes.

The main use cases for Fugue revolve around parallelizing and scaling existing Python and pandas code to run effortlessly across distributed frameworks. By seamlessly transitioning code to Spark, Dask, or Ray, users can take advantage of these systems' scalability and performance benefits without having to rewrite extensive code.

Relevant to our discussion is the fact that Fugue provides a unique feature called FugueSQL that allows users to define end-to-end workflows on pandas, Spark, and Dask DataFrames through an advanced SQL interface. It combines familiar SQL syntax with the ability to call Python code. This gives users a powerful tool to streamline and automate their data processing workflows.

FugueSQL offers a variety of benefits that can be leveraged in multiple scenarios, including parallel code execution as part of the overall goals of the Fugue project or standalone querying on a single machine. Whether we are working with distributed systems or performing data analysis on a local machine, it allows us to efficiently query our DataFrames.

Installing Fugue and FugueSQL

We have several options to install Fugue, depending on our operating system and type of installation. Example 3-67 uses `pip install`.

Example 3-67. Install Fugue

```
pip install fugue
```

Fugue offers various installation extras that enhance its functionality and support different execution engines and data processing libraries. These installation extras include the following:

sql
> This extra enables FugueSQL support. While the non-SQL functionalities of Fugue still work without this extra, installing it is necessary if you intend to use FugueSQL. To achieve that, execute the code snippet in Example 3-68.
>
> *Example 3-68. Install FugueSQL*
>
> ```
> pip install "fugue[sql]"
> ```

spark
> Installing this extra adds support for Spark as the ExecutionEngine in Fugue. With this extra, users can leverage the capabilities of Spark to execute their Fugue workflows. To add this extra, run the code in Example 3-69.
>
> *Example 3-69. Install FugueSpark*
>
> ```
> pip install "fugue[spark]"
> ```

dask

> This extra enables support for Dask as the ExecutionEngine in Fugue. By installing this extra, users can take advantage of Dask's distributed computing capabilities within the Fugue framework.

ray

> Installing this extra adds support for Ray as the ExecutionEngine in Fugue. With this extra, users can leverage Ray's efficient task scheduling and parallel execution capabilities in their Fugue workflows.

duckdb

> This extra enables support for DuckDB as the ExecutionEngine in Fugue. By installing this extra, users can utilize DuckDB's blazing fast in-memory database for efficient query execution within the Fugue framework.

polars

> Installing this extra provides support for Polars DataFrames and extensions using the Polars library. With this extra, users can leverage the features and functionalities of Polars for data processing within Fugue.

ibis

> Enabling this extra allows users to integrate Ibis into Fugue workflows. Ibis provides an expressive and powerful interface for working with SQL-like queries, and by installing this extra, users can incorporate Ibis functionality into their Fugue workflows.

cpp_sql_parser

> Enabling this extra utilizes the CPP (C++) antlr parser for Fugue SQL, which offers significantly faster parsing compared to the pure Python parser. While prebuilt binaries are available for the main Python versions and platforms, this extra may require a C++ compiler to build on-the-fly for other platforms.

We can actually install several of the previous extras in a single `pip install` command. In Example 3-70, we install `duckdb`, `polars`, and `spark` extras with Fugue in a single command.

Example 3-70. Install multiple Fugue extras

```
pip install "fugue[duckdb,spark,polars]"
```

Another interesting extra relates to notebooks. FugueSQL has a notebook extension for both Jupyter Notebooks and JupyterLab. This extension provides syntax highlighting. We can run another `pip install` to install the extension (Example 3-71).

Example 3-71. Install the notebook extension

```
pip install fugue-jupyter

fugue-jupyter install startup
```

The second command, `fugue-jupyter install startup`, registers Fugue in the startup script of Jupyter so that it is available for you whenever you open Jupyter Notebooks or JupyterLab.

If you have installed Fugue and use JupyterLab, the `%%fsql` cell magic is automatically registered by default. This means you can use cell magic directly in your JupyterLab environment without any additional steps. However, if you are using Classic Jupyter Notebooks or the `%%fsql` cell magic is not registered, you can enable it by using the command in Example 3-72 in your notebook.

Example 3-72. Enable notebooks extensions

```
from fugue_notebook import setup
setup(is_lab=True)
```

Running SQL queries with FugueSQL

FugueSQL is designed specifically for SQL users who want to work with Python DataFrames such as pandas, Spark, and Dask. FugueSQL provides a SQL interface that parses and runs on the underlying engine of your choice. This is especially beneficial for data scientists and analysts who prefer to focus on defining logic and data transformations rather than dealing with execution complexity.

But it is also tailored to the needs of SQL enthusiasts, giving them the ability to define end-to-end workflows with SQL across popular data processing engines such as pandas, Spark, and Dask. This way, SQL enthusiasts can leverage their SQL skills and easily orchestrate complex data pipelines without switching between different tools or languages.

Fugue offers a practical solution for data scientists who work primarily with pandas and want to leverage the capabilities of Spark or Dask to process large datasets. Using Fugue, they can effortlessly scale their pandas code and seamlessly transition to Spark or Dask, realizing the potential of distributed computing with minimal effort. For example, if someone uses FugueSQL with Spark, the framework will use SparkSQL and PySpark to execute the queries. Even though FugueSQL supports nonstandard SQL commands, it is important to emphasize that Fugue remains fully compatible with standard SQL syntax. This compatibility ensures that SQL users can seamlessly switch to Fugue and leverage their existing SQL knowledge and skills without major customizations or complications.

Finally, Fugue is proving to be a valuable asset for data teams working on Big Data projects that often face code maintenance issues. By adopting Fugue, these teams can benefit from a unified interface that simplifies the execution of code across distributed computing platforms, ensuring consistency, efficiency, and maintainability throughout the development process.

Example 3-73 shows an end-to-end example using FugueSQL.

Example 3-73. FugueSQL full example

```
import pandas as pd
from pyspark.sql import SparkSession
from fugue.api import fugue_sql_flow

data = [
    {
        'Title': 'Python for Data Analysis',
        'Author': 'Wes McKinney',
        'Publisher': "OReilly",
        'Price': 39.99,
        'UnitsSold': 1000
    },
    {
        'Title': 'Hands-On Machine Learning',
        'Author': 'Aurélien Géron',
        'Publisher': "OReilly",
        'Price': 49.99,
        'UnitsSold': 800
    },
    {
        'Title': 'Deep Learning',
        'Author': 'Ian Goodfellow',
        'Publisher': "OReilly",
        'Price': 59.99,
        'UnitsSold': 1200
    },
    {
        'Title': 'Data Science from Scratch',
        'Author': 'Joel Grus',
        'Publisher': "OReilly",
        'Price': 29.99,
        'UnitsSold': 600
    }
]

# Save the data as parquet
df = pd.DataFrame(data)
df.to_parquet("/tmp/df.parquet")

# Fugue with pandas Engine
import fugue.api as fa
```

```
query = """
LOAD "/tmp/df.parquet"

SELECT Author, COUNT(Title) AS NbBooks
  GROUP BY Author
  PRINT
"""

pandas_df = fa.fugue_sql(query, engine="pandas")

# Fugue with Spark Engine
import fugue.api as fa

query = """
LOAD "/tmp/df.parquet"

SELECT Author, COUNT(Title) AS NbBooks
  GROUP BY Author
  PRINT
"""

spark_df = fa.fugue_sql(query, engine="spark")


# Fugue with DuckDB
import fugue.api as fa
import duckdb

query = """
df = LOAD "/tmp/df.parquet"

res = SELECT *
        FROM df
        WHERE Author = 'Wes McKinney'

SAVE res OVERWRITE "/tmp/df2.parquet"
"""

fa.fugue_sql(query, engine="duckdb")

with duckdb.connect() as conn:
        df2 = conn.execute("SELECT * FROM '/tmp/df2.parquet'").fetchdf()
        print(df2.head())
```

This example creates a FugueSQLWorkflow instance. We register the pandas Data-
Frame df as a table by using the workflow.df() method. Then, we write SQL queries
within the workflow.run() method to perform various operations on the data. This
FugueSQLWorkflow is a class provided by the Fugue library that serves as the entry
point for executing FugueSQL code. It allows us to define and execute SQL queries

on various data sources, as mentioned before, without the need for explicit data transformations or handling the underlying execution engines.

The example demonstrates three queries:

- Calculating the total revenue for O'Reilly books
- Calculating the average price of O'Reilly books
- Retrieving the top-selling O'Reilly books

The results are stored in the `result` object, and we can access the data by using the `first()` and `collect()` methods.

Finally, we print the results to the console. Note that we use two single quotes (") to escape the single quote within the SQL queries for the Publisher name `"O'Reilly"` to ensure proper syntax.

One might wonder if FugueSQL is an alternative to or an evolution of pandas, which has pandasql. We would argue that while pandasql supports only SQLite as a backend, FugueSQL supports multiple local backends, such as pandas, DuckDB, Spark, and SQLite. When using FugueSQL with the pandas backend, SQL queries are directly translated into pandas operations, eliminating the need for data transfer. Similarly, DuckDB has excellent pandas support, resulting in minimal overhead for data transfer. Therefore, both pandas and DuckDB are recommended backends for local data processing in FugueSQL. All in all, FugueSQL is a great framework to take advantage of SQL syntax, with added capabilities for distributed processing and data manipulation at scale.

In general, Fugue, DuckDB, and pandas are powerful tools that offer efficient data processing capabilities. However, regardless of the technology used, it is crucial to recognize that proper data modeling is fundamental for successful scalability. Without a well-designed data model, any system will struggle to handle large-scale data processing efficiently.

The foundation of a robust data model ensures that data is structured, organized, and optimized for analysis and manipulation. By understanding the relationships between data entities, defining appropriate data types, and establishing efficient indexing strategies, we can create a scalable architecture that maximizes performance and enables seamless data operations across platforms and tools. Therefore, while Fugue, DuckDB, and pandas contribute to efficient data processing, the importance of proper data modeling cannot be overstated for achieving scalability. That is also one of the main reasons we covered data modeling in Chapter 2.

Bonus: Training Machine Learning Models with SQL

This header might make you feel that we are pushing the limits with SQL-like capabilities, but the reality is that thanks to a very specific library, *dask-sql*, it is possible to use the Python machine learning ecosystem in SQL.

Dask-sql is a recently developed SQL query engine, in the experimental phase, that builds upon the Python-based Dask distributed library. It offers the unique capability to seamlessly integrate Python and SQL, which gives users the ability to perform distributed and scalable computations. This innovative library opens up opportunities to leverage the strengths of both Python and SQL for data analysis and processing.

We can run a `pip install` to install the extension, as shown in Example 3-74.

Example 3-74. Install dask-sql

```
pip install dask-sql
```

In Example 3-75, we are creating an instance of a `Context` class with the line `c = Context()`. With it, we are initializing a new execution context for SQL queries. This context can be used to execute SQL queries against our data and perform operations like filtering, aggregating, and joining, but it can also apply a special type of command provided by Dask to train and test machine learning models.

Example 3-75. Import the context from dask_sql

```
from dask_sql import Context

c = Context()
```

We now have all the tools to load a dataset to work with. In Example 3-76, we use the `read_csv()` function from Dask and employ it to read the Iris dataset (*https://oreil.ly/vt4-s*). Once the data is loaded, we can access and manipulate the data as a Dask DataFrame.

The next step is registering the loaded Dask DataFrame (`df`) as a table named `iris` in the *dask-sql* `Context`. The `create_table` method of the `Context` class is used to register the table. Once this step is completed, we are able to query the data by using SQL syntax.

Example 3-76. Load the data as a Dask DataFrame and register it as a table

```
# Load data: Download the iris dataset
df = dd.read_csv('https://datahub.io/machine-learning/iris/r/iris.csv')
```

```
# Register a Dask table
c.create_table("iris", df)
```

Let's run a simple select using the `sql()` function of our *dask-sql* Context object, in Example 3-77, and write our SQL query as a parameter.

Example 3-77. Access the dask-sql table

```
# Test accessing the data
c.sql("""
    select * from iris
""")
```

With the data ready, we can now use the training components to train a machine learning model. For that, we start by using the `CREATE OR REPLACE MODEL` statement, which is a *dask-sql* extension that allows you to define and train machine learning models within a SQL context.

In this case, the clustering model is named `clustering`, and the model is created using the KMeans algorithm from the *scikit-learn* library, which is a popular unsupervised learning algorithm for clustering data points. Interestingly enough, *dask-sql* allows us to use model classes from third-party libraries such as *scikit-learn*. The `n_clusters` parameter is set to 3, indicating that the algorithm should identify three clusters in the data.

In Example 3-78, we show that the training data for the model is obtained from the `iris` table registered in the `c` context. The `SELECT` statement specifies the features used for training, which include the `sepallength`, `sepalwidth`, `petallength`, and `petalwidth` columns from the `iris` table.

Example 3-78. Create our clustering model

```
# Train: Create our clustering model using sklearn.cluster.KMeans algorithm
c.sql("""
  CREATE OR REPLACE MODEL clustering WITH (
      model_class = 'sklearn.cluster.KMeans',
      wrap_predict = True,
      n_clusters = 3
  ) AS (
      SELECT sepallength, sepalwidth, petallength, petalwidth
      FROM iris
  )
""")
```

We can now validate that our model was actually created by running a SHOW MODELS command (Example 3-79), which resembles the often-used SHOW TABLES from traditional SQL engines. While the latter shows all tables in a certain schema of a database, the former lists all models created and available to be used in a *dask-sql* context.

Example 3-79. Show the list of models

```
# Show the list of models which are trained and stored in the context.
c.sql("""
  SHOW MODELS
""")
```

Another interesting command is DESCRIBE MODEL *MODEL_NAME* (Example 3-80), which shows all the hyperparameters used to train this model.

Example 3-80. Get all hyperparameters of a certain model

```
# To get the hyperparameters of the trained MODEL
c.sql("""
  DESCRIBE MODEL clustering
""")
```

In Example 3-81, we demonstrate one of the most captivating commands within *dask-sql*—the PREDICT command. It uses the recently created clustering model to predict the cluster classes for the rows of the df DataFrame. The SELECT statement with PREDICT applies trained machine learning models to new data points from a certain table, within a SQL context.

In this case, the PREDICT command is used to apply the clustering model to the first 100 rows of the iris table. The MODEL clause specifies the name of the model to be used, which is clustering. The SELECT statement within the PREDICT command specifies the features to be used for prediction, which are the same features used during the model training step, as demonstrated in Example 3-81.

Example 3-81. Make predictions

```
''' Predict: Test the recently created model by applying
the predictions to the rows of the df—
in this case assign each observation to a cluster'''
c.sql("""
  SELECT * FROM PREDICT (
      MODEL clustering,
      SELECT sepallength, sepalwidth, petallength, petalwidth FROM iris
      LIMIT 100
  )
""")
```

Another interesting capability of *dask-sql* is its experiments component. It runs an experiment to attempt different hyperparameter values for the clustering model by using the CREATE EXPERIMENT statement.

In Example 3-82, the experiment is named first_experiment. It uses the Grid SearchCV class from *scikit-learn*, which is a popular technique for hyperparameter tuning. The hyperparameter being tuned in this case is the number of clusters (n_clusters), and this is only for showing the capability. The tune_parameters parameter specifies the range of values to try for the n_clusters hyperparameter. In this example, the experiment will try three values (2, 3, and 4), meaning the number of clusters we expect to obtain.

In a real-world scenario of a machine learning project, we should focus on selecting the most relevant hyperparameters of our model. This depends on the problem being a classification or regression task and the types of algorithms used.

Example 3-82. Hyperparameter tuning

```
# Hyperparameter tuning: Run an experiment to try different parameters
c.sql("""
  CREATE EXPERIMENT first_experiment WITH (
    model_class = 'sklearn.cluster.KMeans',
    experiment_class = 'GridSearchCV',
    tune_parameters = (n_clusters = ARRAY [2, 3, 4]),
    experiment_kwargs = (n_jobs = -1),
    target_column = 'target'
  ) AS (
      SELECT sepallength, sepalwidth, petallength, petalwidth, class AS target
      FROM iris
      LIMIT 100
  )
""")
```

Last but not least, we have an EXPORT MODEL statement, as seen in Example 3-83. In this case, the model is exported in the pickle format by using the format parameter set to pickle. Pickle is a Python-specific binary serialization format that allows you to save and load Python objects.

The location parameter specifies the path and filename where the exported model file should be saved. In this example, the model is saved in the current directory with the filename *clustering.pkl*.

Example 3-83. Export the model as a pickle file

```
# Export the model: Export as a pickle file to be used in other contexts
c.sql("""
  -- for pickle model serialization
```

```
EXPORT MODEL clustering WITH (
    format ='pickle',
    location = './clustering.pkl'
)
""")
```

Overall, *dask-sql* is a powerful and promising tool for machine learning purposes, offering a SQL interface for data manipulation and machine learning operations on large datasets. With *dask-sql*, we can leverage the familiar SQL syntax to query and transform data, as well as train and evaluate machine learning models by using popular libraries like *scikit-learn*. It allows us to register data tables, apply SQL queries for data preprocessing, and create and train machine learning models within a SQL context.

However, we must highlight that *dask-sql* is still in an experimental phase, and although it's a fascinating tool for SQL lovers who want to explore the machine learning space, it must be used with caution as it grows and matures.

Summary

As we conclude this chapter, let's consider the significant journey of databases and SQL and their undeniable influence on our past and future. SQL remains a reliable and steadfast component in the constantly advancing data landscape, combining proven techniques with modern analytical insights, and thus ensuring an optimistic future.

Our exploration has shown that from clear table structures to sophisticated models that cater to pressing business requirements, SQL's significance continues to endure, with databases experiencing ongoing innovation.

However, it is worth acknowledging that the effectiveness of these tools depends on the skill of those using them. Ongoing education and flexibility are crucial for analytics engineers. SQL, database management, and data analysis fields are constantly evolving. To succeed, we must stay updated, maintain inquisitiveness, and face challenges confidently.

As the data landscape continues to expand rapidly, the distinctions among roles in data engineering, analysis, and data science are becoming more pronounced. While there are certainly areas where these roles overlap and blend, data's sheer volume and complexity drive the need for specialized skills and expertise. This chapter's conclusion is a reminder that the field of analytics engineering is both extensive and captivating. In every query and database, there lies a fresh opportunity for exploration and innovation, driven by the growing demand for specialized roles to navigate the complexities of today's data landscape.

## CHAPTER 4

Data Transformation with dbt

The primary purpose of dbt is to help you *transform* the data of your data platforms in an easy and integrated way by simply writing SQL statements. When we place dbt in an ELT workflow, it matches the activities during the transformation stage, providing you with additional components—such as version control, documentation, tests, or automated deployment—that simplify the overall work of a data specialist. Does this remind you of the actual activities of an analytics engineer? Well, that's because dbt is one of the modern tools that defines what analytics engineers do, giving them the instruments integrated with the platform, which reduces the need to set up additional services to answer specific problems and decreases the overall system complexity.

dbt supports the tasks described for an analytics engineer, empowering them to run the code in their data platform collaboratively for a single source of truth for metrics and business definitions. It promotes central and modular analytics code, leveraging DRY code with Jinja templating language, macros, or packages. In parallel, dbt also provides the security that we typically find in software engineering best practices, such as *collaborate* on data models, *version* them, and *test* and *document* your queries before safely *deploying* them to production, with *monitoring* and *visibility*.

We've provided a thorough introduction to dbt. However, within this chapter, we will delve even deeper into the specifics of dbt and clarify its importance in the world of data analytics. We will discuss the dbt design philosophy, the principles behind this transformation tool, and the data lifecycle with dbt at its core, presenting how dbt transforms raw data into structured models for easy consumption. We will explore the dbt project structure by outlining its various features, such as building models, documentation, and tests, as well as detailing other dbt artifacts, such as YAML files. By the end of this chapter, you will have a comprehensive understanding of dbt and its capabilities, which will enable you to implement it effectively in your data analytics workflow.

dbt Design Philosophy

As data engineering and analytics workflows become increasingly complex, tools that streamline the process while maintaining data quality and reliability are essential. dbt has emerged as a concentrated solution with a well-defined design philosophy that underpins its approach to data modeling and analytics engineering.

In summary, dbt design philosophy relies on the following points:

Code-centric approach
At the core of dbt's design philosophy is a code-centric approach to data modeling and transformation. Instead of relying on GUI-based interfaces or manual SQL scripts, dbt encourages users to define data transformations using code. This shift to code-driven development promotes collaboration, version control, and automation.

Modularity for reusability
dbt promotes modularity, allowing data practitioners to create reusable code components. Models, macros, and tests can be organized into packages, which facilitates code maintenance and scalability. This modular approach aligns with best practices and enhances code reusability.

Transformations as SQL SELECT statements
dbt models are defined as SQL SELECT statements, making them accessible to analysts and engineers with SQL skills. This design choice simplifies development and ensures that data modeling closely follows SQL best practices.

Declarative language
dbt uses a declarative language for defining data transformations. Analysts specify the desired outcome, and dbt handles the underlying implementation. This abstraction reduces the complexity of writing complex SQL code and enhances readability.

Incremental builds
Efficiency is a key focus of dbt's design. It supports incremental builds, which allows data engineers to update only the affected pieces of the data pipeline rather than reprocessing the entire dataset. This accelerates development and reduces processing time.

Documentation as code

dbt advocates for documenting data models and transformations as code. Descriptions, explanations, and metadata are stored alongside the project code, making it easier for team members to understand and collaborate effectively.

Data quality, testing, and validation

dbt places a significant emphasis on data testing. It provides a testing framework that enables analysts to define data quality checks and validation rules. This includes data reliability and quality throughout the pipeline, thus ensuring that data meets predefined criteria and adheres to business rules.

Version control integration

Seamless integration with version control systems like Git is a fundamental aspect of dbt. This feature enables collaborative development, change tracking, and the ability to roll back changes, ensuring that data pipelines remain under version control.

Native integration with data platforms

dbt is designed to work seamlessly with popular data platforms such as Snowflake, BigQuery, and Redshift. It leverages the native capabilities of these platforms for scalability and performance.

Open source and extensible

dbt is an open source tool with a thriving community. Users can extend its functionality by creating custom macros and packages. This extensibility allows organizations to tailor dbt to their specific data needs.

Separation of transformation and loading

dbt separates the transformation and loading steps in the data pipeline. Data is transformed within dbt and then loaded into the data platform.

In essence, dbt's design philosophy is rooted in creating a collaborative, code-centric, and modular environment for data engineers, analysts, and data scientists to efficiently transform data, ensure data quality, and generate valuable insights. dbt empowers organizations to harness the full potential of their data by simplifying the complexities of data modeling and analytics engineering.

dbt Data Flow

Figure 4-1 shows the big picture of a data flow. It identifies where dbt and its features fit in the overall data landscape.

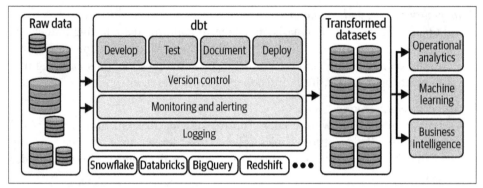

Figure 4-1. Typical data flow with dbt that helps you transform your data from Big-Query, Snowflake, Databricks, and Redshift, among others (see the dbt documentation for supported data platforms (https://oreil.ly/9b8dG))

As mentioned, the primary purpose of dbt is to help you *transform* the data of your data platforms, and for that, dbt offers two tools for achieving that goal:

- dbt Cloud
- dbt Core, an open source CLI tool, maintained by dbt Labs, that you can set up on your managed environments or run locally

Let's look at an example to see how dbt works in real life and what it can do. Imagine that we are working on a pipeline that periodically extracts data from a data platform such as BigQuery. Then, it transforms the data by combining tables (Figure 4-2).

We'll combine the first two tables into one, applying several transformation techniques, such as data cleaning or consolidation. This phase takes place in dbt, so we'll need to create a dbt project to accomplish this merge. We will get there, but let's first get familiar with dbt Cloud and how to set up our working environment.

> For this book, we will use dbt Cloud to write our code since it is the fastest and most reliable way to start with dbt, from development to writing tests, scheduling, deployments, and investigating data models. Also, dbt Cloud runs on top of dbt Core, so while we work on dbt Cloud, we will become familiar with the same commands used in dbt Core's CLI tool.

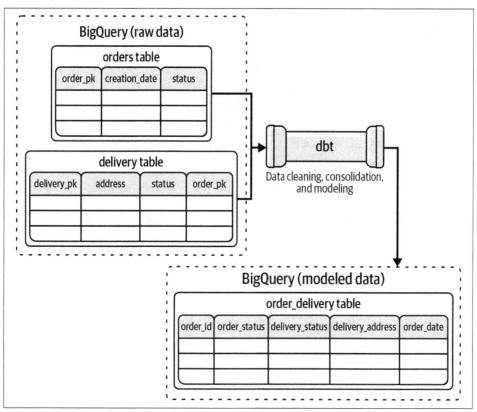

Figure 4-2. Data pipeline use case with dbt

dbt Cloud

dbt Cloud is a cloud-based version of dbt that offers a wide range of features and services to write and productize your analytics code. dbt Cloud allows you to sched-ule your dbt jobs, monitor their progress, and view logs and metrics in real time. dbt Cloud also provides advanced collaboration features, including version control, testing, and documentation. Moreover, dbt Cloud integrates with various cloud data warehouses, such as Snowflake, BigQuery, and Redshift, which allows you to easily transform your data.

You can use dbt Core with the majority of the stated features, but it will require configuration and setup on your infrastructure, similar to running your own server or an Amazon Elastic Compute Cloud (EC2) instance for tools like Airflow. This means you'll need to maintain and manage it autonomously, similar to managing a virtual machine (VM) on EC2.

In contrast, dbt Cloud operates like a managed service, similar to Amazon Managed Workflows for Apache Airflow (MWAA). It offers convenience and ease of use, as many operational aspects are handled for you, allowing you to focus more on your analytics tasks and less on infrastructure management.

Setting Up dbt Cloud with BigQuery and GitHub

There is nothing better than learning a specific technology by practicing it, so let's set up the environment we will use to apply our knowledge. To start, let's first register for a dbt account (*https://oreil.ly/OGGji*).

After registering, we will land on the Complete Project Setup page (Figure 4-3).

Figure 4-3. dbt landing page to complete the project setup

This page has multiple sections to properly configure our dbt project, including connections to our desired data platform and to our code repository. We will use BigQuery as the data platform and GitHub to store our code.

The first step in BigQuery is to set up a new project. In GCP (*https://oreil.ly/EQBXK*), search for Create a Project in the search bar and click it (Figure 4-4).

Create a Project
Search
PRODUCTS & PAGES
Create a Project
IAM & Admin
Manage Resources
IAM & Admin
Welcome
DOCUMENTATION & TUTORIALS

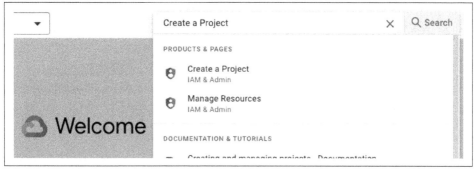

Figure 4-4. BigQuery project setup, step 1

A screen similar to Figure 4-5 is presented, where you can set up the project. We've named it *dbt-analytics-engineer*.

Google Cloud
Search for resources, docs, products, and more
New Project
Project name *
dbt-analytics-engineer
Project ID: dbt-analytics-engineer-365317. It cannot be changed later. EDIT
Organization *
shopai.co
Select an organization to attach it to a project. This selection can't be changed later.
Location *
shopai.co
BROWSE
Parent organization or folder
CREATE
CANCEL

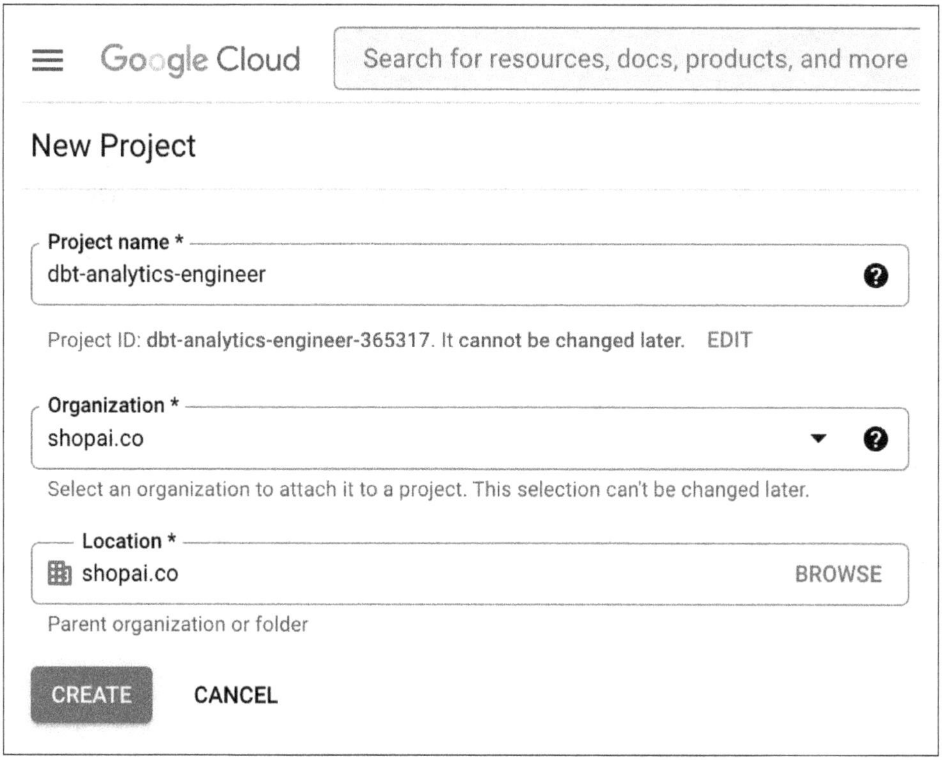

Figure 4-5. BigQuery project setup, step 2

After configuration, go into your BigQuery IDE—you can use the search bar again. It should look similar to Figure 4-6.

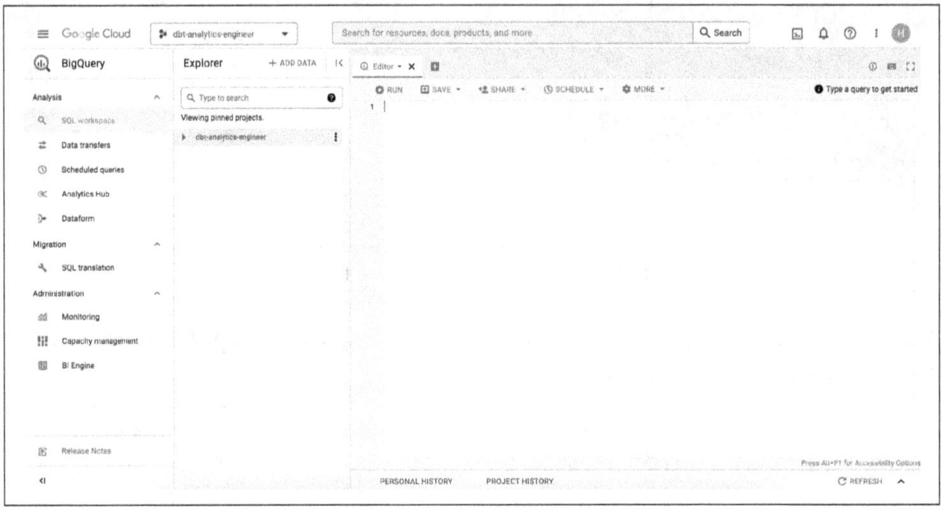

Figure 4-6. BigQuery IDE

Finally, test the dbt public dataset to ensure that BigQuery is working correctly. For that, copy the code in Example 4-1 into BigQuery and then click Run.

Example 4-1. dbt public datasets in BigQuery

```
select * from `dbt-tutorial.jaffle_shop.customers`;
select * from `dbt-tutorial.jaffle_shop.orders`;
select * from `dbt-tutorial.stripe.payment`;
```

If you see the page in Figure 4-7, then you did it!

> Since we've executed three queries simultaneously, we won't see the output results. For that, click View Results to inspect the query output individually.

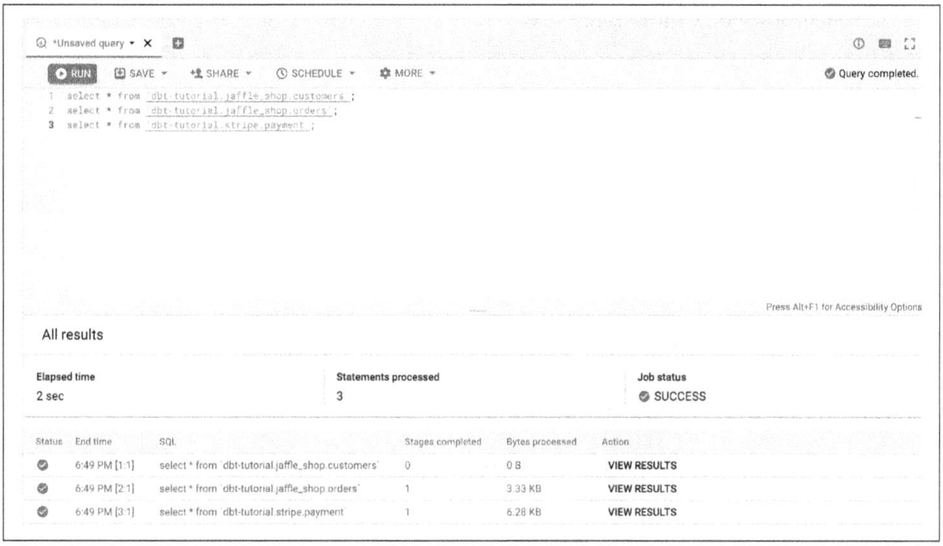

Figure 4-7. BigQuery dataset output

Now let's connect dbt with BigQuery and execute these queries inside the dbt IDE. To let dbt connect to your data platform, you'll need to generate a *keyfile*, similar to using a database username and password in most other data platforms.

Go to the BigQuery console (*https://oreil.ly/EQBXK*). Before proceeding with the next steps, make sure you select the new project in the header. If you do not see your account or project, click your profile picture to the right and verify that you are using the correct email account:

1. Go to IAM & Admin and select Service Accounts.

2. Click Create Service Account.

3. In the name field, type **dbt-user** and then click Create and Continue.

4. On "Grant this service account access to project" select BigQuery Admin in the role field. Click Continue.

5. Leave fields blank in the "Grant users access to this service account" section and click Done.

The screen should look like Figure 4-8.

Figure 4-8. BigQuery Service Accounts screen

Moving on, proceed with the remaining steps:

6. Click the service account that you just created.

7. Select Keys.

8. Click Add Key; then select "Create new key."

9. Select JSON as the key type; then click Create.

10. You should be prompted to download the JSON file. Save it locally to an easy-to-remember spot with a clear filename—for example, *dbt-analytics-engineer-keys.json*.

Now let's get back into the dbt Cloud for the final setup:

11. On the project setup screen, give a more verbose name to your project. In our case, we chose *dbt-analytics-engineer*.

12. On the "Choose a warehouse" screen, click the BigQuery icon and Next.

13. Upload the JSON file generated previously. To do this, click the "Upload a Service Account JSON file" button, visible in Figure 4-9.

Last but not least, after you upload the file, apply the remaining step:

14. Go to the bottom and click "test." If you see "Your test completed successfully," as Figure 4-10 shows, you're good to go! Now click Next. On the other hand, if the test fails, there's a good chance you've encountered an issue with your BigQuery credentials. Try to regenerate them again.

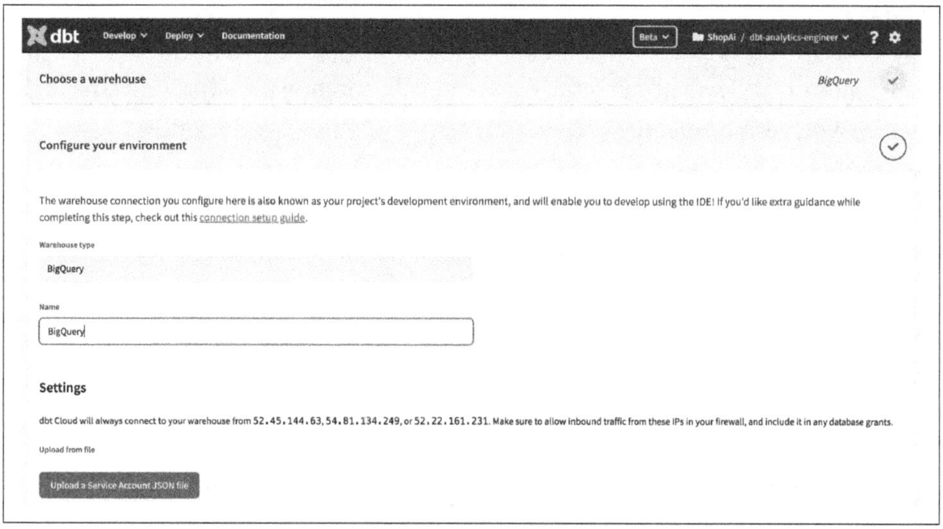

Figure 4-9. dbt Cloud, submit BigQuery Service Account screen

Figure 4-10. dbt and BigQuery connection test

The final step is setting up GitHub, but first, let's understand what we are discussing here. GitHub is a popular version control platform that hosts Git repositories that allow you to track changes in your code and collaborate with others effectively. To correctly use Git, sticking to these principles and best practices is essential:

Commit often, commit early
> Make frequent commits, even for small changes. This helps in tracking your progress and simplifies debugging. Each commit should represent a logical change or feature.

Use meaningful commit messages
> Write concise and descriptive commit messages. A good commit message should explain what was changed and why it was changed.

Follow a branching strategy
> Use branches for different features, bug fixes, or development tasks.

Pull before push
> Always pull the latest changes from the remote repository (e.g., `git pull`) before pushing your changes. This reduces conflicts and ensures that your changes are based on the latest code.

Review code before committing
> If your team practices code reviews, make sure to review and test your changes before committing. It helps maintain code quality.

Use .gitignore
> Create a *.gitignore* file to specify files and directories that should be excluded from version control (e.g., build artifacts, temporary files).

Use atomic commits
> Keep commits focused on a single, specific change. Avoid mixing unrelated changes in the same commit.

Rebase instead of merge
> Use `git rebase` to integrate changes from a feature branch into the main branch instead of traditional merging. This results in a cleaner commit history.

Keep commit history clean
> Avoid committing "work in progress" or debugging statements. Use tools like `git stash` to temporarily save unfinished work.

Use tags
> Create tags, such as version tags, to mark important points in your project's history, like releases or major milestones.

Collaborate and communicate
Communicate with your team about Git workflows and conventions. Establish guidelines for handling issues, pull requests, and conflict resolution.

Know how to undo changes
Learn how to revert commits (`git revert`), reset branches (`git reset`), and recover lost work (`git reflog`) when needed.

Document
Document your project's Git workflow and conventions in a *README* or contributing guidelines to effectively onboard new team members.

Use backup and remote repositories
Regularly back up your Git repositories and use remote repositories like GitHub for collaboration and redundancy.

Continue learning
Git is a great tool with many features. Keep learning and exploring advanced Git concepts like cherry-picking, interactive rebasing, and custom hooks to improve your workflow.

To better understand in practice some of the common Git terms and commands, let's have a look at Table 4-1.

Table 4-1. Git terms and commands

Term/command	Definition	Git command (if applicable)
Repository (repo)	This is similar to a project folder and contains all the files, history, and branches of your project.	-
Branch	A branch is a separate line of development. It allows you to work on new features or fixes without affecting the main codebase.	`git branch <branch_name>`
Pull request (PR)	A pull request is a proposed change that you want to merge into the main branch. It's a way to collaborate and review code changes with your team.	-
Stash	`git stash` is a command that temporarily saves changes you have made in your working directory but do not want to commit yet.	`git stash save "Your stash message here"`
Commit	A commit is a snapshot of your code at a specific point in time. It represents a set of changes you've made to your files.	`git commit -m "Commit message here"`
Add	`git add` is used to stage changes for the next commit. When you modify your files, Git doesn't automatically include them in the next commit. You need to explicitly tell Git which changes to include.	To stage all changes, the git command is `git add .`, but you also specify a file or directory: `git add <path/to/directory/>`
Fork	Forking a repository means creating your copy of someone else's project on GitHub. You can make changes to your forked repository without affecting the original.	-

Term/command	Definition	Git command (if applicable)
Clone	Cloning a repository means making a local copy of a remote repository. You can work on your code locally and push changes to the remote repository.	`git clone <reposi tory_url>`
Push	`git push` uploads your local changes to a remote repository.	`git push <origin branch_name>`
Pull	`git pull` updates your local repository with changes from a remote repository.	`git pull`
Status	`git status` shows the current state of your working directory and staging area.	`git status`
Log	`git log` displays a chronological list of commits in the repository and commits messages, authors, and commit IDs.	`git log`
Diff	The `gitdiff` command shows the differences between two sets of code.	`git diff`
Merge	The `git merge` command combines changes from one branch with another.	`git checkout <tar get_branch>` or `git merge <source_branch>`
Rebase	Rebase allows you to move or combine a sequence of commits to a new base commit.	`git rebase base_branch`
Checkout	The `checkout` command is used for switching between branches or commits.	`git checkout <branch_name>`

These Git commands and terms provide the foundation for version control in your projects. Nevertheless, Git commands often have many additional arguments and options, allowing for fine-tuned control over your version control tasks. While we've covered some essential commands here, it's essential to note that Git's versatility extends far beyond what we've outlined.

For a more comprehensive list of Git commands and the diverse array of arguments they can accept, we recommend referring to the official Git documentation (*https://oreil.ly/kmUcc*).

Now that you understand what Git and GitHub are and their role within the project, let's establish a connection to GitHub. For that, you need to do the following:

1. Register for a GitHub account if you don't already have one.

2. Click New to create a new repository, which is where you will version your analytics code. On the "Create a new repository screen," give your repository a name; then click "Create repository."

3. With the repository created, let's get back to dbt. In the Setup a Repository section, select GitHub and then connect the GitHub account.

4. Click Configure GitHub Integration to open a new window where you can select the location to install the dbt Cloud. Then choose the repository you want to install.

Now click "Start developing in the IDE." Figure 4-11 is what you should expect to see.

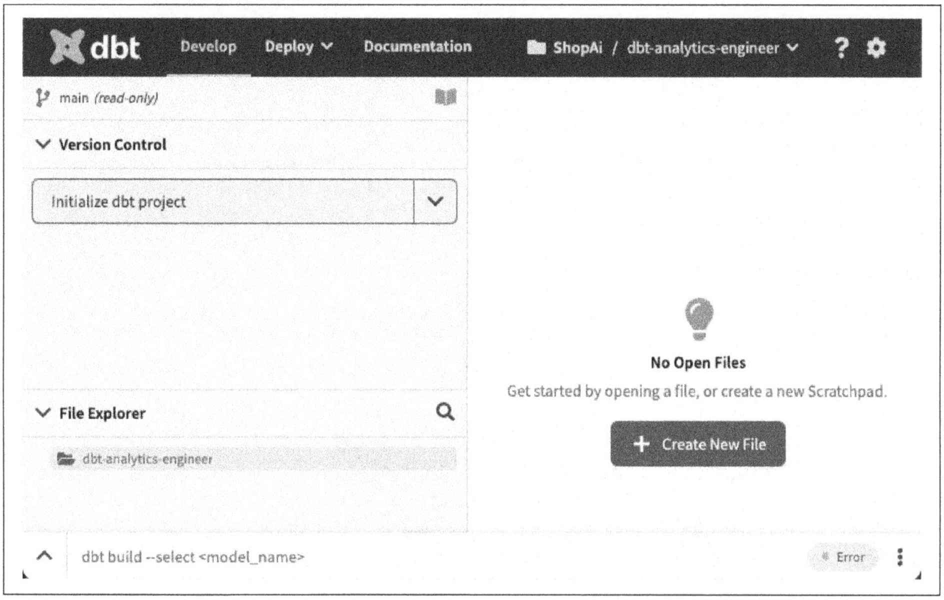

Figure 4-11. dbt IDE

We will give an overview of the dbt Cloud Integrated Development Environment (IDE) in "Using the dbt Cloud IDE" on page 163 and cover it in more detail in "Structure of a dbt Project" on page 165.

Click "Initialize dbt project" on the top left. Now, you should be able to see the screen as it looks in Figure 4-12.

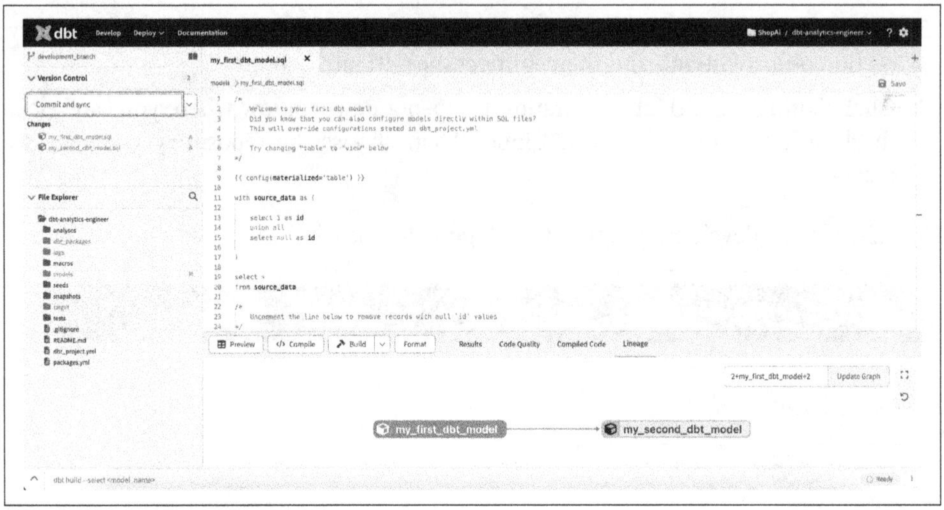

Figure 4-12. dbt after project initialization

We will detail each folder and file in "Structure of a dbt Project" on page 165. For now, let's see if the queries work. Run them again by copying the Example 4-2 code and click Preview.

Example 4-2. dbt public datasets in BigQuery, dbt test

```
--select * from `dbt-tutorial.jaffle_shop.customers`;
--select * from `dbt-tutorial.jaffle_shop.orders`;
select * from `dbt-tutorial.stripe.payment`;
```

If the output looks similar to Figure 4-13, that means your connection works. You can then submit queries to your data platform, which in our case is BigQuery.

> The steps provided here are part of the documentation for the BigQuery adapter in dbt. As technologies evolve and improve, these steps and configurations may also change. To ensure that you have the most up-to-date information, refer to the latest dbt documentation for BigQuery (*https://oreil.ly/og-M8*). This resource will provide you with the most current guidance and instructions for working with dbt and BigQuery.

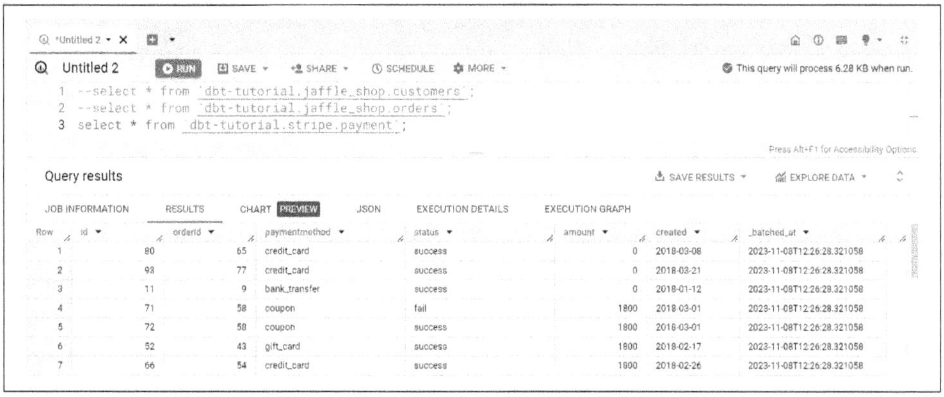

Figure 4-13. dbt output of BigQuery public dataset

Finally, let's test whether your GitHub integration is working as expected by carrying out your first "Commit and push." Click the button with the same description, visible in Figure 4-14, at the left. A popup screen, the image to the right in Figure 4-14, will appear where you can write your commit message. Click Commit Changes.

Figure 4-14. Commit and push to GitHub

Since we didn't create a Git branch, it will version our code inside the main branch. Go into the GitHub repository you made during this setup and see if your dbt project exists. Figure 4-15 should be similar to what you see on your GitHub repository.

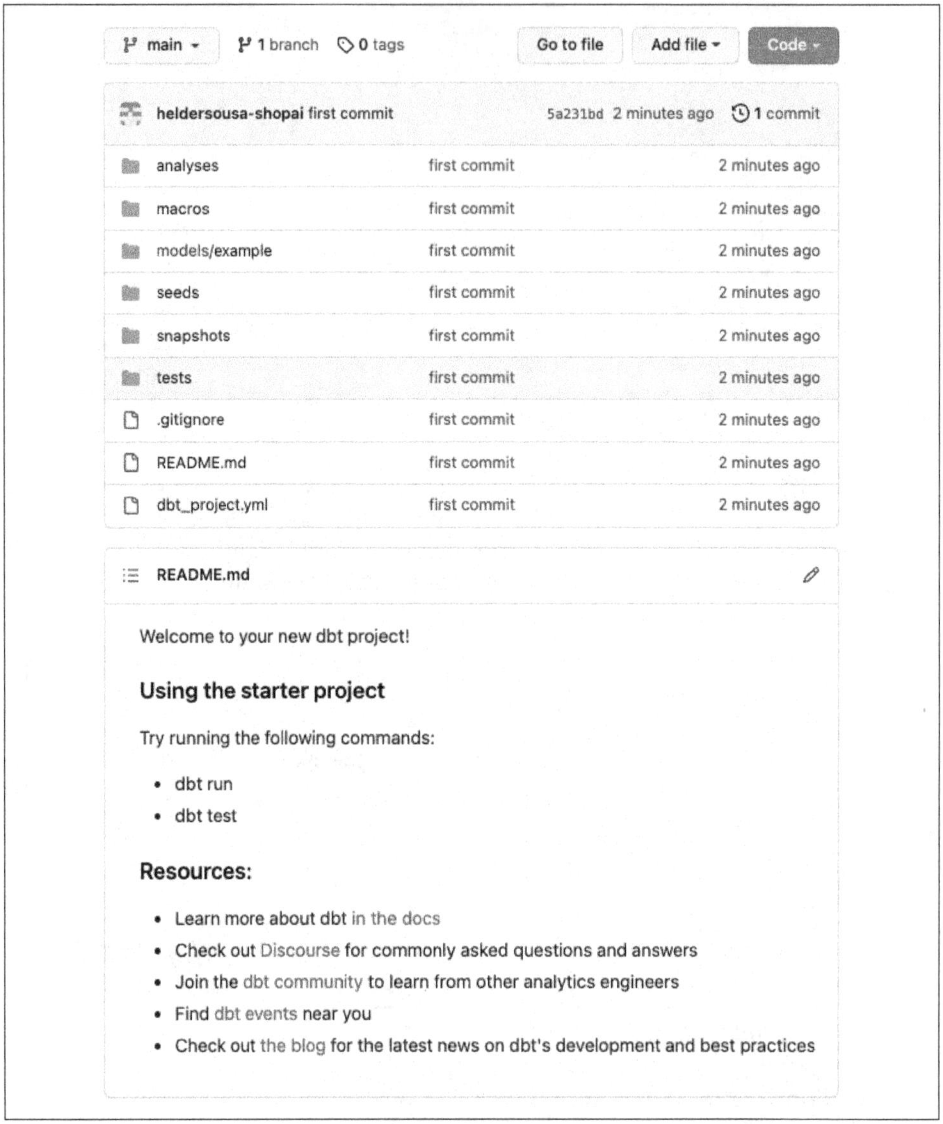

Figure 4-15. dbt GitHub repository, first commit check

Using the dbt Cloud UI

When you sign in to dbt Cloud, the initial page displays a welcome message and a summary of your job's execution history. As Figure 4-16 shows, the page is empty at first but once we create and run our first jobs, we will start seeing information. In "Jobs and Deployment" on page 212, we detail a job's execution in more detail.

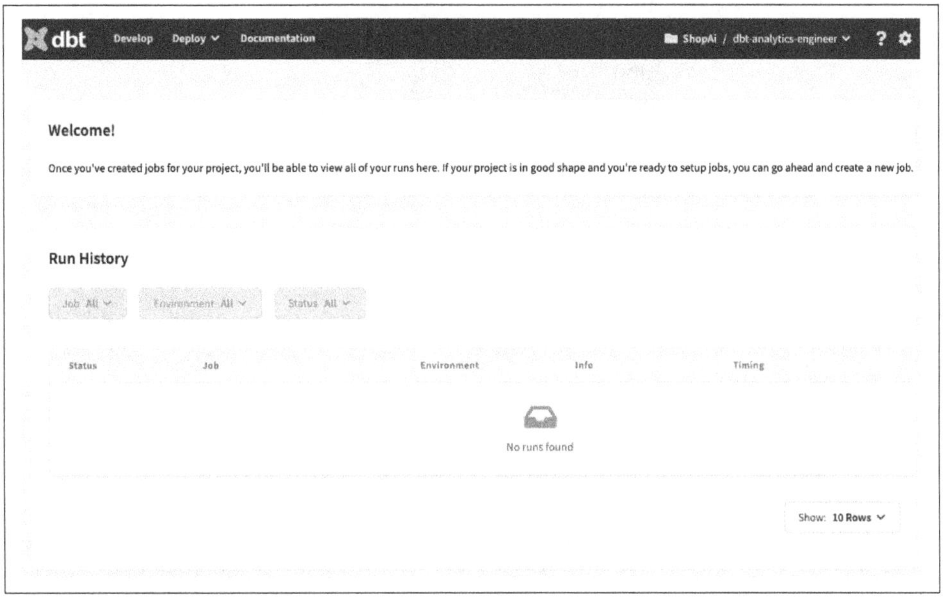

Figure 4-16. dbt landing page

On the top bar, you will see several options. Starting from the left, you can access the Develop page, where you will develop all your analytics code and create your models, tests, and documentation. It is the core of dbt development, and we will give you more insights into this section in "Using the dbt Cloud IDE" on page 163, and deep dive into each component in "Structure of a dbt Project" on page 165.

Right next to the Develop option is the Deploy menu, as shown in Figure 4-17. From this menu, you can configure jobs and monitor their execution via Run History, configure the development environments, and verify the source freshness of your snapshots via Data Sources.

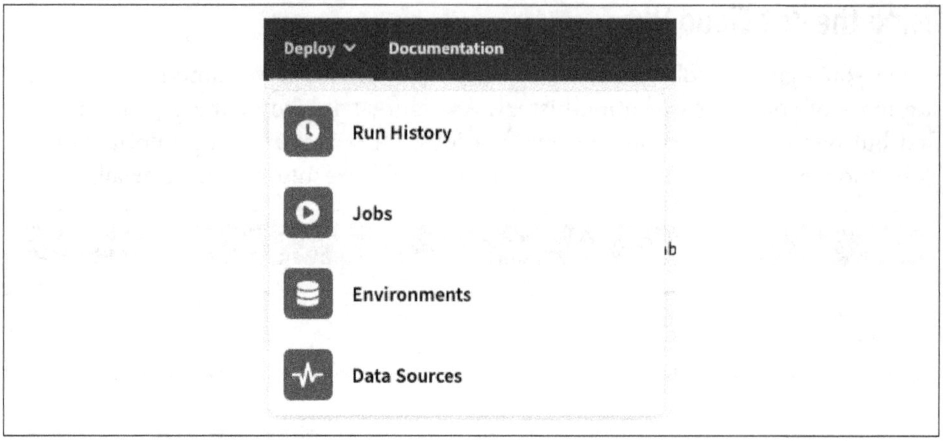

Figure 4-17. dbt Deploy menu

The Deploy menu's first option is Run History, which opens the page shown in Figure 4-18. Here you can see your job's run history. In the context of dbt, *jobs* are automated tasks or processes that you configure to perform specific actions, such as running models, tests, or generating documentation. These jobs are an integral part of orchestrating dbt, which involves managing and automating various data transformation and analytics tasks.

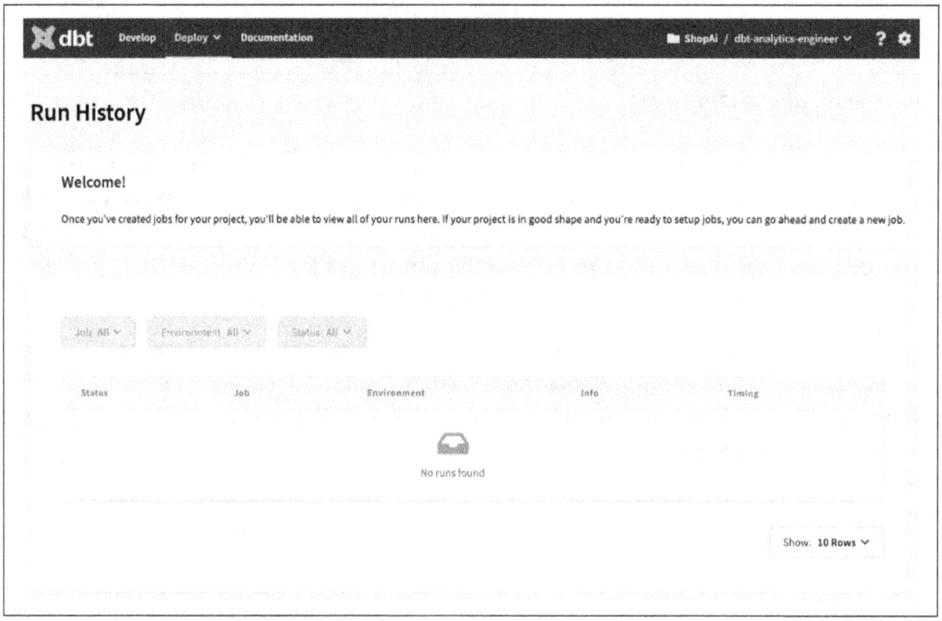

Figure 4-18. dbt Run History page

Suppose you have jobs configured that had executions already in this section. In that case, you can inspect each job's invocation and status. A wealth of information is available in the job's run history, including its status, duration, the environment in which the job executed, and other useful details. You can access information about the steps the job went through, including respective logs for each step. Additionally, you can find artifacts generated by the job, such as models, tests, or documentation.

The Deploy menu's next option is Jobs. This opens a page for configuring all your automation, including CI/CD pipelines, run tests, and other exciting behaviors, without running dbt commands manually from the command line.

Figure 4-19 shows the empty Jobs landing page. We have a whole section dedicated to Jobs in "Jobs and Deployment" on page 212.

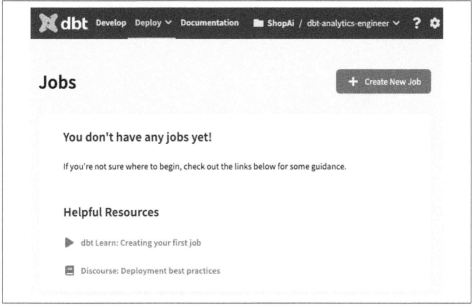

Figure 4-19. dbt Jobs page

The third Deploy menu option is Environments. Inside dbt, we have two main types of environment: development and deployment. Out of the box, dbt configures the development environment for you, which is visible right after you set up your dbt project. Figure 4-20 shows you the Environments landing page, which should be similar to yours if you followed the steps in "Setting Up dbt Cloud with BigQuery and GitHub" on page 140.

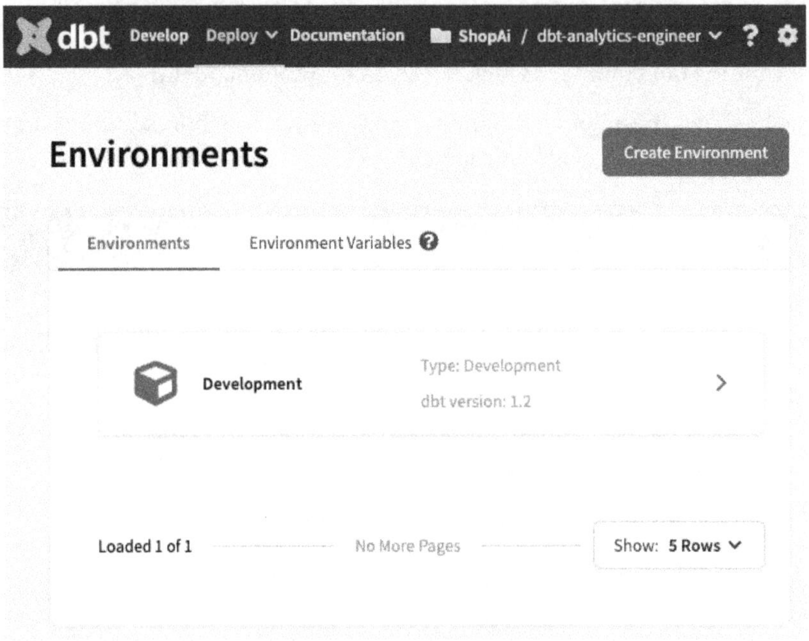

Figure 4-20. dbt Environments page

Finally, we have the Data Sources option. This page, shown in Figure 4-21, is populated automatically by dbt Cloud once you configure a job to snapshot source-data freshness. Here you will see the state of the most recent snapshots, allowing you to analyze if your source data freshness is meeting the service-level agreements (SLAs) you've defined with your organization. We will give you a better idea of data freshness in "Source freshness" on page 187 and how to test it in "Testing sources" on page 195.

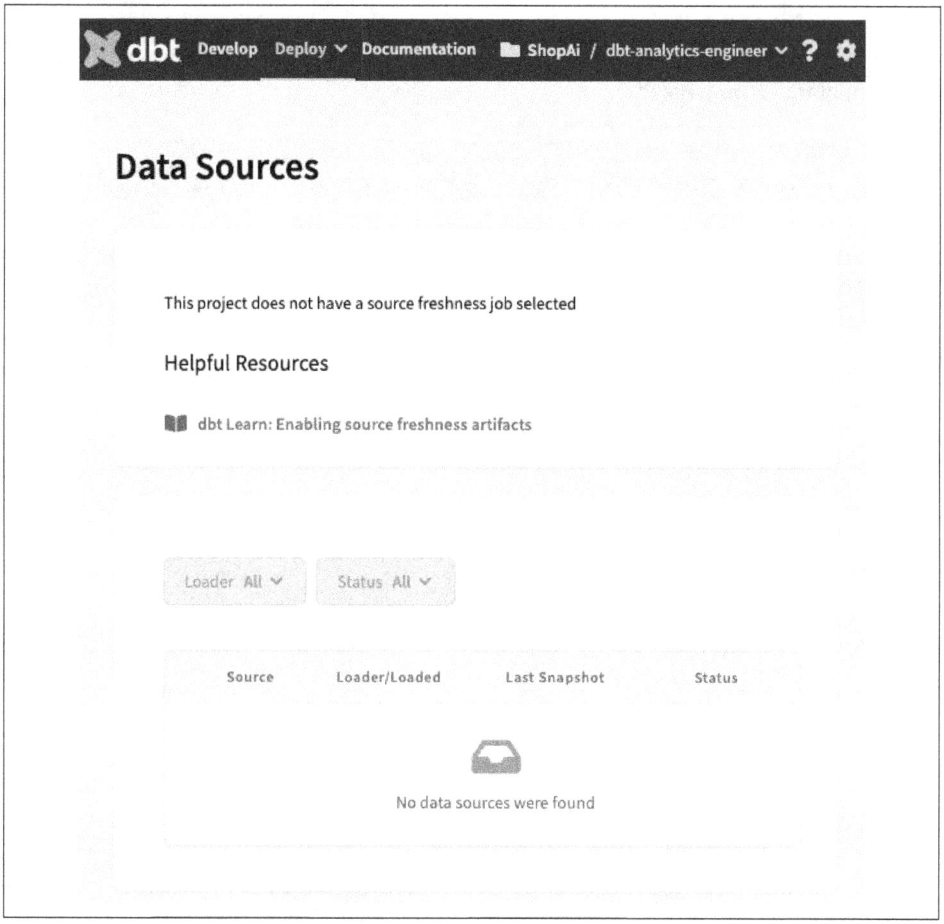

Figure 4-21. dbt Data Sources page

Next is the Documentation option, and as long as you and your team create routines to ensure that your dbt project is correctly documented, this step will have a particular level of significance. Proper documentation can answer questions like these:

- What does this data mean?
- Where does this data come from?
- How are these metrics calculated?

Figure 4-22 shows the Documentation page for your project. We will explain how to leverage and write documentation inside your dbt project while writing your code in "Documentation" on page 200.

Figure 4-22. dbt Documentation page

The top-right menu allows you to select your dbt project (Figure 4-23). This short menu makes it simple to move around between dbt projects.

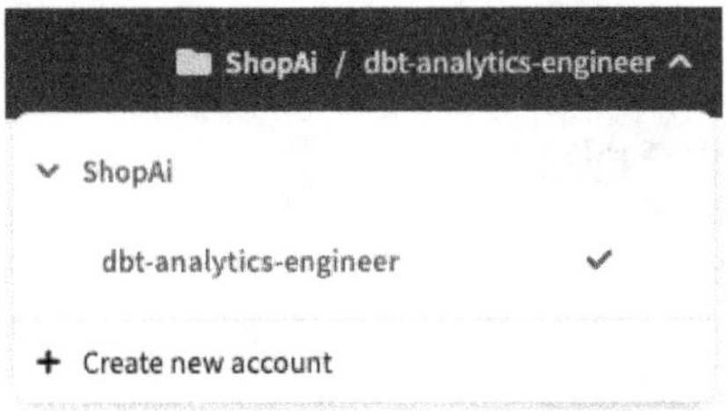

Figure 4-23. dbt Select Account menu

The dbt Help menu (Figure 4-24) can be found by clicking the question mark symbol. Here you can speak directly with the dbt team through chat, provide feedback, and access dbt documentation. Finally, via the Help menu, you can join the Slack dbt community or GitHub dbt discussions.

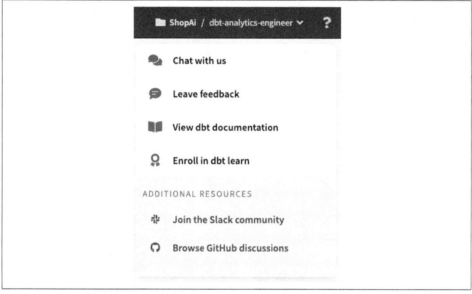

Figure 4-24. dbt Help menu

The Settings menu, Figure 4-25, is where you can configure everything related to your account, profile, or even notifications.

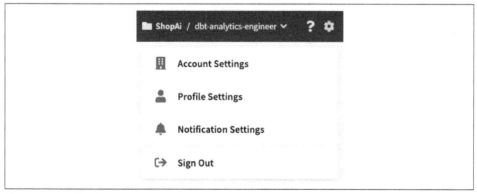

Figure 4-25. dbt Settings menu

Once you click one of the three options, you will land on the Settings page, similar to Figure 4-26. On the first page, Account Settings, you can edit and create new dbt projects, manage users and their access control level (if you are an owner), and manage the billing.

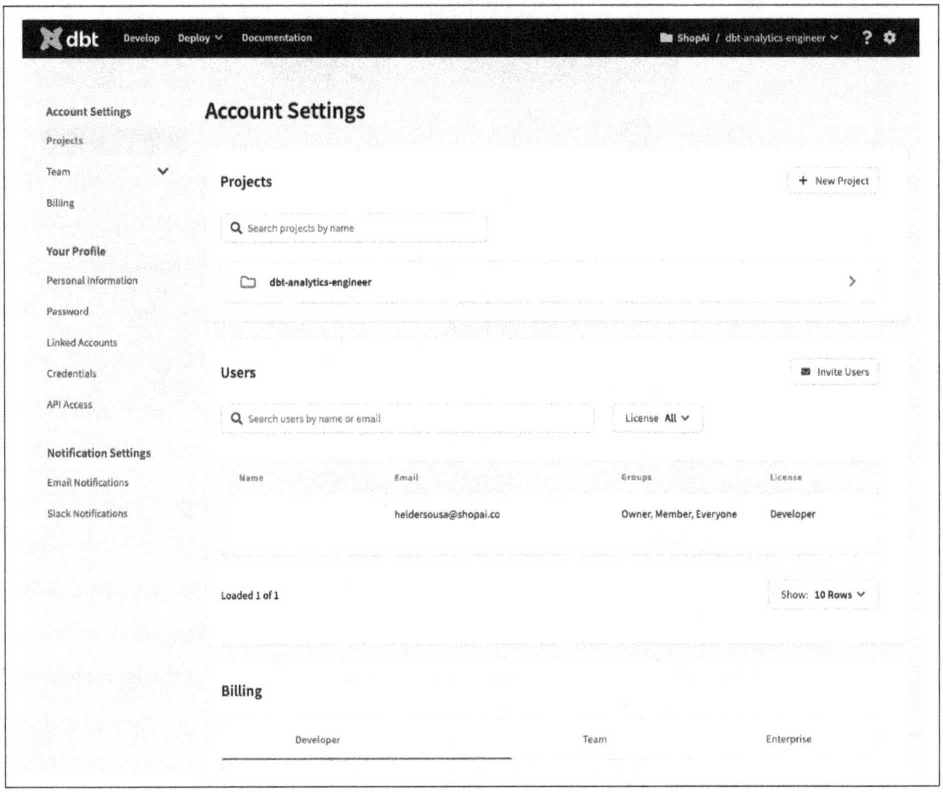

Figure 4-26. dbt Account Settings page

The second menu option, Profile Settings, accesses the Your Profile page (Figure 4-27). On this page, you can review all your personal information and manage linked accounts, such as GitHub or GitLab, Slack, and single sign-on (SSO) tools. You can also review and edit the credentials you defined for your data platform and the API access key.

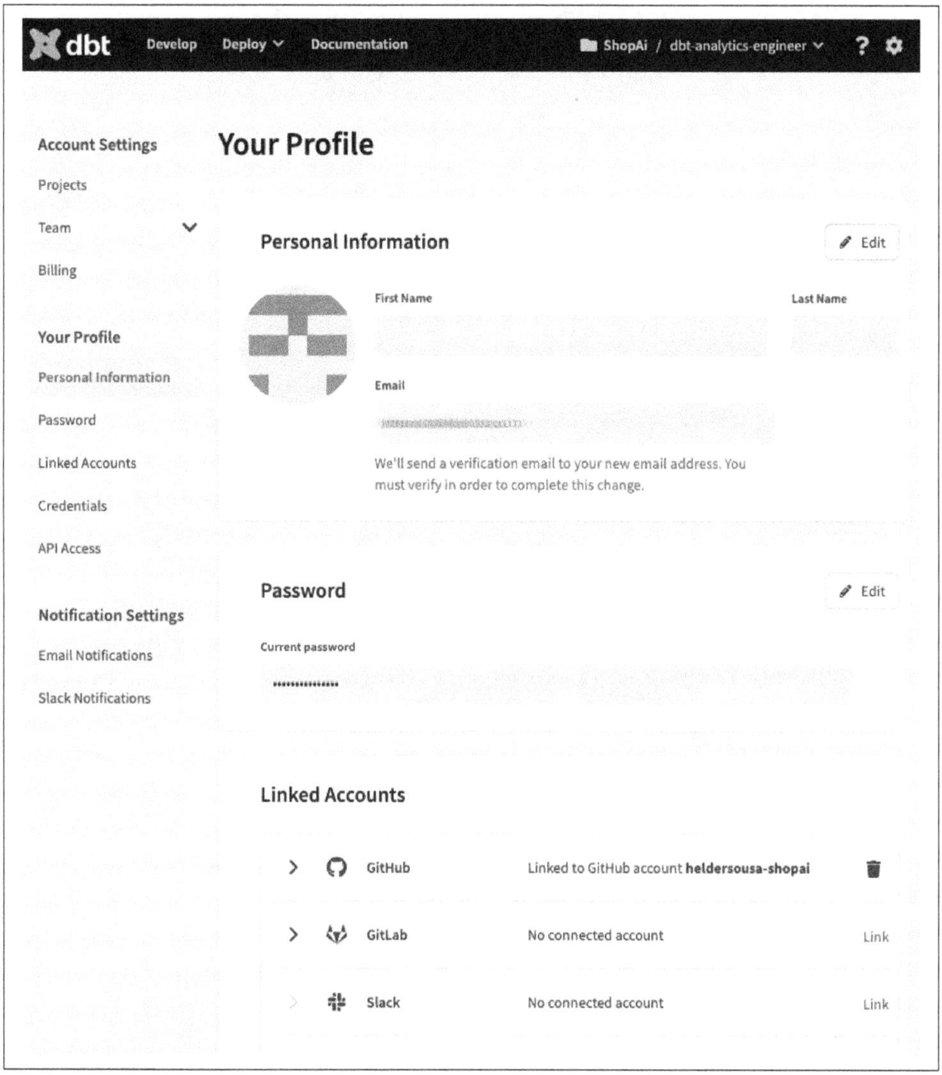

Figure 4-27. dbt Your Profile page

Finally, the Notification Settings option accesses the Notifications center (Figure 4-28), where you can configure alerts to be received in a chosen Slack channel or email when a job run succeeds, fails, or is canceled.

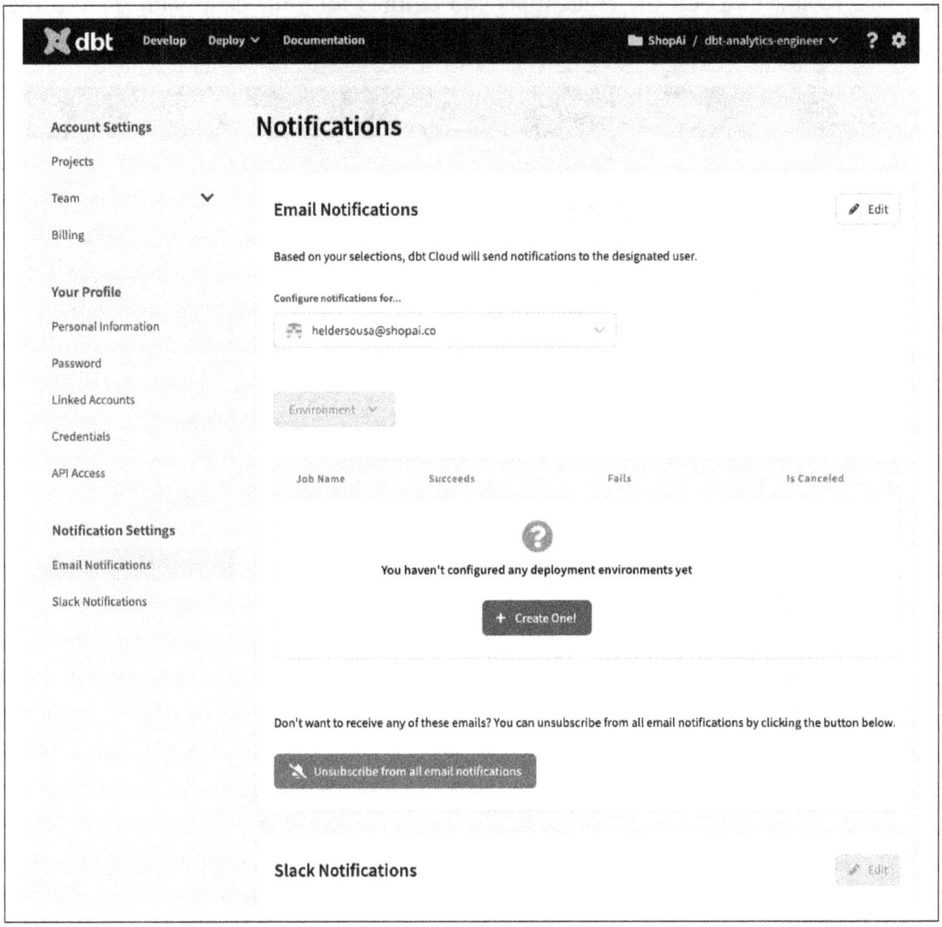

Figure 4-28. dbt Notifications center

Using the dbt Cloud IDE

One of the essential parts of the dbt Cloud is the IDE, where all your analytics code can be written, along with tests and documentation. Figure 4-29 shows the main sections of the dbt IDE.

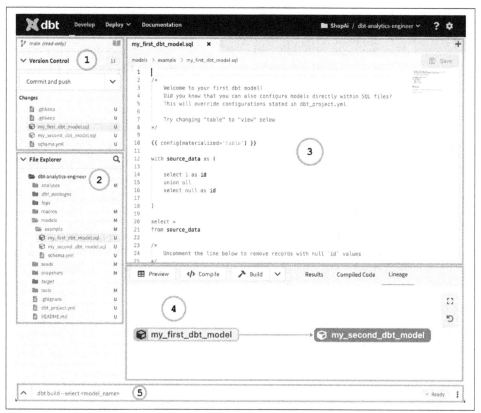

Figure 4-29. dbt IDE—annotated

Next, you can find a detailed explanation of what each section represents and its relevance inside the integrated development environment:

1. Git controls and documentation

    This menu is where you interact with Git. Here you can see what changed since your previous commit and what's new. All Git commands in the IDE are here, and you can decide whether to commit and push or revert your code. Also, in the top right of this window, you can see the documentation icon. Once documentation is generated, you can click this shortcut to access your project documentation.

2. File Explorer

   The File Explorer gives you the main overview of your dbt project. Here you can check how your dbt project is built—generally in the form of *.sql*, *.yml*, and other compatible file types.

3. Text editor

   This section of the IDE is where your analytics code is written and becomes mature. Here you can also edit and create other relevant files for your project, such as the YAML files. If you select those files from File Explorer, they will pop up here. Multiple files can be opened simultaneously.

4. Information window and code Preview, Compile, and Build

   This menu will show your results once you click the Preview or Compile buttons. Preview will compile and run your query against your data platform and display the results in the Results tab at the bottom of your screen. On the other hand, Compile will convert any Jinja into pure SQL. This will be displayed in the information window in the Compiled Code tab at the bottom of your screen. Preview or Compile buttons apply to statements and SQL files.

   Build is a special button that pops up only in specific files. Depending on what type of build you choose, the run results will include information about all models, tests, seeds, and snapshots that were selected to build, combined into one file.

   The information window is also helpful for troubleshooting errors during development or using the Lineage tab to check the data lineage of the model currently open in the text editor and its ancestors and dependencies.

5. Command line

   The command line is where you can execute specific dbt commands such as dbt run or dbt test. During or after the execution of the command, it also displays a pop-up screen to show the results as they are processed—for that, click the arrow at the beginning of the command line. Logs can also be viewed here. Figure 4-30 shows the command line expanded; the command to be executed is at the top, and the log of the execution follows.

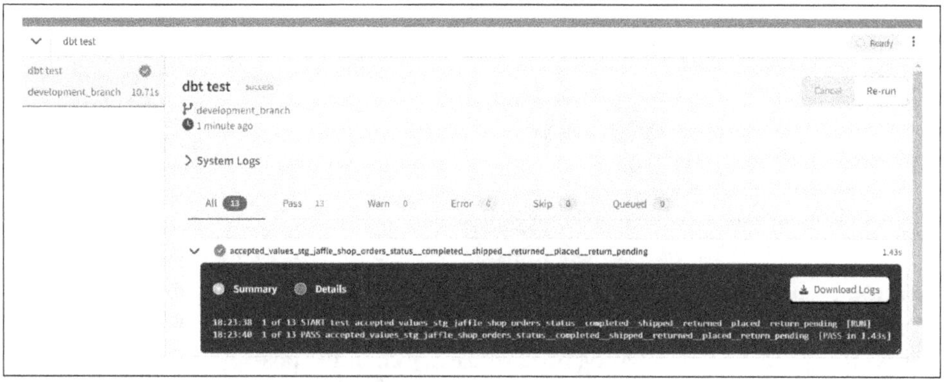

Figure 4-30. dbt command line expanded

Structure of a dbt Project

A dbt *project* is a directory composed of folders and files, programming patterns, and naming conventions. All your analytics code, tests, documentation, and parametrizations that will tell dbt how to operate will be in those files and folders. It will use those naming conventions and programming patterns. The way you organize your folders and file directory is your dbt project structure.

Building a proper dbt project takes effort. To be well implemented, it needs to bring together the company domains and departments, leveraging their particular expertise to map the goals and needs of the whole company. As such, defining a set of conventions and patterns that are clear, comprehensive, and consistent is relevant. Accomplishing that will ensure that the project remains accessible and maintainable as your company scales, while using dbt to empower and benefit as many people as possible.

How you organize your dbt project can vary and might be subject to changes defined by you or company guidelines. That's not a problem. What's important is that you explicitly declare those changes in a rigorous and accessible way for all contributors and, above all, stay consistent with it. For the sake of this book, we will keep the basic structure of the dbt project that you encounter once you initialize (Example 4-3).

Example 4-3. Initial structure of a dbt project

```
root/
├─ analyses/
├─ dbt_packages/
├─ logs/
├─ macros/
├─ models/
│   ├─ example/
│   │   ├─ schema.yml
```

```
|   |   ├─ my_second_dbt_model.sql
|   |   ├─ my_first_dbt_model.sql
├─ seeds/
├─ snapshots/
├─ target/
├─ tests/
├─ .gitignore
├─ dbt_project.yml
├─ README.md
```

Each folder and file will be explained in the subsequent sections in this chapter and Chapter 5. Some will have more emphasis and will be used more regularly than others. Yet, it is essential to have a broader idea of their purpose:

analyses folder
> Detailed in "Analyses" on page 197, this folder is commonly used to store queries for auditing purposes. For example, you may want to find discrepancies during logic migration from another system into dbt and still leverage the capabilities of dbt, such as the use of Jinja and version control, without including it in your built models inside your data platform.

dbt_packages folder
> Is where you will install your dbt packages. We will cover the concept of packages in "dbt Packages" on page 242. Still, the idea is that packages are standalone dbt projects that tackle specific problems and can be reused and shared across organizations. This promotes a DRY-er code since you aren't implementing the same logic over and over.

logs folder
> Is where all your project logs will be written by default, unless you configure them differently in your *dbt_project.yml*.

macros folder
> Is where your DRY-ing up transformations code will be stored. Macros, analogous to functions in other programming languages, are pieces of Jinja code that can be reused multiple times. We will devote an entire section in "Using SQL Macros" on page 236 to detailing them.

models folder
> Is one of the mandatory folders in dbt. Generally speaking, a *model* is a SQL file that contains a SELECT statement with a modular piece of logic that will take your raw data and build it into the final transformed data. In dbt, the model's name indicates the name of a future table or view, or neither if configured as an ephemeral model. This subject will be detailed in "Models" on page 174.

---

seeds folder

Is where our lookup tables will be stored. We will discuss this in "Seeds" on page 198. The general idea is that seeds are CSV files that change infrequently, and are used for modeling data that doesn't exist in any source system. Some helpful use cases could be mapping zip codes to states or a list of test emails we need to exclude from the analysis.

snapshots folder

Contains all snapshot models for your project, which must be separated from the models folder. The dbt snapshot feature records change to a mutable table over time. It applies the type 2 slowly changing dimension (SCDs), which identifies how a row in a table changes during the time. This is covered in detail in "Snapshots" on page 230.

target folder

Contains the compiled SQL files that will be written when you run the `dbt run`, `dbt compile`, or `dbt test` commands. You can optionally configure in *dbt_project.yml* to be written into another folder.

tests folder

Serves the purpose of testing multiple specific tables simultaneously. This will not be the solo folder where your tests will be written. A good number will still be under your model's folder inside the YAML files, or through macros. Yet, the tests folder is more suited for singular tests, which report the results of how several specific models interact or relate to one another. We will cover this topic in depth in "Tests" on page 189.

dbt_project.yml

Is the core of every dbt project. This is how dbt knows a directory is a dbt project, and it contains important information that tells dbt how to operate on your project. We will cover this file throughout the course of this book. It's also covered in "dbt_project.yml" on page 170.

.gitignore and README.md

Are files typically used for your Git projects. While *gitignore* specifies intentional files that Git should ignore during your commit and push, the *README* file is an essential guide that gives other developers a detailed description of your Git project.

We'll cover these folders in more detail in this chapter and Chapter 5 while going deeper into the dbt project and features.

Jaffle Shop Database

In this book, we will give a set of practical examples of how to work with the components and features of dbt. In most cases, we will need to develop SQL queries to give you the best idea of what we want to show. So, it is essential to have a database that we can work with. That database is the Jaffle Shop.

The *Jaffle Shop database* is a simple database composed of two tables, for customers and orders. To give more context, we will have a side database, from Stripe, with the payments connected with the orders. All three tables will be our raw data.

The reason we use this database is that it is already publicly available, in BigQuery, by dbt Labs. It is one of the main databases used for their documentation and courses, so we hope it will simplify the overall learning curve of the dbt platform at this stage of the book.

Figure 4-31 shows you the ERD representing our raw data with customers, orders, and payments.

jaffle_shop.customers		jaffle_shop.orders		stripe.payment	
ID	INTEGER	ID	INTEGER	id	INTEGER
FIRST_NAME	STRING	USER_ID	INTEGER	orderid	INTEGER
LAST_NAME	STRING	ORDER_DATE	DATE	paymentmethod	STRING
		STATUS	STRING	status	STRING
		_etl_loaded_at	DATETIME	amount	INTEGER
				created	DATE
				_batched_at	DATETIME

Figure 4-31. A Jaffle Shop raw data ERD, which we read as follows: single customer (1) can have multiple orders (N), and a single order (1) can have multiple processing payments (N)

YAML Files

YAML is a human-readable data-serialization language commonly used for configuration files and in applications where data is being stored or transmitted. In dbt, YAML is used to define properties and some configurations of the components of your dbt project: models, snapshots, seeds, tests, sources, or even the actual dbt project, *dbt_project.yml*.

Apart from the top-level YAML files, such as *dbt_project.yml* and *packages.yml*, that need to be specifically named and in specific locations, the way you organize the other YAML files inside your dbt project is up to you. Remember that, as with other aspects of structuring your dbt project, the most important guidelines are to keep consistent, be clear on your intentions, and document how and why it is organized that way. It is important to balance centralization and file size to make specific configurations as easy to find as possible. Following are a set of recommendations on how to organize, structure, and name your YAML files:

- As mentioned, balancing the configuration's centralization and file size is particularly relevant. Having all configurations within a single file might make it challenging to find a specific one as your project scales (though you technically can use one file). Change management with Git will also be complicated because of the repetitive nature of the file.

- As per the previous point, if we follow a config per folder approach, it is better to maintain all your configurations in the long run. In other words, in each model's folder directory, it is recommended to have a YAML file that will facilitate the configurations of all the models in that directory. Extend this rule by separating the model's configuration file, having a specific file for your sources configurations inside the same directory (Example 4-4).

In this structure, we've used the staging models to represent what's being discussed, since it covers most cases, such as sources, YAML files. Here you can see the config per folder system, where source and model configurations are divided. It also introduces the Markdown files for documentation, which we will discuss in more detail in "Documentation" on page 200. Finally, the underscore at the beginning puts all these files at the top of their respective directory so they are easier to find.

Example 4-4. dbt YAML files in the model directory

```
root/
├─ models/
│  ├─ staging/
│  │  ├─ jaffle_shop/
│  │  │  ├─ _jaffle_shop_docs.md
│  │  │  ├─ _jaffle_shop_models.yml
│  │  │  ├─ _jaffle_shop_sources.yml
│  │  │  ├─ stg_jaffle_shop_customers.sql
│  │  │  ├─ stg_jaffle_shop_orders.sql
│  │  ├─ stripe/
│  │  │  ├─ _stripe_docs.md
│  │  │  ├─ _stripe_models.yml
│  │  │  ├─ _stripe_sources.yml
```

```
|   |   |   ⊢ stg_stripe_order_payments.sql
⊢ dbt_project.yml
```

- When using documentation blocks, also follow the same approach by creating one Markdown file (.md) per models directory. In "Documentation" on page 200, we will get to know this type of file better.

It is recommended that you set up default configurations of your dbt project in your *dbt_project.yml* file at the directory level and use the cascading scope priority to define variations of these configurations. This can help you streamline your dbt project management and ensure that your configurations are consistent and easily maintainable. For example, leveraging Example 4-4, imagine that all our staging models would be configured to be materialized as a view by default. That would be in your *dbt_project.yml*. But if you have a specific use case where you need to change the materialization configuration for your `jaffle_shop` staging models, you can do so by modifying the *_jaffle_shop_models.yml* file. This way, you can customize the materialization configuration for this specific set of models while keeping the rest of your project configurations unchanged.

The ability to override the default configurations for specific models is made possible by the cascading scope priority used in the dbt project build. While all staging models would be materialized as views because this is the default configuration, the staging `jaffle_shop` models would be materialized as tables because we overrode the default by updating the specific *_jaffle_shop_models.yml* YAML file.

dbt_project.yml

One of the most critical files in dbt is *dbt_project.yml*. This file must be in the root of the project and it is the main configuration file for your project, containing pertinent information for dbt to properly operate.

The *dbt_project.yml* file also has some relevancy while writing your DRY-er analytics code. Generally speaking, your project default configurations will be stored here, and all objects will inherit from it unless overridden at the model level.

Here are some of the most important fields that you will encounter in this file:

name
> (Mandatory.) The name of the dbt project. We recommend changing this configuration to your project name. Also, remember to change it in the model's section and the *dbt_project.yml* file. In our case, we name it *dbt_analytics_engineer_book*.

version
> (Mandatory.) Core version of your project. Different from *dbt version*.

config-version
> (Mandatory.) Version 2 is the currently available version.

profile
> (Mandatory.) Profile within dbt is used to connect to your data platform.

[folder]-paths
> (Optional.) Where [folder] is the list of folders in the dbt project. It can be a model, seed, test, analysis, macro, snapshot, log, etc. For example, the *model-paths* will state the directory of your models and sources. The *macro-paths* is where your macros code lives, and so on.

target-path
> (Optional.) This path will store the compiled SQL file.

clean-targets
> (Optional.) List of directories containing artifacts to be removed by the dbt `clean` command.

models
> (Optional.) Default configuration of the models. In Example 4-5, we want all models inside the staging folder to be materialized as views.

Example 4-5. dbt_project.yml, model configuration

```
models:
  dbt_analytics_engineer_book:
    staging:
      materialized: view
```

packages.yml

Packages are standalone dbt projects that tackle specific problems and can be reused and shared across organizations. They are projects with models and macros; by adding them to your project, those models and macros will become part of it.

To access those packages, you first need to define them in the *packages.yml* file. The detailed steps are as follows:

1. You must ensure that the *packages.yml* file is in your dbt project. If not, please create it at the same level as your *dbt_project.yml* file.

2. Inside the dbt *packages.yml* file, define the packages you want to have available for use inside your dbt project. You can install packages from sources like the dbt Hub (*https://hub.getdbt.com*); Git repositories, such as GitHub or GitLab; or even packages you have stored locally. Example 4-6 shows you the syntax required for each of these scenarios.

3. Run `dbt deps` to install the defined packages. Unless you configure differently, by default those packages get installed in the *dbt_packages* directory.

Example 4-6. Syntax to install packages from the dbt hub, Git, or locally

```
packages:
  - package: dbt-labs/dbt_utils
    version: 1.1.1

  - git: "https://github.com/dbt-labs/dbt-utils.git"
    revision: 1.1.1

  - local: /opt/dbt/bigquery
```

profiles.yml

If you decide to use the dbt CLI and run your dbt project locally, you will need to set up a *profiles.yml*, which is not needed if you use dbt Cloud. This file contains the database connection that dbt will use to connect to the data platform. Because of its sensitive content, this file lives outside the project to avoid credentials being versioned into your code repository. You can safely use code versioning if your credentials are stored under environment variables.

Once you invoke dbt from your local environment, dbt parses your *dbt_project.yml* file and gets the profile name, which dbt needs to connect to your data platform. You can have multiple profiles as needed, yet it is common to have one profile per dbt project or per data platform. even using dbt Cloud for this book, and the profiles configuration not being necessary. We're showing a sample of the *profiles.yml* if you are curious or prefer to use dbt CLI with BigQuery.

The typical YAML schema file for *profiles.yml* is shown in Example 4-7. We are using dbt Cloud for this book, meaning the profiles configuration is not necessary. However, we're showing a sample of *profiles.yml* if you are curious or prefer to use the dbt CLI with BigQuery.

Example 4-7. profiles.yml

```
dbt_analytics_engineer_book:
  target: dev
  outputs:
    dev:
      type: bigquery
      method: service-account
      project: [GCP project id]
      dataset: [the name of your dbt dataset]
      threads: [1 or more]
```

```
keyfile: [/path/to/bigquery/keyfile.json]
<optional_config>: <value>
```

The most common structure of *profiles.yaml* has the following components:

profile_name
> The profile's name must be equal to the name found in your *dbt_project.yml*. In our case, we've named it `dbt_analytics_engineer_book`.

target
> This is how you have different configurations for different environments. For instance, you would want separate datasets/databases to work on when developing locally. But when deploying to production, it is best to have all tables in a single dataset/database. By default, the target is set up to be `dev`.

type
> The type of data platform you want to connect: BigQuery, Snowflake, Redshift, among others.

database-specific connection details
> Example 4-7 includes attributes like `method`, `project`, `dataset`, and `keyfile` that are required to set up a connection to BigQuery, using this approach.

threads
> Number of threads the dbt project will run on. It creates a DAG of links between models. The number of threads represents the maximum number of paths through the graph that dbt may work in parallel. For example, if you specify `threads: 1`, dbt will start building only one resource (models, tests, etc.) and finish it before moving on to the next. On the other hand, if you have `threads: 4`, dbt will work on up to four models at once without violating dependencies.

> The overall idea of the *profiles.yml* file is presented here. We will not go further than this nor give a detailed setup guide on configuring your dbt local project with BigQuery. Most of the tasks were already described, such as keyfile generation in "Setting Up dbt Cloud with BigQuery and GitHub" on page 140, but there might be some nuances. If you want to learn more, dbt provides a comprehensive guide (*https://oreil.ly/BeMDc*).

Models

Models are where you, as a data specialist, will spend most of your time inside the dbt ecosystem. They are typically written as `select` statements, saved as *.sql*, and are one of the most important pieces in dbt that will help you transform your data inside your data platform.

To properly build your models and create a clear and consistent project structure, you need to be comfortable with the data modeling concept and techniques. This is core knowledge if your goal is to become an analytics engineer or, generically speaking, someone who wants to work with data.

As we saw in Chapter 2, *data modeling* is the process that, by analyzing and defining the data requirements, creates data models that support the business processes in your organization. It shapes your source data, the data your company collects and produces, into transformed data, answering the data needs of your company domains and departments and generating added value.

In line with data modeling, and also as introduced in Chapter 2, modularity is another concept that is vital to properly structuring your dbt project and organizing your models while keeping your code DRY-er. Conceptually speaking, *modularity* is the process of decomposing a problem into a set of modules that can be separated and recombined, which reduces the overall complexity of the system, often with the benefit of flexibility and variety of use. In analytics, this is no different. While building a data product, we don't write the code all at once. Instead, we make it piece by piece until we reach the final data artifacts.

Since we will try to have modularity present from the beginning, our initial models will also be built with modularity in mind and in accordance with what we've discussed in Chapter 2. Following a typical dbt data transformation flow, there will be three layers in our model's directory:

Staging layer
> Our initial modular building blocks are within the staging layer of our dbt project. In this layer, we establish an interface with our source systems, similar to how an API interacts with external data sources. Here, data is reordered, cleaned up, and prepared for downstream processing. This includes tasks like data standardization and minor transformations that set the stage for more advanced data processing further downstream.

Intermediate layer
> This layer consists of models between the staging layer and the marts layer. These models are built on top of our staging models and are used to conduct extensive data transformations, as well as data consolidation from multiple sources, which creates varied intermediate tables that will serve distinct purposes.

Marts layer

Depending on your data modeling technique, marts bring together all modular pieces to give a broader vision of the entities your company cares about. If, for example, we choose a dimensional modeling technique, the marts layer contains your fact and dimension tables. In this context, *facts* are occurrences that keep happening over time, such as orders, page clicks, or inventory changes, with their respective measures. *Dimensions* are attributes, such as customers, products, and geography, that can describe those facts. *Marts* can be described as subsets of data inside your data platform that are oriented to specific domains or departments, such as finance, marketing, logistics, customer service, etc. It can also be a good practice to have a mart called "core," for example, that isn't oriented to a specific domain but is instead the core business facts and dimensions.

With the introductions made, let's now build our first models, initially only on our staging layer. Create a new folder inside your models folder, named *staging*, and the respective folders per source, *jaffle_shop* and *stripe*, inside the *staging* folder. Then create the necessary SQL files, one for *stg_stripe_order_payments.sql* (Example 4-8), another for *stg_jaffle_shop_customers.sql* (Example 4-9), and finally one for *stg_jaffle_shop_orders.sql* (Example 4-10). In the end, delete the example folder inside your models. It is unnecessary, so it would create unneeded visual noise while coding. The folder structure should be similar to Example 4-11.

Example 4-8. stg_stripe_order_payments.sql

```
select
    id as payment_id,
    orderid as order_id,
    paymentmethod as payment_method,
    case
        when paymentmethod in ('stripe'
                               , 'paypal'
                               , 'credit_card'
                               , 'gift_card')
        then 'credit'
        else 'cash'
    end as payment_type,
    status,
    amount,
    case
        when status = 'success'
        then true
        else false
    end as is_completed_payment,
    created as created_date
from `dbt-tutorial.stripe.payment`
```

Example 4-9. stg_jaffle_shop_customers.sql

```
select
    id as customer_id,
    first_name,
    last_name
from `dbt-tutorial.jaffle_shop.customers`
```

Example 4-10. stg_jaffle_shop_orders.sql

```
select
    id as order_id,
    user_id as customer_id,
    order_date,
    status,
    _etl_loaded_at
from `dbt-tutorial.jaffle_shop.orders`
```

Example 4-11. Staging models' folder structure

```
root/
├ models/
│   ├ staging/
│   │   ├ jaffle_shop/
│   │   │   ├ stg_jaffle_shop_customers.sql
│   │   │   ├ stg_jaffle_shop_orders.sql
│   │   ├ stripe/
│   │   │   ├ stg_stripe_order_payments.sql
├ dbt_project.yml
```

Now let's execute and validate what we did. Typically, typing dbt run in your command line is enough, but at BigQuery, you may need to type **dbt run --full-refresh**. After, look at your logs by using the arrow to the left of your command line. The logs should look similar to Figure 4-32.

```
dbt run   success                                                    Cancel    Re-run

 development_branch
 2 minutes ago

 System Logs

    Summary      Details                                         Download Logs

   16:20:19  [WARNING]: Configuration paths exist in your dbt_project.yml file which do not apply to any resources.
   There are 1 unused configuration paths:
   - models.dbt_analytics_engineer_book.example
   16:20:19  Found 3 models, 0 tests, 0 snapshots, 0 analyses, 319 macros, 0 operations, 0 seed files, 0 sources, 0 exposures, 0 metrics
   16:20:19
   16:20:19  Concurrency: 4 threads (target='default')
   16:20:19
   16:20:19  1 of 3 START sql view model dbt_heldersousashopai.stg_jaffle_shop_customers .... [RUN]
   16:20:19  2 of 3 START sql view model dbt_heldersousashopai.stg_jaffle_shop_orders ....... [RUN]
   16:20:19  3 of 3 START sql view model dbt_heldersousashopai.stg_stripe_order_payments .... [RUN]
   16:20:20  1 of 3 OK created sql view model dbt_heldersousashopai.stg_jaffle_shop_customers  [CREATE VIEW (0 processed) in 1.07s]
   16:20:21  2 of 3 OK created sql view model dbt_heldersousashopai.stg_jaffle_shop_orders .. [CREATE VIEW (0 processed) in 1.10s]
   16:20:21  3 of 3 OK created sql view model dbt_heldersousashopai.stg_stripe_order_payments  [CREATE VIEW (0 processed) in 1.10s]
   16:20:21
   16:20:21  Finished running 3 view models in 0 hours 0 minutes and 1.56 seconds (1.56s).
   16:20:21
   16:20:21  Completed successfully
   16:20:21
   16:20:21  Done. PASS=3 WARN=0 ERROR=0 SKIP=0 TOTAL=3


   All  3      Pass  3      Warn  0      Error  0      Skip  0      Queued  0


    stg_jaffle_shop_customers                                              1.07s

    stg_jaffle_shop_orders                                                 1.10s

    stg_stripe_order_payments                                              1.10s
```

Figure 4-32. dbt system logs

Your logs should also give you a good idea of the issue if something goes wrong. In Figure 4-32, we present a logs summary, but you can also check the detailed logs for more verbosity.

Expecting that you have received the "Completed successfully" message, let's now take a look at BigQuery, where you should see all three models materialized, as Figure 4-33 shows.

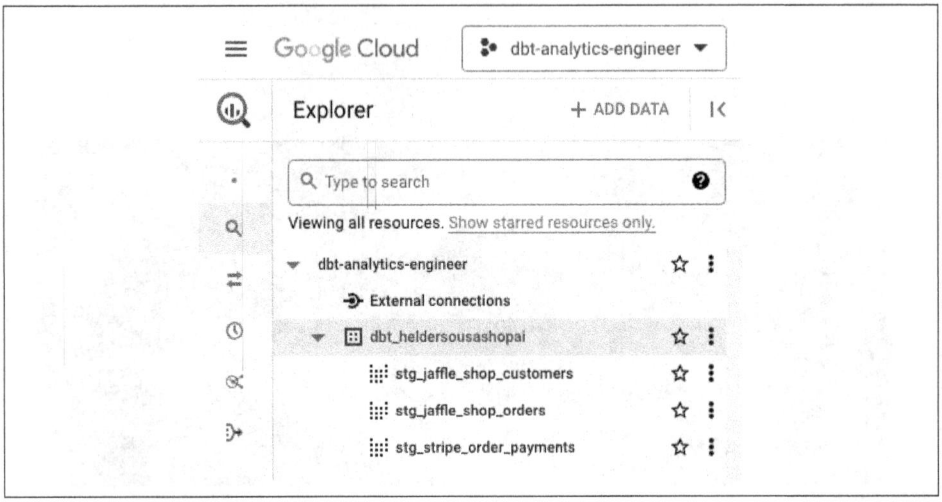

Figure 4-33. dbt BigQuery models

By default, dbt materializes your models inside your data platform as views. Still, you can easily configure this in the configuration block at the top of the model file (Example 4-12).

Example 4-12. Materialization config inside the model file

```
{{
    config(
        materialized='table'
    )
}}

SELECT
    id as customer_id,
    first_name,
    last_name
FROM `dbt-tutorial.jaffle_shop.customers`
```

Now that we have created our first models, let's move to the next steps. Rearrange the code using the YAML files, and follow the best practices recommended in "YAML Files" on page 168. Let's take the code block from there and configure our materializations inside our YAML files (Example 4-12). The first file we will change is *dbt_project.yml*. This should be the core YAML file for default configurations. As such, let's change the model's configuration inside with the code presented in Example 4-13 and then execute **dbt run** again.

Example 4-13. Materialize models as views and as tables

```
models:
  dbt_analytics_engineer_book:
    staging:
      jaffle_shop:
        +materialized: view
      stripe:
        +materialized: table
```

 The + prefix is a dbt syntax enhancement, introduced with dbt v0.17.0, designed to clarify resource paths and configurations within *dbt_project.yml* files.

Since Example 4-13 forced all staging Stripe models to be materialized as a table, BigQuery should look like Figure 4-34.

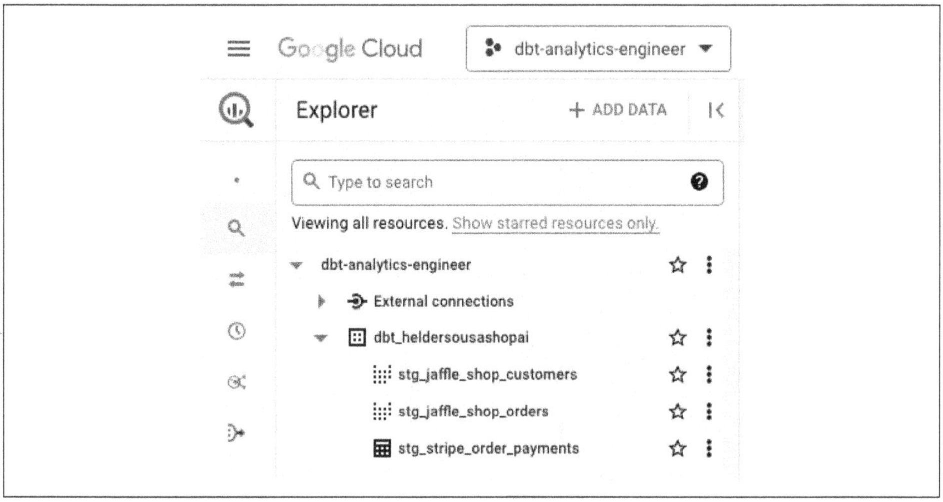

Figure 4-34. dbt BigQuery models with materialized table

Example 4-13 shows how to configure, per folder, the specific desired materializations inside *dbt_project.yml*. Your staging models will be kept by default as views, so overriding this configuration can be done at the model's folder level, leveraging the cascading scope priority on the project build. First, let's change our *dbt_project.yml* to set all staging models to be materialized as views, as Example 4-14 shows.

Example 4-14. Staging models to be materialized as views

```
models:
  dbt_analytics_engineer_book:
```

```
staging:
  +materialized: view
```

Now let's create the separate YAML file for `stg_jaffle_shop_customers`, stating that it needs to be materialized as a table. For that, create the respective YAML file, with the name *_jaffle_shop_models.yml*, inside the *staging/jaffle_shop* directory and copy the code in Example 4-15.

Example 4-15. Defining that the model will be materialized as a table

```
version: 2

models:
  - name: stg_jaffle_shop_customers
    config:
      materialized: table
```

After you rerun dbt, take a look at BigQuery. It should be similar to Figure 4-35.

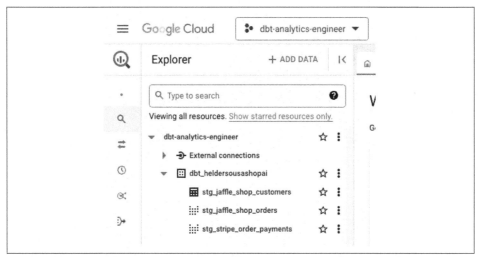

Figure 4-35. dbt BigQuery customers model materialized into a table

This is a simple example of using the YAML files, playing with table materializations, and seeing what the cascading scope priority means in practice. There is still a lot to do and see, and some of what we're discussing will have even more applicability as we move onward. For now, we would just ask you to change your model inside *_jaffle_shop_models.yml* to be materialized as a view. This will be your default configuration.

Hopefully, at this stage, you've developed your first models and understand roughly the overall purpose of the YAML files and the cascading scope priority. The following steps will be to create our intermediate and mart models while learning about `ref()` functions. This will be our first use of Jinja, which we will cover in more detail in "Dynamic SQL with Jinja" on page 233.

First things first: our use case. With our models inside our staging area, we need to know what we want to do with them. As we mentioned at the start of this section, you need to define the data requirements that support the business processes in your organization. As a business user, multiple streams can be taken from our data. One of them, which will be our use case, is to analyze our orders per customer, presenting the total amount paid per successful order and the total amount per successful order type (cash and credit).

Since we have some transformations here that require a granularity change from payment type level to order grain, it justifies isolating this complex operation before we reach the marts layer. This is where the intermediate layer lands. In your models folder, create a new folder named *intermediate*. Inside, create a new SQL file named *int_payment_type_amount_per_order.sql* and copy the code in Example 4-16.

Example 4-16. int_payment_type_amount_per_order.sql

```
with order_payments as (
    select * from {{ ref('stg_stripe_order_payments') }}
)

select
    order_id,
    sum(
        case
            when payment_type = 'cash' and
                status = 'success'
            then amount
            else 0
        end
        ) as cash_amount,
    sum(
        case
            when payment_type = 'credit' and
                status = 'success'
            then amount
            else 0
        end
        ) as credit_amount,
    sum(case
            when status = 'success'
            then amount
        end
        ) as total_amount
from order_payments
group by 1
```

As you can see while creating the `order_payments` CTE, we gather the data from `stg_stripe_order_payments` by using the `ref()` function. This function references the upstream tables and views that were building your data platform. We'll use this function as a standard while we implement our analytics code due to the benefits, such as:

- It allows you to build dependencies among models in a flexible way that can be shared in a common codebase since it compiles the name of the database object during the `dbt run`, gathering it from the environment configuration when you create the project. This means that in your environment, the code will be compiled considering your environment configurations, available in your particular development environment, but different from that of your teammate who is using a different development environment but shares the same codebase.

- You can build lineage graphs in which you can visualize a specific model's data flow and dependencies. We will discuss this later in this chapter, and it's also covered in "Documentation" on page 200.

Finally, while acknowledging that the preceding code may seem like an antipattern, because of the sense of repetitiveness of `CASE WHEN` conditions, it's essential to clarify that the entire dataset includes all orders, regardless of their payment status. However, for this example, we chose to conduct financial analysis only on payments associated with orders that have reached the "success" status.

With the intermediate table built, let's move to the final layer. Considering the use case described, we need to analyze the orders from the customer's perspective. This means we must create a customer dimension that connects with our fact table. Since the current use case can fulfill multiple departments, we will not create a specific department folder but one named *core*. So, to start, let's create, in our models folder, the *marts/core* directory. Then copy Example 4-17 into a new file named *dim_customers.sql* and Example 4-18 into a new file named *fct_orders.sql*.

Example 4-17. dim_customers.sql

```
with customers as (
    select * from {{ ref('stg_jaffle_shop_customers')}}
)

select
    customers.customer_id,
    customers.first_name,
    customers.last_name
from customers
```

Example 4-18. fct_orders.sql

```
with orders as  (
    select * from {{ ref('stg_jaffle_shop_orders' )}}
),

payment_type_orders as  (
    select * from {{ ref('int_payment_type_amount_per_order' )}}
)

select
    ord.order_id,
    ord.customer_id,
    ord.order_date,
    pto.cash_amount,
    pto.credit_amount,
    pto.total_amount,
    case
        when status = 'completed'
        then 1
        else 0
    end as is_order_completed

from orders as ord
left join payment_type_orders as pto ON ord.order_id = pto.order_id
```

With all files created, let's just set our default configurations inside *dbt_project.yml*, as shown in Example 4-19, and then execute dbt run, or potentially dbt run --full-refresh on BigQuery.

Example 4-19. Model configuration, per layer, inside dbt_project.yml

```
models:
  dbt_analytics_engineer_book:
    staging:
      +materialized: view
    intermediate:
      +materialized: view
    marts:
      +materialized: table
```

> If you are receiving an error message similar to "Compilation Error in rpc request...depends on a node named *int_payment_type_amount_per_order* which was not found," this means that you have a model, dependent on the one that you are trying to preview, that is not yet inside your data platform—in our case int_payment_type_amount_per_order. To solve this, go to that particular model and execute the dbt run --select *MODEL_NAME* command, replacing *MODEL_NAME* with the respective model name.

If everything ran successfully, your data platform should be fully updated with all dbt models. Just look at BigQuery, which should be similar to Figure 4-36.

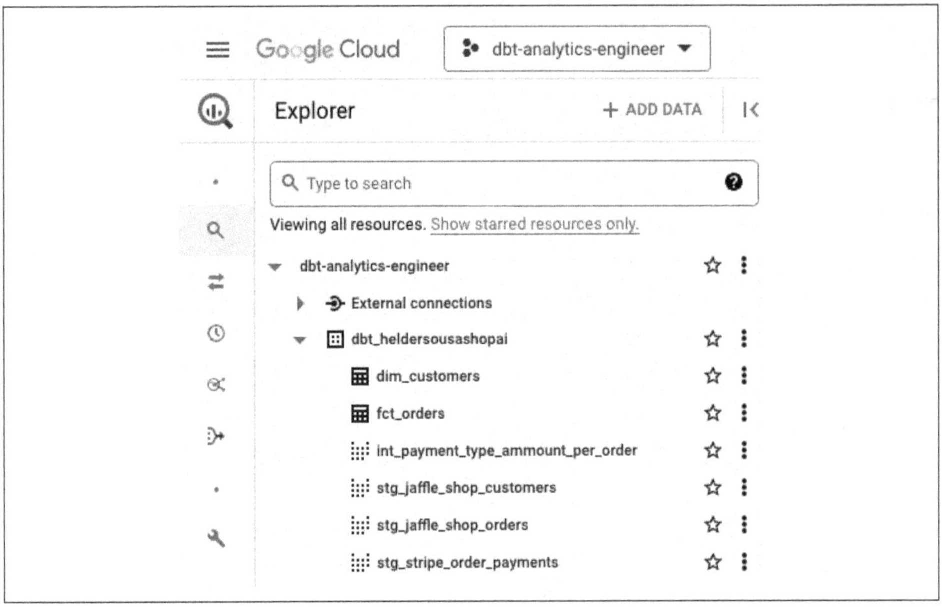

Figure 4-36. dbt BigQuery with all models

Finally, open *fct_orders.sql* and look at the Lineage option inside the information window (Figure 4-37). This is one of the great features we will cover in "Documentation" on page 200, giving us a good idea of the data flow that feeds a specific model and its upstream and downstream dependencies.

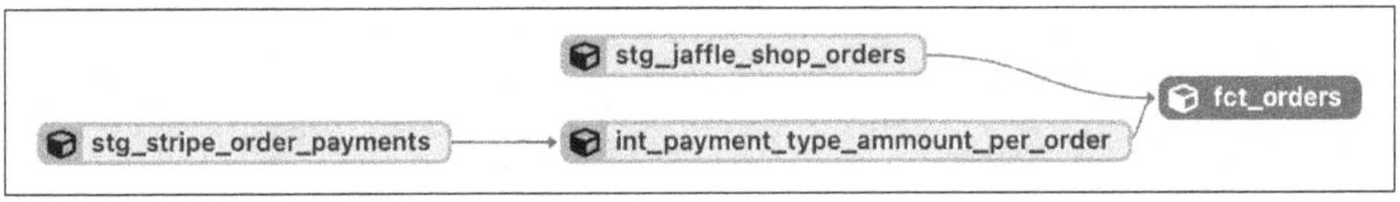

Figure 4-37. dbt fct_orders data lineage

Sources

In dbt, *sources* are the raw data available in your data platform, captured using a generic extract-and-load (EL) tool. It is essential to distinguish dbt sources from traditional data sources. A traditional data source can be either internal or external. *Internal data sources* provide the transactional data that supports the daily business operations inside your organization. Customer, sales, and product data are examples of potential content from an internal data source. On the other hand, *external data sources* provide data that originated outside your organization, such as data collected from your business partners, the internet, and market research, among others. Often this is data related to competitors, economics, customer demographics, etc.

dbt sources rely on internal and external data upon business demand but differ in definition. As mentioned, dbt sources are the raw data inside your data platform. This raw data is typically brought by the data engineering teams, using an EL tool, into your data platform and will be the foundation that allows your analytical platform to operate.

In our models, from "Models" on page 174, we've referred to our sources by using hardcoded strings such as `dbt-tutorial.stripe.payment` or `dbt-tutorial.jaffle _shop.customers`. Even if this works, consider that if your raw data changes, such as its location or the table name to follow specific naming conventions, making the changes across multiple files can be difficult and time-consuming. This is where dbt sources come in. They allow you to document those source tables inside a YAML file, where you can reference your source database, the schema, and tables.

Let's put this into practice. By following the recommended best practices in "YAML Files" on page 168, let's now create a new YAML file in the *models/staging/jaffle_shop* directory, named *_jaffle_shop_sources.yml,* and copy the code from Example 4-20. Then create another YAML file, now in the *models/staging/stripe* directory, named *_stripe_sources.yml,* copying the code in Example 4-21.

Example 4-20. _jaffle_shop_sources.yml—sources parametrization file for all tables under the Jaffle Shop schema

```
version: 2

sources:
  - name: jaffle_shop
    database: dbt-tutorial
    schema: jaffle_shop
    tables:
      - name: customers
      - name: orders
```

Example 4-21. _stripe_sources.yml—sources parametrization file for all tables under the stripe schema

```
version: 2

sources:
  - name: stripe
    database: dbt-tutorial
    schema: stripe
    tables:
      - name: payment
```

With our YAML files configured, we need to make a final change inside our models. Instead of having our sources hardcoded, we will use a new function named source(). This works like the ref() function that we introduced in "Referencing data models" on page 50, but instead of {{ ref("stg_stripe_order_payments") }}, to configure a source we now pass something like {{ source("stripe", "payment") }}, which, in this particular case, will reference the YAML file that we've created in Example 4-21.

Let's now get our hands dirty. Take all the SQL staging model code you created earlier, and replace it with the respective code in Example 4-22.

Example 4-22. Payments, orders, and customers staging models with the source() function

```sql
-- REPLACE IT IN stg_stripe_order_payments.sql
select
    id as payment_id,
    orderid as order_id,
    paymentmethod as payment_method,
    case
        when paymentmethod in ('stripe'
                            ,'paypal'
                            , 'credit_card'
                            , 'gift_card')
        then 'credit'
        else 'cash'
    end as payment_type,
    status,
    amount,
    case
        when status = 'success'
        then true
        else false
    end as is_completed_payment,
    created as created_date
from {{ source('stripe', 'payment') }}

-- REPLACE IT IN stg_jaffle_shop_customers.sql file
select
    id as customer_id,
    first_name,
    last_name
from {{ source('jaffle_shop', 'customers') }}

-- REPLACE IT IN stg_jaffle_shop_orders.sql
select
    id as order_id,
    user_id as customer_id,
    order_date,
    status,
```

```
    _etl_loaded_at
from {{ source('jaffle_shop', 'orders') }}
```

After you switch your models with our `source()` function, you can check how your code executes in your data platform by running `dbt compile` or clicking the Compile button in your IDE. In the backend, dbt will look to the referenced YAML file and replace the `source()` function with the direct table reference, as shown in Figure 4-38.

Figure 4-38. dbt customers staging model with source() *function and respective code compiled. The compiled code is what will run inside your data platform.*

Another benefit of using the `source()` function is that now you can see the sources in the lineage graph. Just take a look, for example, at the *fct_orders.sql* lineage. The same lineage shown in Figure 4-37 should now look like Figure 4-39.

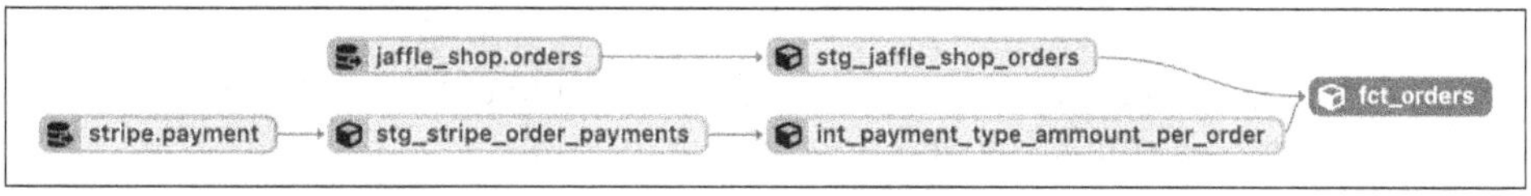

Figure 4-39. dbt fct_orders *data lineage with sources*

Source freshness

The freshness of your data is an essential aspect of data quality. If the data isn't up-to-date, it is obsolete, which could cause significant issues in your company's decision-making process since it could lead to inaccurate insights.

dbt allows you to mitigate this situation with the source freshness test. For that, we need to have an audit field that states the loaded timestamp of a specific data artifact in your data platform. With it, dbt will be able to test how old the data is and trigger a warning or an error, depending on the specified conditions.

To achieve this, let's get back to our source YAML files. For this particular example, we will use the orders data in our data platform, so by inference, we will replace the code in _jaffle_shop_sources.yml with the code in Example 4-23.

Example 4-23. _jaffle_shop_sources.yml—sources parametrization file for all tables under Jaffle Shop schema, with source freshness test

```
version: 2

sources:
  - name: jaffle_shop
    database: dbt-tutorial
    schema: jaffle_shop
    tables:
      - name: customers
      - name: orders
        loaded_at_field: _etl_loaded_at
        freshness:
          warn_after: {count: 12, period: hour}
          error_after: {count: 24, period: hour}
```

As you can see, we've used the _etl_loaded_at field in our data platform. We didn't have to bring it to our transformation process since it had no added value for forward models. This isn't an issue because we are testing our upstream data, which in our case is our raw data. In the YAML file, we've created two additional properties: loaded_at_field, which represents the field to be monitored under the source freshness test, and freshness, with the actual rules to monitor the source freshness. Inside the freshness property, we've configured it to raise a warning if the data is 12 hours outdated with the warn_after property and raise an actual error if the data wasn't refreshed in the past 24 hours with the error_after property.

Finally, let's see what happens if we execute the command **dbt source freshness**. In our case, we got a warning, as you can see in Figure 4-40.

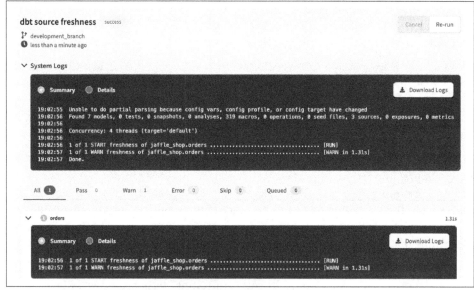

Figure 4-40. dbt orders raw data and source freshness test logs

If you check the log details, you can see the query executed in your data platform and troubleshoot. This particular warning was expected. The _etl_loaded_at was built to take 16 hours from the current time, so anything lower than that will raise a warning. If you want to keep playing around, change your warn_after to something higher, like 17 hours. All your tests should pass.

Hopefully, the source freshness concept is now clear. We will get back to it later in the book and show you how to automate and snapshot the source freshness tests. In the meantime, it is essential to understand its purpose in the overall test landscape, how to configure it, and how important this test could be to mitigate data quality issues.

Tests

As an analytics engineer, you must ensure that data is accurate and reliable to build trust in the analytics you deliver and provide objective insights for your organization. Everyone agrees with this, yet even if you follow all the engineering state-of-the-art best practices, there will always be exceptions—even more so when you have to deal with the volatility that is working with data, its variations, type, structure, etc.

There are many ways to capture those exceptions. Nonetheless, when you work with significant amounts of data, you need to think of a scalable approach to analyzing large datasets and quickly identifying those exceptions. This is where dbt comes in.

dbt allows you to rapidly and easily scale tests across your data workflow so that you can identify when things break before anyone else does. In a development environment, you can use tests to ensure that your analytics code produces the desired output. In a deployment/production environment, you can automate tests and set up an alert to tell you when a specific test fails so you can quickly react to it and fix it before it generates a more extreme consequence.

As a data practitioner, it's important to understand that tests in dbt can be summarized as assertions about your data. When you run tests on top of your data models, you assert that those data models produce the expected output, which is a crucial step in ensuring data quality and reliability. These tests are a form of verification similar to confirming that your data follows specific patterns and meets predefined criteria.

However, it's essential to note that dbt tests are just one type of testing within the broader landscape of data testing. In software testing, tests are often differentiated between verification and validation. dbt tests primarily focus on verification by confirming that data adheres to established patterns and structures. They are not designed for testing the finer details of logic within your data transformations, comparable to what unit tests do in software development.

Furthermore, dbt tests can assist with the integration of data components to some extent, particularly when multiple components are run together. Nevertheless, it's crucial to recognize that dbt tests have their limitations and may not cover all testing use cases. For comprehensive testing in data projects, you may need to employ other testing methods and tools tailored to specific validation and verification needs.

With this in mind, let's focus on which tests can be employed with dbt. There are two main classifications of tests in dbt: singular and generic. Let's get to know a bit more about both types, their purpose, and how we can leverage them.

Generic tests

The simplest yet highly scalable tests in dbt are *generic tests*. With these tests, you usually don't need to write any new logic, yet custom generic tests are also an option. Nevertheless, you typically write a couple of YAML lines of code and then test a particular model or column, depending on the test. dbt comes with four built-in generic tests:

unique *test*

Verifies that every value in a specific column is unique

not_null *test*

Verifies that every value in a specific column is not null

accepted_values *test*

Ensures that every value in a specific column exists in a given predefined list

relationships *test*

Ensures that every value in a specific column exists in a column in another model, and so we grant referential integrity

Now that we have some context about the generic tests, let's try them. We can choose the model we want, but to simplify, let's pick one to which we can apply all the tests. For that, we've chosen the *stg_jaffle_shop_orders.sql* model. Here we will be able to test unique and not_null in fields like customer_id and order_id. We can use accepted_values to check whether all orders status are in a predefined list. Finally, we will use the relationships test to check whether all values from the customer_id are in the *stg_jaffle_shop_customers.sql* model. Let's start by replacing our *_jaffle_shop_models.yml* with the code in Example 4-24.

Example 4-24. _jaffle_shop_models.yml parametrizations with generic tests

```
version: 2

models:
  - name: stg_jaffle_shop_customers
    config:
      materialized: view
    columns:
      - name: customer_id
        tests:
          - unique
          - not_null

  - name: stg_jaffle_shop_orders
    config:
      materialized: view
    columns:
      - name: order_id
        tests:
          - unique
          - not_null
      - name: status
        tests:
          - accepted_values:
              values:
```

```
                           - completed
                           - shipped
                           - returned
                           - placed
              - name: customer_id
                tests:
                  - relationships:
                      to: ref('stg_jaffle_shop_customers')
                      field: customer_id
```

Now, in your command line, type **dbt test** and take a look at the logs. If the test failed in the accepted_values, you did everything right. It was supposed to fail. Let's debug to understand the potential root cause of the failure. Open the logs and expand the test that failed. Then click Details. You'll see the query executed to test the data, as Figure 4-41 shows.

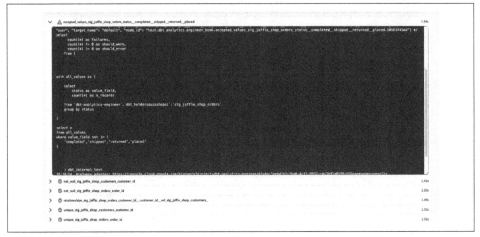

Figure 4-41. Generic test, dbt logs with accepted_values *failed test*

Let's copy this query to your text editor—keep only the inner query and then execute it. You should have a similar output as in Figure 4-42.

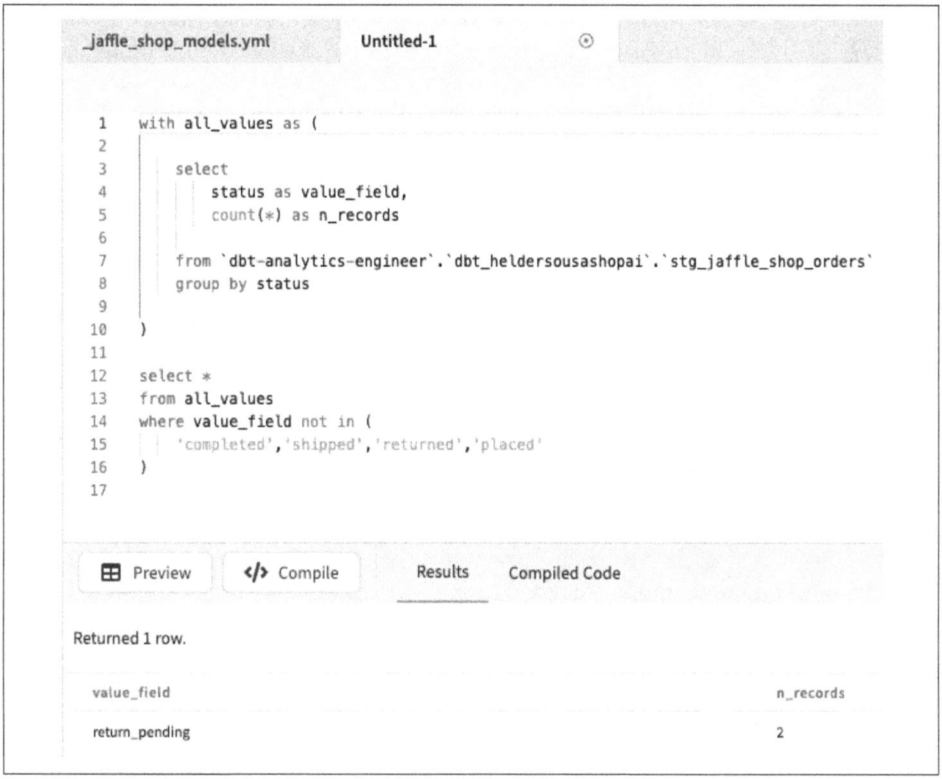

```
1    with all_values as (
2
3        select
4            status as value_field,
5            count(*) as n_records
6
7        from `dbt-analytics-engineer`.`dbt_heldersousashopai`.`stg_jaffle_shop_orders`
8        group by status
9
10   )
11
12   select *
13   from all_values
14   where value_field not in (
15       'completed','shipped','returned','placed'
16   )
17
```

Preview </> Compile   Results   Compiled Code

Returned 1 row.

value_field	n_records
return_pending	2

Figure 4-42. Generic test debug

And voilá. We found the issue. The additional status return_pending is missing from our test list. Let's add it and rerun our **dbt test** command. All the tests should pass now, as shown in Figure 4-43.

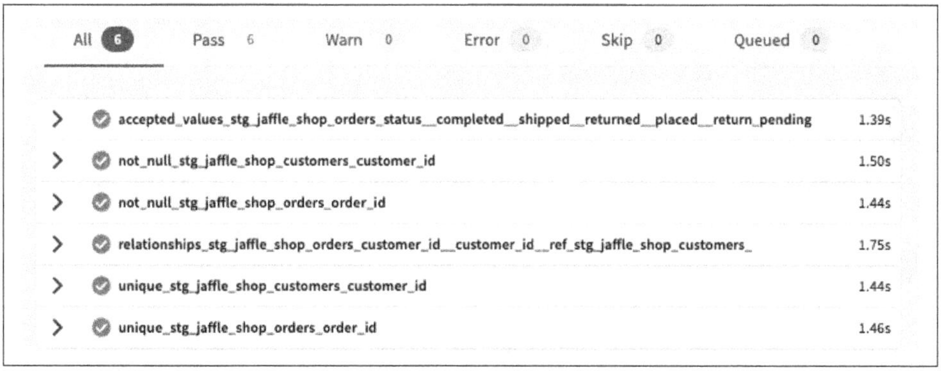

Figure 4-43. Generic test with all tests being successfully executed

In addition to the generic tests within dbt Core, a lot more are in the dbt ecosystem. These tests are found in dbt packages because they are an extension of the generic tests built inside dbt. "dbt Packages" on page 242 will detail the concept of packages and how to install them, but for extended testing capabilities, packages such as *dbt_utils* (*https://oreil.ly/MwqgC*) from the dbt team, or *dbt_expectations* (*https://oreil.ly/bmrqJ*) from the Python library Great Expectations, are clear examples of the excellent usage of packages and a must-have in any dbt project. Finally, custom generic tests are another dbt feature that enables you to define your own data validation rules and checks, tailored to your specific project requirements.

Singular tests

Unlike the generic tests, *singular tests* are defined in *.sql* files under the *tests* directory. Typically, these tests are helpful when you want to test a specific attribute inside a particular model, but the traditional tests built inside dbt don't fit your needs.

Looking into our data model, a good test is to check that no order has a negative total amount. We could perform this test in one of the three layers—staging, intermediate, or marts. We've chosen the intermediate layer since we did some transformations that could influence the data. To start, create a file named *assert_total_payment_amount_is_positive.sql* in the *tests* directory and copy the code in Example 4-25.

Example 4-25. assert_total_payment_amount_is_positive.sql singular test to check if the `total_amount` attribute inside int_payment_type_amount_per_order has only non-negative values

```
select
    order_id,
    sum(total_amount) as total_amount
from {{ ref('int_payment_type_amount_per_order') }}
group by 1
having total_amount < 0
```

Now you can execute one of the following commands to run your test, which should pass:

`dbt test`
    Executes all your tests

`dbt test --select test_type:singular`
    Executes only singular tests

```
dbt test --select int_payment_type_amount_per_order
```
   Executes all tests for the `int_payment_type_amount_per_order` model

```
dbt test --select assert_total_payment_amount_is_positive
```
   Executes only the specific test we created

These commands offer the ability to selectively run tests according to your requirements. Whether you need to run all tests, tests of a specific type, tests for a particular
model, or even a single specific test, dbt allows you to leverage various selection
syntax options within your commands. This variety of choices ensures that you can
precisely target the tests, along with other dbt resources, that you wish to execute. In
"dbt Commands and Selection Syntax" on page 209, we'll provide a comprehensive
overview of the available dbt commands and investigate how to efficiently use selection syntax to specify resources.

Testing sources

To test your models in your dbt project, you can also extend those tests to your
sources. You already did this with the source freshness test in "Source freshness" on
page 187. Still, you can also potentiate generic and singular tests for that purpose.
Using the test capabilities in your sources will give us confidence that the raw data is
built to fit our expectations.

In the same way that you configure tests in your models, you can also do so for your
sources. Either in YAML files for generic tests, or *.sql* files for singular tests, the norm
remains the same. Let's take a look at one example for each type of test.

Starting with generic tests, you will need to edit the specific YAML file of the sources.
Let's keep the same `unique`, `not_null`, and `accepted_values` tests as we have for
the customers and orders staging tables, but now you will test their sources. So,
to make this happen, replace the *_jaffle_shop_sources.yml* code with the code from
Example 4-26.

Example 4-26. _jaffle_shop_sources.yml—parametrizations with generic tests

```
version: 2

sources:
  - name: jaffle_shop
    database: dbt-tutorial
    schema: jaffle_shop
    tables:
      - name: customers
        columns:
            - name: id
              tests:
                - unique
```

```
              - not_null
  - name: orders
    loaded_at_field: _etl_loaded_at
    freshness:
      warn_after: {count: 17, period: hour}
      error_after: {count: 24, period: hour}
    columns:
          - name: id
            tests:
              - unique
              - not_null
          - name: status
            tests:
              - accepted_values:
                  values:
                    - completed
                    - shipped
                    - returned
                    - placed
                    - return_pending
```

Once you have your new code in the YAML file, you can run dbt test or, to be more exact, execute the command that will test only the source for which we've created these tests, dbt test --select source:jaffle_shop. All your tests should pass.

Finally, you can also implement singular tests as you did before. Let's replicate the singular test we performed earlier in Example 4-25. Create a new file named *assert_source_total_payment_amount_is_positive.sql* in your *tests* directory and copy the code from Example 4-27. This test checks whether the sum of the amount attribute, per order, inside the payment source table has only nonnegative values.

Example 4-27. assert_source_total_payment_amount_is_positive.sql singular test

```
select
    orderid as order_id,
    sum(amount) as total_amount
from {{ source('stripe', 'payment') }}
group by 1
having total_amount < 0
```

Execute dbt test or dbt test --select source:stripe, since we look into the Stripe source in this case. Everything should pass as well.

Analyses

The *analyses* folder can store your ad hoc queries, audit queries, training queries, or refactoring queries, used, for example, to check how your code will look before affecting your models.

Analyses are templated SQL files that you can't execute during `dbt run`, but since you can use Jinja on your analyses, you can still use `dbt compile` to see how your code will look while preserving your code under version control. Considering its purpose, let's look into one use case where we can leverage the *analyses* folder.

Imagine that you don't want to build a whole new model but still want to keep a piece of information for future needs by leveraging the code versioning. With analyses, you can do just that. For our use case, let's analyze the top 10 most valuable customers in terms of the total amount paid, considering only orders "completed" status. To see this, inside the *analyses* directory, create a new file named *most_valuable_customers.sql* and copy the code from Example 4-28.

Example 4-28. most_valuable_customers.sql analyses, which output the top 10 most valuable customers based on completed orders

```
with fct_orders as (
    select * from {{ ref('fct_orders')}}
),

dim_customers as  (
    select * from {{ ref('dim_customers' )}}
)

select
    cust.customer_id,
    cust.first_name,
    SUM(total_amount) as global_paid_amount
from fct_orders as ord
left join dim_customers as cust ON ord.customer_id = cust.customer_id
where ord.is_order_completed = 1
group by cust.customer_id, first_name
order by 3 desc
limit 10
```

Now execute the code and check the results. It will give you the top 10 most valuable customers if everything goes well, as Figure 4-44 shows.

customer_id	first_name	global_paid_amount
51.0	Howard	9900.0
3.0	Kathleen	6500.0
50.0	Billy	4700.0
8.0	Frank	4500.0
71.0	Gerald	4400.0
99.0	Mary	4400.0
54.0	Rose	4100.0
53.0	Anne	3900.0
69.0	Janet	3200.0
32.0	Thomas	3000.0

Figure 4-44. Top 10 most valuable customers, based on the total global amount paid with completed orders

Seeds

Seeds are CSV files within your dbt platform with a small amount of nonvolatile data to be materialized as a table inside your data platform. By simply typing dbt seed in your command line, seeds can be used in your models in the standard way, like all the other models, using the ref() function.

We can find multiple applications for seeds, from mapping country codes (for example, PT to Portugal or US to United States), zip codes to states, dummy email addresses to be excluded from our analyses, or even other complex analyses, like price range classification. What's important is to remember that seeds shouldn't have large or frequently changing data. If that is the case, rethink your data capture approach—for example, using an SFTP (SSH File Transfer Protocol) or an API.

To better understand how to use seeds, let's follow the next use case. Taking into account what we did in "Analyses" on page 197, we want to not only see the top 10 most valuable customers, based on paid orders completed, but also classify all customers with orders as *regular*, *bronze*, *silver*, or *gold*, considering the total_amount paid. As a start, let's create our seed. For that, create a new file named *customer_range_per_paid_amount.csv* in your seeds folder and copy the Example 4-29 data.

Example 4-29. seed_customer_range_per_paid_amount.csv with ranges mapping

```
min_range,max_range,classification
0,9.999,Regular
10,29.999,Bronze
30,49.999,Silver
50,9999999,Gold
```

After you complete this, execute **dbt seed**. It will materialize your CSV file into a table in your data platform. Finally, in the *analyses* directory, let's make a new file named *customer_range_based_on_total_paid_amount.sql* and copy the code from Example 4-30.

Example 4-30. customer_range_based_on_total_paid_amount.sql shows you, based on the completed orders and the total amount paid, the customer classification range

```
with fct_orders as (
    select * from {{ ref('fct_orders')}}
),

dim_customers as  (
    select * from {{ ref('dim_customers' )}}
),

total_amount_per_customer_on_orders_complete as (
    select
        cust.customer_id,
        cust.first_name,
        SUM(total_amount) as global_paid_amount
    from fct_orders as ord
    left join dim_customers as cust ON ord.customer_id = cust.customer_id
    where ord.is_order_completed = 1
    group by cust.customer_id, first_name
),

customer_range_per_paid_amount as (
    select * from {{ ref('seed_customer_range_per_paid_amount' )}}
)

select
        tac.customer_id,
        tac.first_name,
        tac.global_paid_amount,
        crp.classification
from total_amount_per_customer_on_orders_complete as tac
left join customer_range_per_paid_amount as crp
```

```
on tac.global_paid_amount >= crp.min_range
    and tac.global_paid_amount <= crp.max_range
```

Let's now execute our code and see the results. It will give each customer the total amount paid and its corresponding range (Figure 4-45).

4.61s	Returned 48 rows.		
customer_id	first_name	global_paid_amount	classification
92.0	Willie	1700.0	Gold
28.0	Lisa	300.0	Gold
39.0	Louise	1000.0	Gold
54.0	Rose	4100.0	Gold
31.0	Jane	1800.0	Gold
51.0	Howard	9900.0	Gold
53.0	Anne	3900.0	Gold
35.0	Sara	1500.0	Gold
32.0	Thomas	3000.0	Gold
13.0	Kathleen	2600.0	Gold
26.0	Aaron	800.0	Gold
8.0	Frank	4500.0	Gold
59.0	Adam	100.0	Gold
3.0	Kathleen	6500.0	Gold

Figure 4-45. Customers' range, based on the total global amount paid with completed orders

Documentation

Documentation is critical in the global software engineering landscape, yet it seems like a taboo. Some teams do it, others don't, or it is incomplete. It can become too bureaucratic or complex, or be seen as an overhead to the developer's to-do list, and thus avoided at all costs. You might hear a giant list of reasons to justify not creating documentation or postponing it to a less demanding time. No one says documentation is nonessential. It's just that "we won't do it," "not now," or "we don't have time."

Here are several reasons to justify creating and using documentation:

- Facilitates the onboarding, handover, and hiring processes. With proper documentation, any new team member will have the safeguard that they are not being "thrown to the wolves." The new colleague will have the onboarding process and technical documentation in writing, which reduces their learning curve on the current team processes, concepts, standards, and technological developments. The same applies to employee turnover and the knowledge-sharing transition.

- It will empower a single source of the truth. From business definitions, processes, and how-to articles, to letting users answer self-service questions, having documentation will save your team time and energy trying to reach that information.

- Sharing knowledge through documentation will mitigate duplicate or redundant work. If the documentation was done already, it could be reused without the need to start from scratch.

- It promotes a sense of shared responsibility, ensuring that critical knowledge is not confined to a single individual. This shared ownership is crucial in preventing disruptions when key team members are unavailable.

- It is essential when you want to establish quality, process control, and meet compliance regulations. Having documentation will enable your team to work toward cohesion and alignment across the company.

One reason that justifies the lack of motivation to create documentation is that it is a parallel stream from the actual development flow, like using one tool for development and another for the documentation. With dbt, this is different. You build your project documentation while developing your analytics code, tests, and connecting to sources, among other tasks. Everything is inside dbt, not in a separate interface.

The way dbt handles documentation enables you to create it while building your code. Typically, a good part of the documentation is already dynamically generated, such as the lineage graphs we've introduced before, requiring only that you configure your `ref()` and `source()` functions appropriately. The other part is partially automated, needing you to give your manual inputs of what a particular model or column represents. Yet, once again, everything is done inside dbt, directly in the YAML or Markdown files.

Let's get started with our documentation. The use case we want to achieve is to document our models and respective columns of `fct_orders` and `dim_customers`. We will use the models' YAML files, and for richer documentation, we will use doc blocks inside the Markdown files. Since we still need to create a YAML file for the core models inside the *marts* directory, let's do so with the name *_core_models.yml*.

Copy Example 4-31. Then, create a Markdown file in the same directory folder named *_code_docs.md*, copying Example 4-32.

Example 4-31. _core_models.yml—YAML file with `description` parameter

```
version: 2

models:
  - name: fct_orders
    description: Analytical orders data.
    columns:
      - name: order_id
        description: Primary key of the orders.
      - name: customer_id
        description: Foreign key of customers_id at dim_customers.
      - name: order_date
        description: Date that order was placed by the customer.
      - name: cash_amount
        description: Total amount paid in cash by the customer with "success" payment
        status.
      - name: credit_amount
        description: Total amount paid in credit by the customer with "success"
        payment status.
      - name: total_amount
        description: Total amount paid by the customer with "success" payment status.
      - name: is_order_completed
        description: "{{ doc('is_order_completed_docblock') }}"

  - name: dim_customers
    description: Customer data. It allows you to analyze customers perspective linked
    facts.
    columns:
      - name: customer_id
        description: Primary key of the customers.
      - name: first_name
        description: Customer first name.
      - name: last_name
        description: Customer last name.
```

Example 4-32. _core_doc.md—markdown file with a doc block

```
{% docs is_order_completed_docblock %}

Binary data which states if the order is completed or not, considering the order
status. It can contain one of the following values:

| is_order_completed | definition                                            |
|--------------------|-------------------------------------------------------|
| 0                  | An order that is not completed yet, based on its status  |
| 1                  | An order which was completed already, based on its status |

{% enddocs %}
```

Before generating the documentation, let's try to understand what we did. By ana-lyzing the YAML file *_core_models.yml*, you can see we've added a new property: description. This basic property allows you to complement the documentation with your manual inputs. These manual inputs can be text, as we used in most cases, but can also reference doc blocks inside Markdown files, as done in fct_orders, column is_order_completed. We first created the doc block inside the Markdown file _code_docs.md and named it is_order_completed_docblock. This name is the one that we've used to reference the doc block inside the description field: "{{ doc('is_order_completed_docblock') }}".

Let's generate our documentation by typing **dbt docs generate** in your command line. After it finishes successfully, you can navigate through the documentation page.

Reaching the documentation page is simple. After you execute dbt docs generate successfully, inside the IDE, at the top left of the screen, you can click the Documentation site book icon right next to the Git branch information (Figure 4-46).

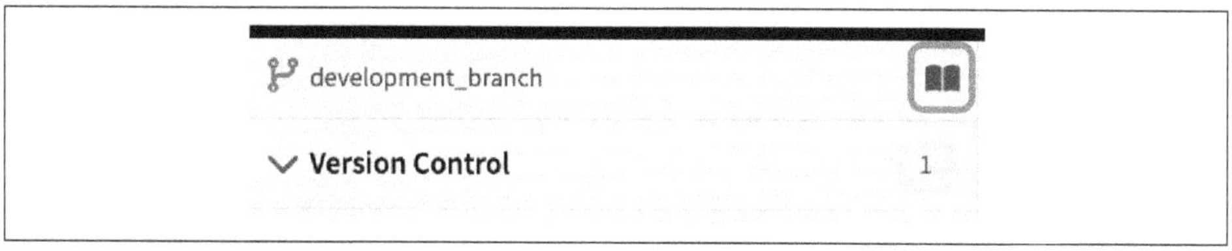

Figure 4-46. View documentation

Once you enter the documentation page, you will see the overview page, similar to Figure 4-47. For now, you have the default information provided by dbt, but this page is also fully customizable.

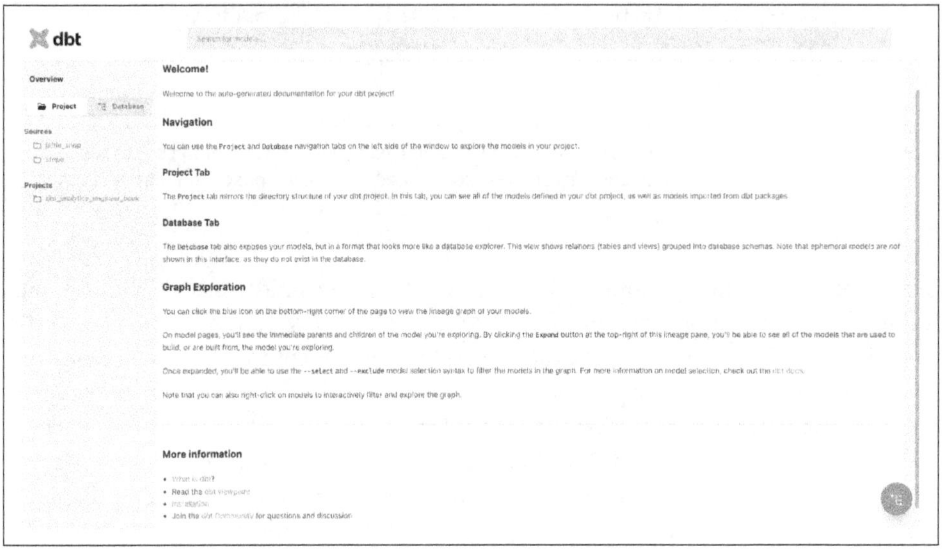

Figure 4-47. Documentation landing page

Looking on the overview page, you can see your project structure to the left (Figure 4-48) with tests, seeds, and models, among others, that you can navigate freely.

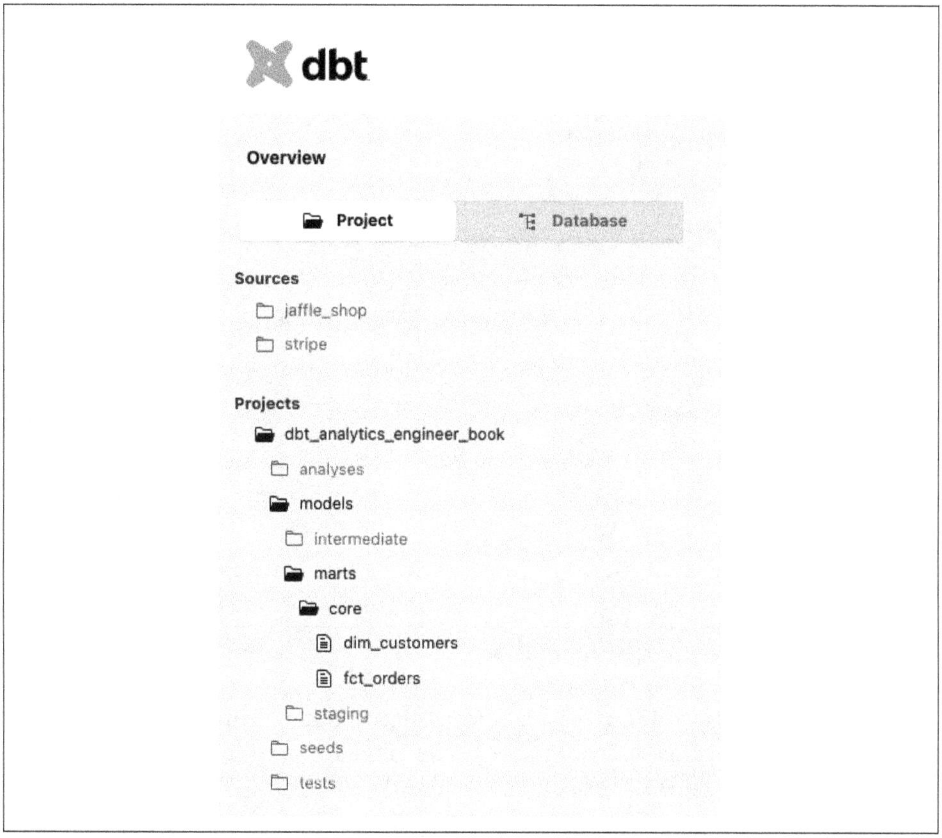

Figure 4-48. dbt project structure inside the documentation

Now choose one of our developed models and look at its respective documentation. We've selected the fct_orders model. Once we click its file, the screen will show you several layers of information on the model, as shown in Figure 4-49.

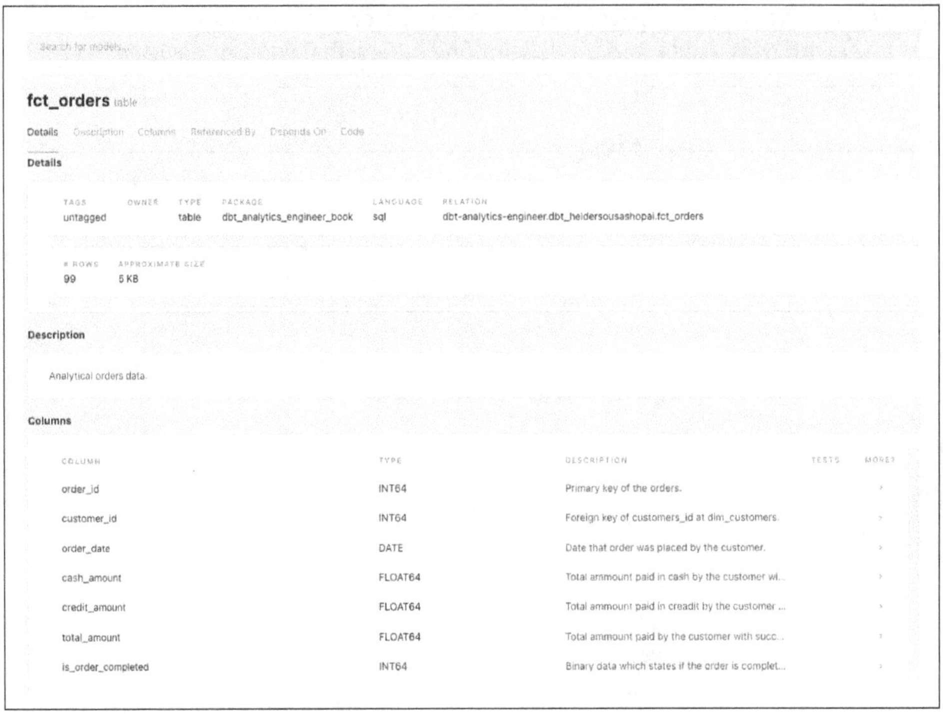

Figure 4-49. `fct_orders` documentation page

At the top, the Details section gives you information about table metadata, such as the table type (also known as *materialization*). The language used, the number of rows, and the approximate table size are other available details.

Right after, we have the Description of the model. As you may recall, it was the one we configured in the *_core_models.yml* file for the `fct_orders` table.

Finally, we have the Columns information related to `fct_orders`. This documentation is partially automated (for example, the column type), but also receives manual inputs (such as the column descriptions). We gave those inputs already filling the description properties and provided comprehensive information using doc blocks for the `is_order_completed` attribute. To see the written doc block on the documentation page, click in the `is_order_completed` field, which should expand and present the desired information (Figure 4-50).

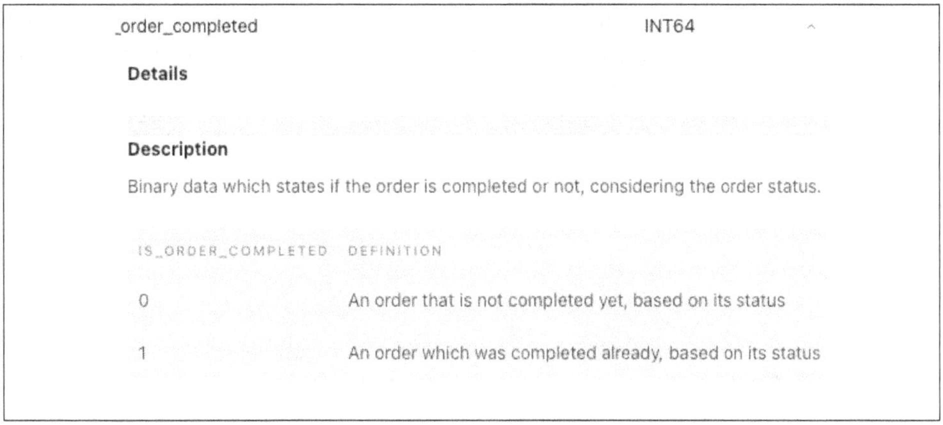

Figure 4-50. `is_order_completed` *column showing the configured doc block*

After the Columns information, we have the downstream and upstream dependencies of the model, with the Referenced By and Depends On sections, respectively. These dependencies are also shown in Figure 4-51.

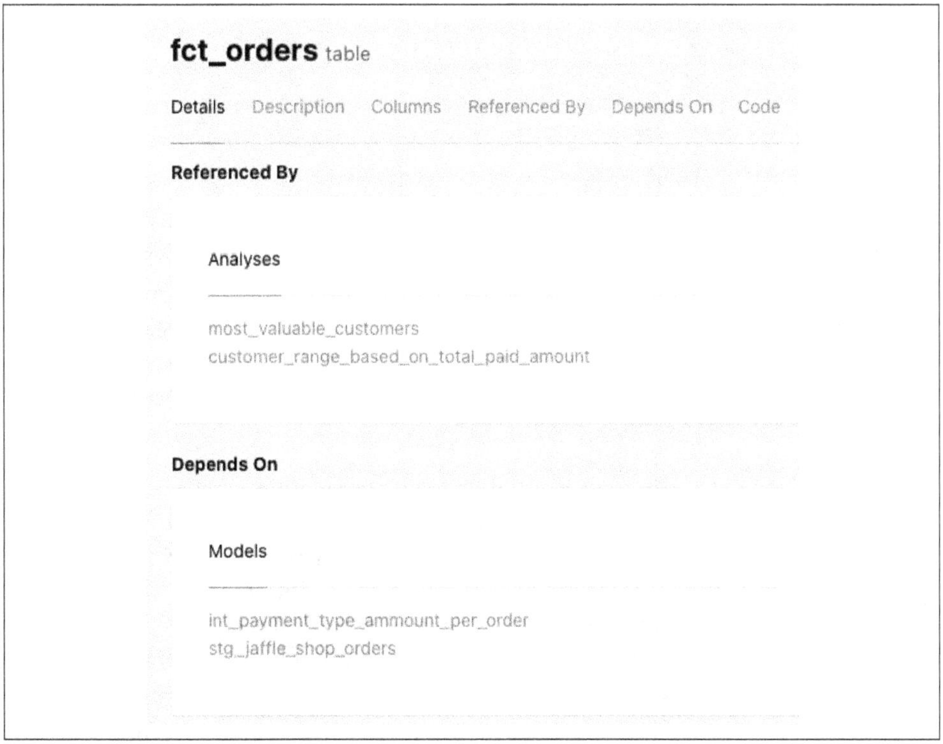

Figure 4-51. `fct_orders` *dependencies in the documentation*

At the bottom of the `fct_orders` documentation page is the Code that generated the specific model. You can visualize the source code in a raw format, with Jinja, or the compiled code. Figure 4-52 shows its raw form.

```
Code

Source   Compiled                                            copy to clipboard
_____

1   with orders as (
2       select * from {{ ref('stg_jaffle_shop_orders' )}}
3   ),
4
5   payment_type_orders as (
6       select * from {{ ref('int_payment_type_ammount_per_order' )}}
7   )
8
9   select
10      ord.order_id,
11      ord.customer_id,
12      ord.order_date,
13      pto.cash_amount,
14      pto.credit_amount,
15      pto.total_amount,
16      case
17          when status = 'completed'
18          then 1
19          else 0
20      end as is_order_completed
21
22  from orders as ord
23  left join payment_type_orders as pto ON ord.order_id = pto.order_id
```

Figure 4-52. `fct_orders` source code

Finally, if you look at the bottom right of your documentation page, you'll see a blue button. Clicking this button accesses the lineage graph for the respective model you are visualizing. We have selected the `fct_orders` lineage graph, where you can see the upstream dependencies, such as the source tables or the intermediate tables, as well as the downstream dependencies, like the analysis files shown in Figure 4-53. The lineage graph is powerful since it provides a holistic view of how data moves from the moment you consume it until you transform and serve it.

Another interesting aspect of dbt documentation worth mentioning is the ability to persist column- and table-level descriptions directly to the database by using the `per sist_docs` configuration. This feature is valuable for all users of your data warehouse, including those who may not have access to dbt Cloud. It ensures that essential metadata and descriptions are readily available to data consumers, facilitating better understanding and utilization of your data assets.

Figure 4-53. fct_orders lineage graph

dbt Commands and Selection Syntax

We've already introduced several dbt commands, such as dbt run and dbt test, and how we interact with the CLI to execute them. In this section, we'll explore the essential dbt commands and selection syntax that allow you to execute, manage, and control various aspects of your dbt project. Whether running transformations, executing tests, or generating documentation, these commands are your toolkit for effective project management.

Let's start at the beginning. At its core, dbt is a command-line tool designed to streamline your data transformation workflows. It provides a set of commands that enable you to interact with your dbt project efficiently. Let's explore each of these commands in more detail.

dbt run

The dbt run command is your go-to tool for executing data transformations defined in your dbt models. It works with your project's configuration files, such as *dbt_project.yml*, to understand which models to run and in what order. This command will identify the models that must be executed based on their dependencies and run them in the appropriate order.

dbt test

Ensuring the quality and reliability of your data is essential. The dbt test command lets you define and execute tests on your data models, verifying that they meet your business rules and expectations.

dbt docs

Adequate documentation is essential for collaborative data projects. dbt docs automates the documentation generation for your dbt project, including model descriptions, column descriptions, and relationships between models. To generate the documentation, you need to execute dbt docs generate.

dbt build

Before running your dbt project, compiling it is often necessary. The `dbt build` command performs this task, creating the required artifacts for execution. This step is essential for optimizing the execution process and ensuring everything is in its proper place. Once your project compiles successfully, you can proceed with other commands like `dbt run` with more confidence.

Other commands

Although the preceding commands may be the most used, you should be aware of other dbt commands, such as these:

`dbt seed`
Loads raw data or reference data into your project

`dbt clean`
Deletes artifacts generated by `dbt build`

`dbt snapshot`
Takes a snapshot of your data for versioning

`dbt archive`
Archives tables or models to cold storage

`dbt deps`
Installs project dependencies defined in *packages.yml*

`dbt run-operation`
Runs a custom operation defined in your project

`dbt source snapshot-freshness`
Checks the freshness of your source data

`dbt ls`
Lists resources defined in a dbt project

`dbt retry`
Re-runs the last run dbt command from the point of failure

`dbt debug`
Runs dbt in debug mode, providing detailed debugging information

`dbt parse`
Parses dbt models without running them, which is helpful for syntax checking

`dbt clone`
Clones selected models from the specified state

```
dbt init
```
Creates a new dbt project in the current directory

Selection syntax

As your dbt projects grow, you'll need to target specific models, tests, or other resources for execution, testing, or documentation generation instead of running them all every time. This is where selection syntax comes into play.

Selection syntax allows you to precisely specify which resources to include or exclude when running dbt commands. Selection syntax includes various elements and techniques, such as the following.

Wildcard *. The asterisk (*) represents any character or sequence of characters. Let's have a look at Example 4-33.

Example 4-33. Selection syntax with * wildcard

```
dbt run --select models/marts/core/*
```

Here, we're using the * wildcard along with the `--select` flag to target all resources or models within the *core* directory. This command will execute all models, tests, or other resources located within that directory.

Tags. *Tags* are labels you can assign to models, macros, or other resources in your dbt project—in particular, inside the YAML files. You can use selection syntax to target resources with specific tags. For instance, Example 4-34 shows how to select resources based on the `marketing` tag.

Example 4-34. Selection syntax with a tag

```
dbt run --select tag:marketing
```

Model name. You can precisely select a single model by using its name in the selection syntax, as shown in Example 4-35.

Example 4-35. Selection syntax with a model

```
dbt run --select fct_orders
```

Dependencies. Use the + and - symbols to select models that depend on or are depended upon by others. For example, `fct_orders+` selects models that depend on `fct_orders`, while `+fct_orders` selects models that `fct_orders` depends on (Example 4-36).

Example 4-36. Selection syntax with dependencies

```
# run fct_orders upstream dependencies
dbt run --select +fct_orders

# run fct_orders downstream dependencies
dbt run --select fct_orders+

# run fct_orders both up and downstream dependencies
dbt run --select +fct_orders+
```

Packages.   If you organize your dbt project into packages, you can use package syntax to select all resources within a specific package, as shown in Example 4-37.

Example 4-37. Selection syntax with a package

```
dbt run --select my_package.some_model
```

Multiple selections.   You can combine elements of selection syntax to create complex selections, as shown in Example 4-38.

Example 4-38. Selection syntax with multiple elements

```
dbt run --select tag:marketing fct_orders
```

In this example, we combined elements such as tagging and model selection. It will run the dbt model named `fct_orders` only if it has the tag `marketing`.

Selection syntax allows you to control which dbt resources run based on various criteria, including model names, tags, and dependencies. You can use selection syntax with the `--select` flag to tailor your dbt operations to specific subsets of your project.

Additionally, dbt offers several other selection-related flags and options, such as `--selector`, `--exclude`, `--defer`, and more, which provide even more fine-grained control over how you interact with your dbt project. These options make it easier to manage and execute dbt models and resources in a way that aligns with your project's requirements and workflows.

Jobs and Deployment

Until now, we've been covering how to develop using dbt. We've learned about models and how to implement tests and write documentation, among other relevant components that dbt provides. We accomplished and tested all of this by utilizing our development environment and manually executing our dbt commands.

Using a development environment shouldn't be minimized. It allows you to continue building your dbt project without affecting the deployment/production environment until you are ready. But now we have reached the stage where we need to productionize and automate our code. For that, we need to deploy our analytics code into a production branch, typically named the main branch, and into a dedicated production schema, such as `dbt_analytics_engineering.core` in BigQuery, or the equivalent production target in your data platform.

Finally, we need to configure and schedule a job to automate what we want to roll into production. Configuring a job is an essential part of the CI/CD process. It allows you to automate the execution of your commands in a cadence that fits your business needs.

To begin, let's commit and sync everything we did until now into our development branch and then merge with the main branch. Click the "Commit and sync" button (Figure 4-54). Don't forget to write a comprehensive message.

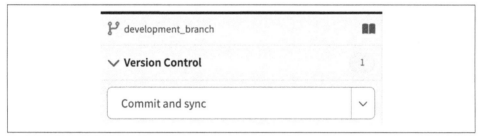

Figure 4-54. "Commit and sync" button

You may need to make a pull request. As explained briefly in "Setting Up dbt Cloud with BigQuery and GitHub" on page 140, pull requests (PRs) play an essential role in collaborative development. They serve as a fundamental mechanism for communicating your proposed changes to your team. However, it's crucial to understand that PRs are not just about notifying your colleagues of your work; they are a critical step in the review and integration process.

When you create a PR, you are essentially inviting your team to review your code, provide feedback, and collectively decide whether these changes align with the project's goals and quality standards.

Getting back to our code, after your PR, merge it with your main branch in GitHub. Your final screen in GitHub should be similar to Figure 4-55.

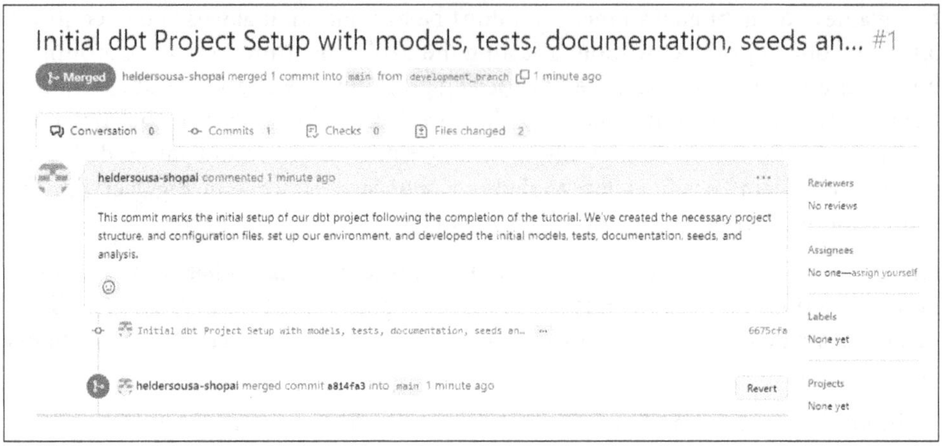

Figure 4-55. Pull request screen after merging with the main branch

At this stage, your main branch should equal your development branch. Now it is time to deploy it into your data platform. Before creating a job, you need to set up your deployment environment:

1. From the Deploy menu, click the Environments option and then click the Create Environment button. A screen will pop up where you can configure your deployment environment.

2. Keep the latest dbt Version, and don't check the option to run on a custom branch since we've merged our code into the main branch.

3. Name the environment "Deployment."

4. In the Deployment Credentials section, write the dataset that will link your deployment/production environment. We've named it `dbt_analytics_engineer_prod`, but you can use the name that best suits your needs.

If everything goes well, you should have a deployment environment set up with configurations similar to those in Figure 4-56.

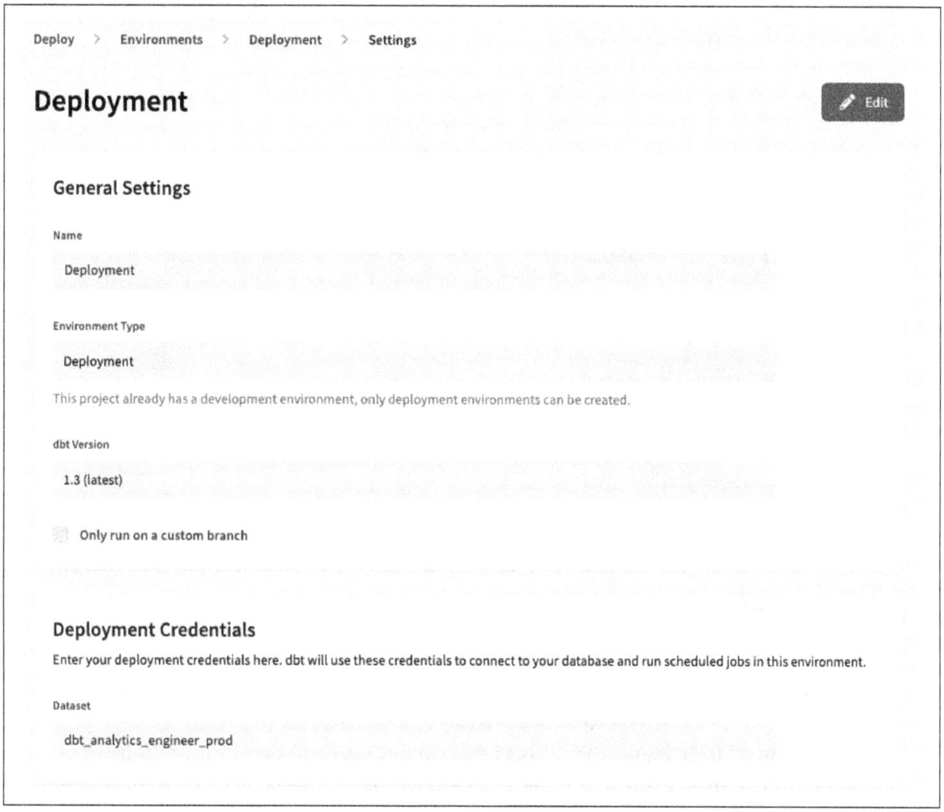

Figure 4-56. Deployment environment settings

Now it is time to configure your job. Inside the dbt Cloud UI, click the Jobs option in your Deploy menu and then click the Create New Job button. Creating a job can range from simple concepts to more complex ones. Let's set up a job that will cover the main ideas that we've discussed:

1. Name the job (Figure 4-57).

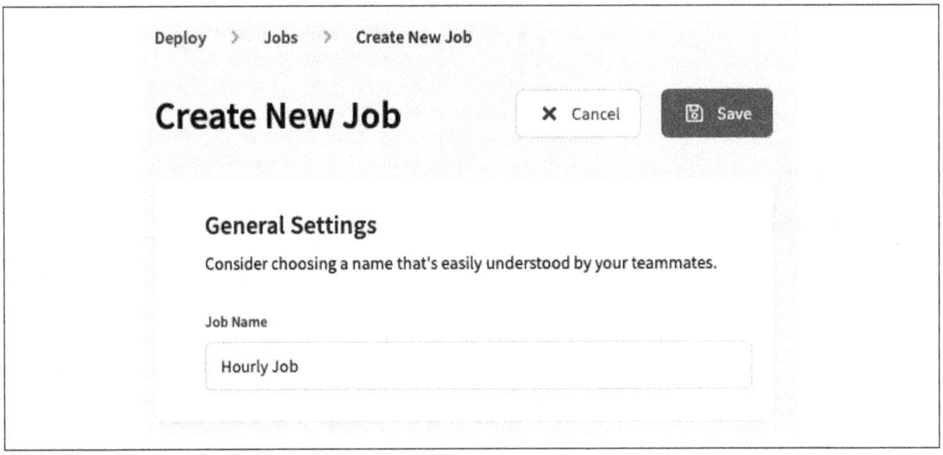

Figure 4-57. Defining the job name

2. In the Environment section, we will point to the Deployment environment. Configure the dbt version to inherit from the version defined in the Deployment environment. Then leave the Target Name set as default. This is helpful if you would like to define conditions based on your work environment (for example: if in the deployment environment, do this; if in development, do that). Finally, we covered the Threads in "profiles.yml" on page 172. Let's keep it set to the default configuration. We didn't create any Environment Variables, so this section will be left empty. Figure 4-58 presents the overall Environment section configuration.

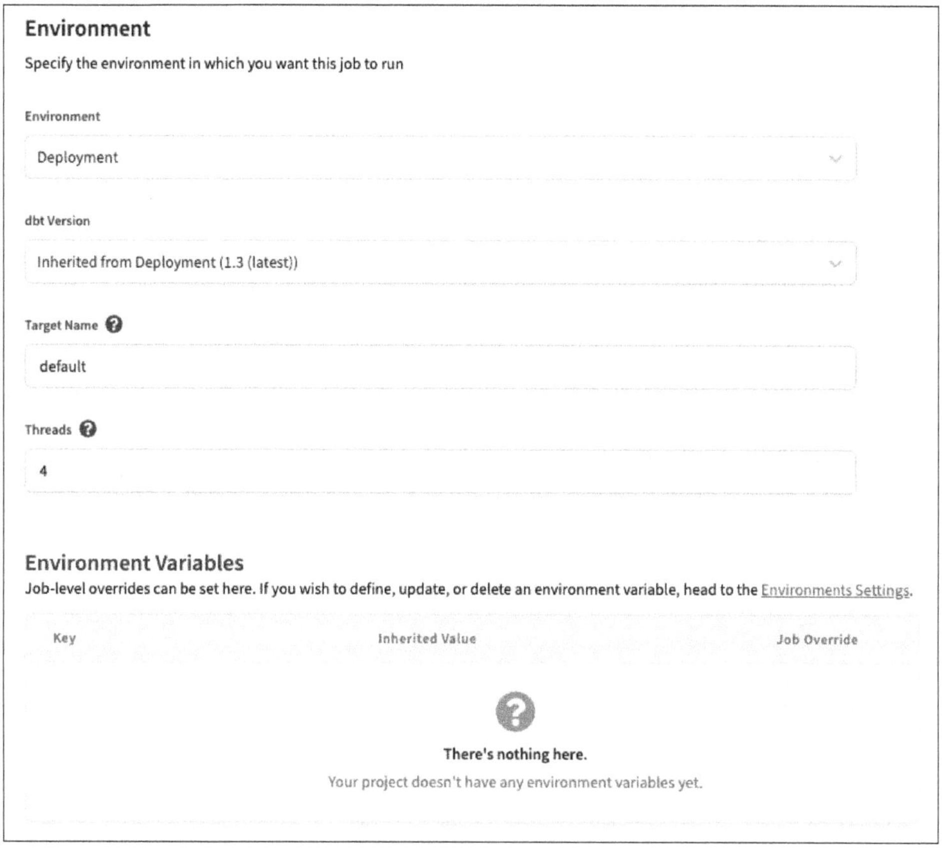

Environment

Specify the environment in which you want this job to run

Environment

| Deployment | ∨ |

dbt Version

| Inherited from Deployment (1.3 (latest)) | ∨ |

Target Name ❓

| default |

Threads ❓

| 4 |

Environment Variables

Job-level overrides can be set here. If you wish to define, update, or delete an environment variable, head to the Environments Settings.

Key	Inherited Value	Job Override

❓

There's nothing here.

Your project doesn't have any environment variables yet.

Figure 4-58. Defining the job environment

3. Figure 4-59 shows the global configurations of the Execution Settings. We've set Run Timeout to 0, so dbt will never kill the job if it runs for more than a certain amount of time. Then we've also chosen "do not defer to another run." Finally, we've selected the "Generate docs on run" and "Run source freshness" boxes. This configuration will reduce the number of commands you need to write in the Commands section. For this use case, we kept the default dbt build only.

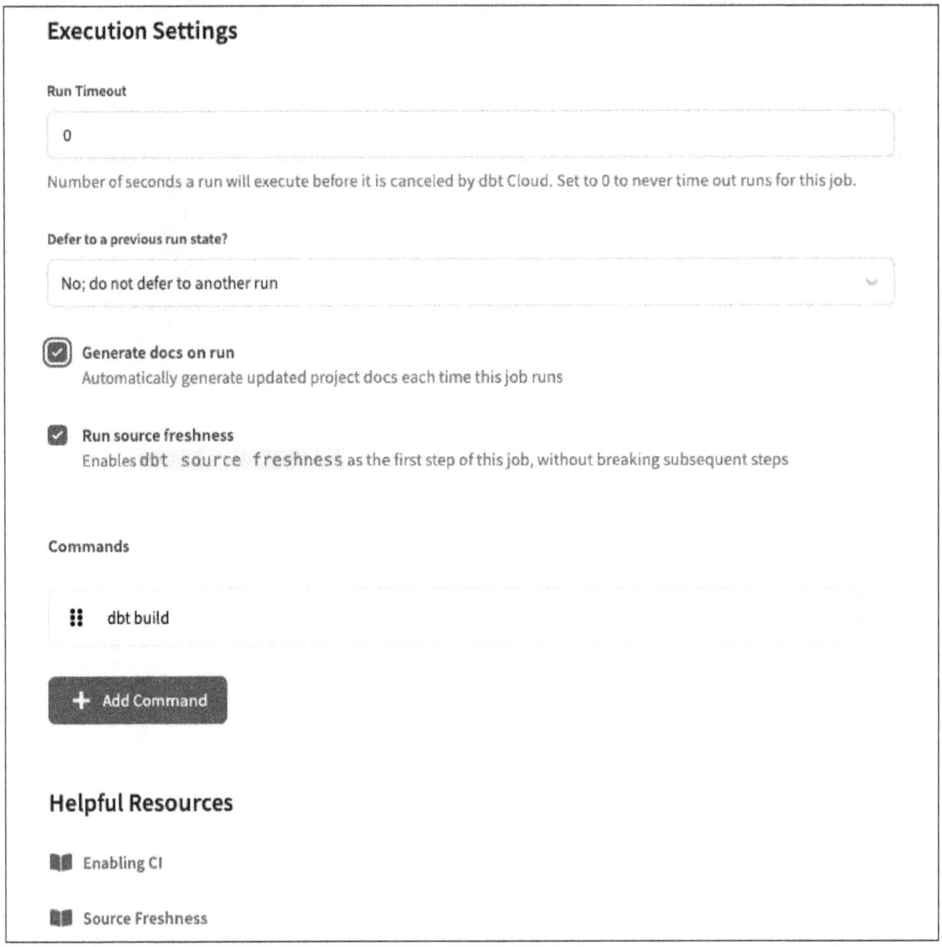

Execution Settings

Run Timeout

```
0
```

Number of seconds a run will execute before it is canceled by dbt Cloud. Set to 0 to never time out runs for this job.

Defer to a previous run state?

```
No; do not defer to another run
```

☑ **Generate docs on run**
Automatically generate updated project docs each time this job runs

☑ **Run source freshness**
Enables `dbt source freshness` as the first step of this job, without breaking subsequent steps

Commands

⠿   dbt build

+ Add Command

Helpful Resources

📖 Enabling CI

📖 Source Freshness

Figure 4-59. Defining job settings

4. The last configuration setting is Triggers, in which you configure how to launch the job. There are three options to trigger a job:

- A configured schedule inside dbt
- Through Webhooks
- Through an API call

For this use case, we've chosen the Schedule option and set the schedule to run on an hourly basis, as shown in Figure 4-60.

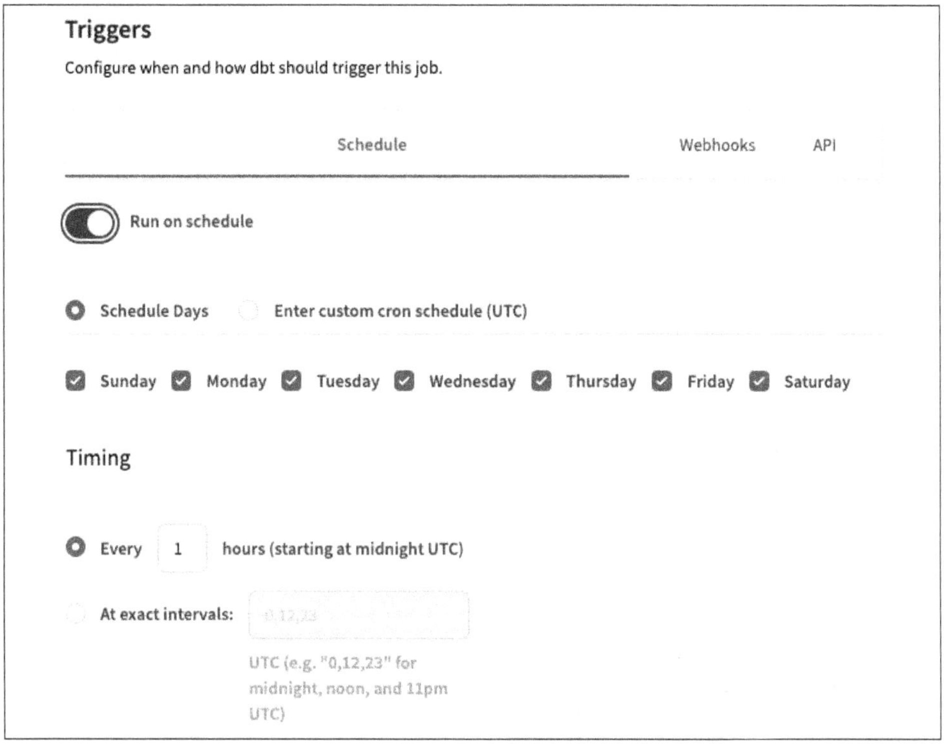

Figure 4-60. Defining the job trigger

It's time to execute and see what happens. Save your job; then select Run Now or wait for the job to be automatically triggered after it hits the configured schedule.

While the job runs, or after it finishes, you can always inspect the status and what was executed. From the Deploy menu, select the Run History option. You will see your job executions. Select one and take a look at the Run Overview. Figure 4-61 is what you should expect to see.

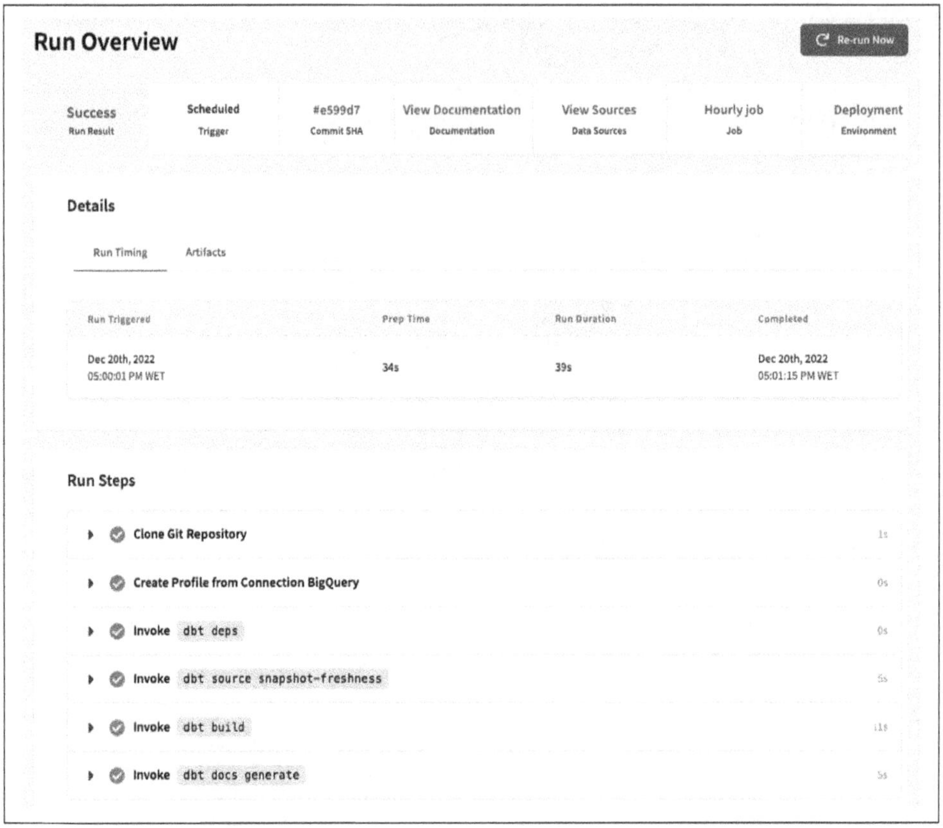

Figure 4-61. The job's Run Overview screen

Once inside the Run Overview, you have relevant information about the specific job execution, which could be helpful with potential troubleshooting issues. At the top is a summary of the job execution status, the person or system who triggered the job, the Git commit indexed to this job execution, the generated documentation, sources, and the environment where this job ran.

Right after the job summary, you can find the execution details, such as the time it took to execute the job and when it started and finished. Finally, one of the essential pieces of information that the Run Overview gives you is the Run Steps, which detail all the commands executed during the job execution and allow you to inspect each isolated step and its logs, as shown in Figure 4-62. Exploring each step's logs will enable you to understand what ran in each and look up issues during its execution.

Figure 4-62. The job's Run Steps details

By using dbt jobs, you can easily automate your transformations and deploy your projects to production in an efficient and scalable way. Whether you are a data analyst, data engineer, or analytics engineer, dbt can help you address the complexity of your data transformations and ensure that your data models are always accurate and up-to-date.

Summary

This chapter demonstrates that analytics engineering is an ever-evolving field that is always influenced by innovations. dbt is not just one aspect of this story; it is a crucial tool in the field.

The primary objective of analytics engineering is to convert raw data into valuable insights, and this tool plays a crucial role in simplifying the complexities of data transformation and promoting cooperation among a wide range of stakeholders. dbt ensures that data transformation is not just a technical change but also places great emphasis on openness, inclusivity, and knowledge sharing.

dbt is renowned for its capacity to streamline complicated processes by effortlessly integrating with large data warehouses. It also promotes a collaborative approach to data transformation by ensuring optimal traceability and accuracy. Furthermore, it highlights the significance of thoroughly testing data processes to guarantee dependability. Its user-friendly interface reinforces the notion that analytics engineering is an inclusive field, welcoming contributions from individuals of all competency levels.

To conclude, we strongly encourage analytics engineers who want to stay at the forefront of the industry to take a deep dive into this transformational tool. As dbt is increasingly important and unequivocally beneficial, being proficient in this tool can not only improve your skill set but also facilitate smoother and more cooperative data transformations in the future.

dbt Advanced Topics

dbt is a tool that focuses on the transformation part of the ELT process. With only SQL experience, we can develop all our analytical code with this tool. At the same time, in parallel, we can still encapsulate it under a set of best practices and standards typically found in software engineering, such as test development, automatic deployment, or even documentation built side by side while we develop.

In this chapter, our journey through dbt takes a more advanced and subtle turn. We will dig into the diverse collection of model materializations in dbt. Beyond the traditional views and tables, we'll explore the potential of ephemeral models, leverage materialized views, capture data snapshots at precise moments, and even use incremental models, which free you from recurrent, resource-intensive full data loads.

But that's not all. We'll elevate your analytics code to the next level with Jinja, macros, and packages. We're on a mission to transform your codebase, making it more efficient and DRY-er. By the end of this chapter, you'll be supplied with the knowledge and tools to level up your analytics workflow, enabling you to deliver insights faster and with even greater precision.

Model Materializations

Materializations are strategies for persisting dbt models in a data platform. In dbt, materializations can be used to improve the performance and scalability of a data model by reducing the need to compute queries and views on the fly.

In dbt, various types of materializations can be used, depending on the needs and requirements of the project. For example, you might use incremental materializations to store the results of queries that need to be updated only incrementally. Additionally, you might use snapshots, which are similar to materializations in dbt, but with distinct characteristics. Snapshots are used to store the results of a query or view at a specific point in time, yet snapshots are not models in dbt. They are intentionally designed to be non-idempotent, which sets them apart from most other aspects of dbt.

We've used materialization strategies already in Chapter 4, such as views and tables. However, it is important to be familiar with all types of materializations available, from ephemeral models to incremental data loads or even materialized views, so you can take advantage of them while optimizing your analytics code and provide accurate and prompt responses to your company's data consumers.

Tables, Views, and Ephemeral Models

We've been using view or table materializations to implement our models. This chapter aims to dig into both types of materializations and introduce the ephemeral models. But let's first look at Figure 5-1, which presents the current lineage of dim_customers already built earlier. In this use case, we will test the various materialization strategies—in particular, by changing the materialization type of the *stg_jaffle_shop_customers.sql* model.

Figure 5-1. dim_customers data lineage

Let's start with the tables' materialization type. In dbt, tables are structures used to store and organize data, and consist of rows and columns; each row represents a record or piece of data, while each column represents a specific attribute or field of the data. When you choose this type of materialization, internally, you are parameterizing dbt to render the referenced model to be physically created in your data platform, with data stored on disk; therefore, it will be slow to build. Typically, these materializations are used downstream on the marts layer and are recommended when we deal with huge amounts of data and multiple queries to our models that require fast response times.

To test the table materialization, let's change your YAML file *_jaffle_shop_models.yml*, setting the materialization to table for the stg_jaffle_shop_customers model. If you run your code, it should be similar to Figure 5-2 in BigQuery.

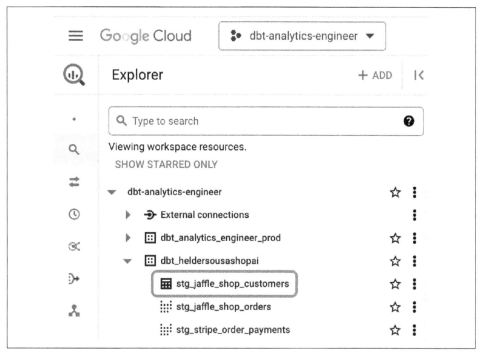

Figure 5-2. stg_jaffle_shop_customers materialized as a table

Views are virtual tables created by selecting and combining data from one or more upstream models. A view does not store any data on its own but instead retrieves data from the underlying tables when accessed. Typically, we will use views in dbt to simplify complex queries and facilitate the overall transformation process or to provide security by hiding specific columns or rows of data from users. When we set a model as a view, it will be built as a view in your data platform. It is the query itself that is stored in the disk, so only in runtime is the data captured and the transformations implemented, which can lead to slower query response times.

To test the usage of views, let's change your YAML file *_jaffle_shop_models.yml*, setting the materialization to view for the stg_jaffle_shop_customers model. Again, run your code. It should be similar to Figure 5-3 in BigQuery.

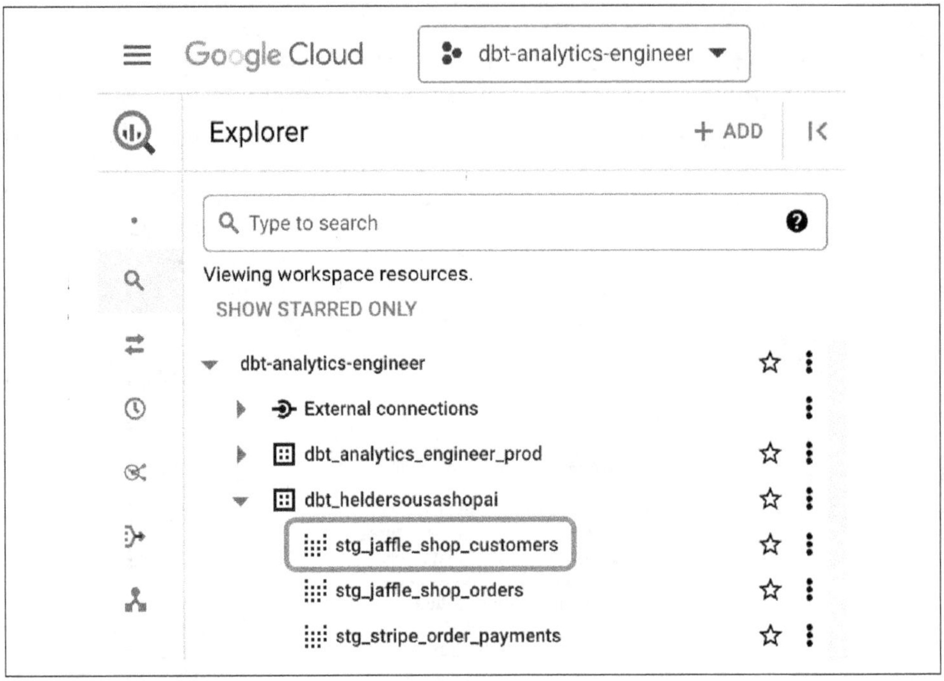

Figure 5-3. `stg_jaffle_shop_customers` materialized as a view

Finally, we have the *ephemeral* models. dbt builds these temporary data models on the fly, not persisting them in a database. It's best to use ephemeral models for lightweight data manipulation or analysis tasks that do not require the data to be permanently stored. When we go with this strategy, it is essential to remember that dbt will interpret this as CTEs in downstream models, which could also increase the overall building time of those models. Also, it could bring some complexity while debugging your code if we overuse ephemeral models because you cannot query them directly in your data platform since they will not exist there.

To test the ephemeral model, and following the previous examples, change your YAML file *_jaffle_shop_models.yml*, setting the materialization to `ephemeral` for the `stg_jaffle_shop_customers` model. Since, in this case, you will not have an actual materialization in your data platform, look at the `dim_product` compiled code. Figure 5-4 shows the difference between your code compiled with the `stg_jaffle_shop_customers` model as a view and as an ephemeral model.

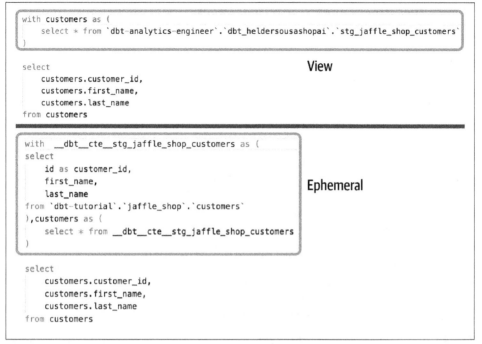

```
with customers as (
    select * from `dbt-analytics-engineer`.`dbt_heldersousashopai`.`stg_jaffle_shop_customers`
)

select                                          View
    customers.customer_id,
    customers.first_name,
    customers.last_name
from customers
```

```
with __dbt__cte__stg_jaffle_shop_customers as (
select
    id as customer_id,
    first_name,                                 Ephemeral
    last_name
from `dbt-tutorial`.`jaffle_shop`.`customers`
),customers as (
    select * from __dbt__cte__stg_jaffle_shop_customers
)

select
    customers.customer_id,
    customers.first_name,
    customers.last_name
from customers
```

Figure 5-4. dim_customer code compiled with the stg_jaffle_shop_customers model using a view (top) and an ephemeral model (bottom)

Incremental Models

In a dbt project, an *incremental model* is designed to process only new or changed data rather than all the data in a source. These models can be used to improve the efficiency and speed of a data pipeline, especially when working with large datasets that are updated frequently.

To test incremental models, first you need to configure your model's YAML file, setting the desired model as incremental. We will use an already created model, `stg_jaffle_shop_orders`, for our test case. Looking into its YAML file *_jaffle_shop_models*, we see it is materialized as `view`, as earlier configured. Since we want to make it incremental, the change is straightforward, yet we will also embed it with additional capacities, such as the `incremental_type`. So, let's update our model's YAML file with the code in Example 5-1.

Example 5-1. Incremental model, YAML file configuration

```
version: 2

models:
  - name: stg_jaffle_shop_orders
    config:
      materialized: incremental
      incremental_strategy: merge
      unique_key: order_id
```

First, we changed the model materialization type to incremental. This is the core of the incremental models and a mandatory configuration to make an incremental model work. In parallel, we've included two additional configurations: incremental_strategy: merge and unique_key: order_id. These configurations help you optimize and enhance your incremental loads. The incremental strategy is defined as merge (yet in dbt, you have more options, such as append or insert_overwrite), where each incremental run merges new rows with existing rows based on the identified unique key. In this case, if there's a match for order_id, the existing rows will be updated with the new information. Otherwise, if there is no match, new rows are created. In a standard incremental load, both scenarios occur in parallel.

The final step is to arrange the model code to make it compatible with incremental loads. In Example 5-2, you can see how we implement this in our stg_jaffle_shop_orders model.

Example 5-2. Incremental model, sample code

```
select
    id as order_id,
    user_id as customer_id,
    order_date,
    status,
    _etl_loaded_at
from {{ source('jaffle_shop', 'orders') }}

{% if is_incremental() %}

  where _etl_loaded_at >= (select max(_etl_loaded_at) from {{ this }} )

{% endif %}
```

By analyzing the query, we leverage Jinja to make our incremental models. Moving directly to the if statement, we see the usage of the is_incremental() macro. This macro will return true if the running model is configured with materialized= 'incremental', the dbt model already exists, and the dbt is not running in full-refresh mode. With is_incremental() returning true, inside the if code block, we have the `where` condition that filters rows based on the timestamp column `_etl_loaded_at`. It compares this timestamp to the maximum `_etl_loaded_at` timestamp from the current table (`{{ this }}`), which effectively checks whether the row's load timestamp is greater than or equal to the maximum load timestamp in the current table.

Incremental models play an essential role in optimizing data pipelines within a dbt project. One of their standout advantages is cost efficiency. By adopting incremental models, you can significantly reduce the computational resources required to process data. This efficiency not only speeds up your data transformation processes but also leads to cost savings, as you don't need to redo unnecessary work.

Moreover, incremental models ensure that your dbt project always operates with the most up-to-date data. This type of synchronization with data sources enhances the reliability and accuracy of your analytics. Whether you're dealing with streaming data or periodic updates, incremental models keep your analytical insights in sync with the evolving data landscape.

Materialized Views

Materialized views, at their core, are specialized database objects designed to store the results of a query as a physically materialized table. Their dynamic nature sets them apart from regular tables; the data within a materialized view is periodically refreshed to reflect the latest changes in the underlying dataset. This refreshing process ensures that materialized views remain up-to-date without the need for reprocessing, which makes them ideal when low-latency data access is critical.

Interestingly, materialized views share some common ground with dbt's incremental models, and this resemblance is no coincidence. In many ways, materialized views can be considered as successors to incremental models, offering an alternative approach to data optimization. Depending on your project's requirements and your chosen data platform, you might even consider replacing all your incremental dbt models with materialized view models. This shift simplifies your workflow, eliminating the need for manual incremental strategies that detail how dbt should update the base table—the data platform handles these tasks seamlessly.

However, it's essential to acknowledge the trade-offs that come with this transition. While materialized views offer efficiency, they might result in less fine-grained control over your incremental logic and orchestration. By entrusting the data platform with defining the logic and execution of updates, you gain convenience but may lose some of the specific control that incremental models can provide.

The way you test a dbt materialized view may vary depending on your data platform. The following method applies if you are using Postgres, Redshift, Databricks, or BigQuery (in dbt 1.7) and assumes you want to keep testing the `stg_jaffle_shop_customers` model. In the _jaffle_shop_models.yml_ file, change the materialization to `materialized_view`, as shown in Example 5-3.

Example 5-3. Materialized view, YAML file configuration

```
models:
  - name: stg_jaffle_shop_customers
    config:
      materialized: materialized_view
```

However, if you are using Snowflake instead, the concept varies slightly. Instead of materialized views, Snowflake has a distinct concept: *dynamic tables*. The basic configuration to use a dynamic table is presented in Example 5-4.

Example 5-4. Dynamic table, YAML file configuration

```
models:
  - name: stg_jaffle_shop_customers
    config:
      materialized: dynamic_table
```

In summary, materialized views are an integral part of data optimization, offering the benefits of performance improvement and data currency. Their role intersects with that of incremental models in dbt, presenting a choice for data engineers who want to simplify their workflows while considering the trade-offs in control and customization.

Snapshots

A *snapshot* is a copy of a dataset saved at a specific point in time. Typically, we use these snapshots when our analysis needs to look at the previous data states in continually updated tables. For example, you can use a snapshot to track the history of a dataset, allowing you to see how it has evolved over time. In addition, snapshots can be helpful for testing and debugging, as they enable you to compare the current state of a dataset to a previous state to identify any changes or discrepancies.

dbt snapshots are implemented by applying type 2 slowly changing dimensions (SCDs) over mutable source tables. These SCDs identify how a row in a table changes over time. Let's take a look at an example. Using the `jaffle_shop` database, imagine that you want to keep a record of the status transition of your orders so that you can monitor and inspect the lead times and identify potential bottlenecks in a particular status. By looking at the `stg_jaffle_shop_orders` model, we can see in Figure 5-5 that we already have the order status, but we need visibility of all statuses that the order moved through until it reached the current status.

order_id	customer_id	order_date	status	_etl_loaded_at
84.0	70.0	2018-03-26	placed	2023-10-01T04:42...
86.0	68.0	2018-03-26	placed	2023-10-01T04:42...
87.0	46.0	2018-03-27	placed	2023-10-01T04:42...
89.0	21.0	2018-03-28	placed	2023-10-01T04:42...
91.0	47.0	2018-03-31	placed	2023-10-01T04:42...
92.0	84.0	2018-04-02	placed	2023-10-01T04:42...
93.0	66.0	2018-04-03	placed	2023-10-01T04:42...

Figure 5-5. `stg_jaffle_shop_orders` transactional dataset

To allow us to track the status transition, we first need to retain the snapshots, which in dbt are **select** statements defined within a snapshot block inside a *.sql*, in our snapshot folder. So to start, let's create, in the *snapshots* directory, a file named *snap_order_status_transition.sql*, and copy the code from Example 5-5.

Example 5-5. snap_order_status_transition.sql snapshot creation

```
{% snapshot orders_status_snapshot %}

{{
    config(
      target_schema='snapshots',
      unique_key='id',

      strategy='timestamp',
      updated_at='_etl_loaded_at',
    )
}}

select * from {{ source('jaffle_shop', 'orders') }}

{% endsnapshot %}
```

Before executing the code, let's outline what those configurations mean:

target_schema

This is the schema that dbt should render the snapshot table into. In other words, dbt allows you to store your snapshots in a different schema in your data platform, separate from the actual production environment. It gives you the flexibility to take them out and back them up in another place. You can also leverage this field with the complement of target_database to store those snapshots not only in a different schema but also in a different database.

unique_key

Typically, this is the record's primary-key column or expression. It must point to a key that is unique.

strategy

This indicates the snapshot strategy to use, either timestamp or check. In the preceding example, we've used the timestamp strategy. It is the recommended strategy since it is scalable for new column addition. Sometimes the timestamp is unreliable, and in that case, we can use the check strategy to compare the current and historical values of a list of columns.

updated_at

When using the timestamp strategy, we need to declare which column we need to look at in the dataset.

check_cols

Used only with the check strategy, this is the columns that dbt will need to check to generate the snapshot.

Now that we understand what those configurations represent, let's execute the snapshot and see its output. For that, in the CLI, run **dbt snapshot**. After it finishes successfully, take a look at BigQuery. A new schema was created, named snapshots, with the actual snapshot materialized, as shown in Figure 5-6.

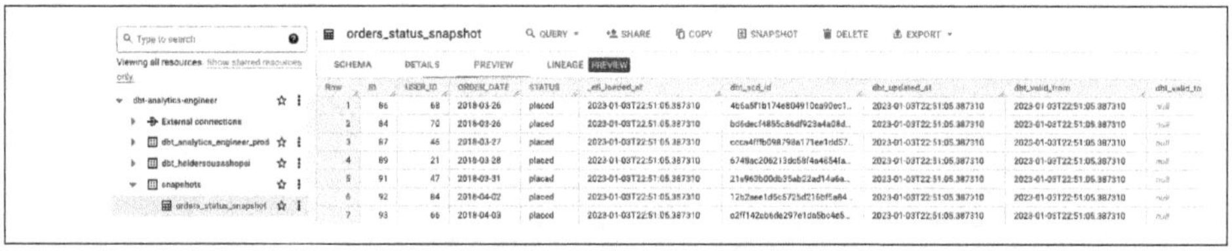

Figure 5-6. snap_order_status_transition snapshot table inside BigQuery

As you can see, dbt created the snapshot orders_status_snapshot inside your data platform, producing four additional columns:

dbt_scd_id

Used internally by dbt, a unique key is generated for each record snapshotted.

dbt_updated_at

Also used internally by dbt, this field was the updated_at timestamp of the source record when this snapshot row was inserted.

dbt_valid_from

The timestamp when this snapshot row was first inserted. It can be used to order the different "versions" of a record.

dbt_valid_to

The timestamp when this row became invalidated. It will show null if the record is still the most recent/valid record.

Suppose you want to keep exploring the concept of a snapshot. In that case, dbt provides comprehensive documentation that covers what we've mentioned here and additional content, such as best practices and how to handle hard deletes from source systems. Just search Snapshots (*https://oreil.ly/541Xm*) in the dbt Developer Hub (*https://docs.getdbt.com*).

Dynamic SQL with Jinja

Jinja is a templating language for Python widely used in web development. It allows you to create dynamic HTML pages by using variables and expressions and easily customize your website's appearance and behavior. You can also leverage it to level up your SQL code with dbt.

One of the key features of Jinja is its ability to insert variables and expressions into templates, allowing you to create customized templates for different users or contexts without hardcoding the values into the template itself. For example, you might want to define some behaviors based on your working environment, like limiting the amount of data while working in the development environment. For this case, we use the target name property in dbt, and then in our SQL code, and by leveraging Jinja, we can define the rule to handle it, as shown in Example 5-6.

Example 5-6. Jinja sample with the target name property

```
select *
from {{ ref('fct_orders' )}}

-- limit the amount of data queried in dev
{% if target.name != 'prod' %}
```

```
where order_date > DATE_SUB(CURRENT_DATE(), INTERVAL 3 MONTH)
{% endif %}
```

Note that we are using BigQuery and BigQuery syntax. Some functions and syntax may differ if you use a different data platform. Now, looking at the preceding code, we can see some Jinja notation already being used:

`{% … %}`

Used for statements, these perform any function programming, such as setting a variable or starting a for loop. In this particular example, we are using an `if` statement that checks if the property name is different (`!=`) from the `prod` field.

Jinja also provides a range of control structures, such as loops and conditional statements, that allow you to create more complex templates that can adapt to different data and contexts. You might use a loop to iterate over a list of items and dynamically generate your SQL code instead of manually doing it, field by field.

An ideal example can be demonstrated using the *int_payment_type_amount_per_order.sql* model you created earlier in Example 4-16. Instead of manually writing the amount metrics per type, you could generate them automatically and make them scalable, handling the current and future payment types. Look at Example 5-7 and see how we can leverage Jinja to do that.

Example 5-7. `int_payment_type_amount_per_order` model with dynamic Jinja

```
{# declaration of payment_type variable. Add here if a new one appears #}
{%- set payment_types= ['cash','credit'] -%}

with

payments as (

    select * from {{ ref('stg_stripe_order_payments') }}

),

pivot_and_aggregate_payments_to_order_grain as (

    select
        order_id,
        {% for payment_type in payment_types -%}

        sum(
            case
                when payment_type = '{{ payment_type }}' and
                     status = 'success'
                then amount
                else 0
            end
```

```
   ) as {{ payment_type }}_amount,

   {%- endfor %}
   sum(case when status = 'success' then amount end) as total_amount

 from payments

 group by 1

)

select * from pivot_and_aggregate_payments_to_order_grain
```

The preceding code is a more complex usage of Jinja, with loops and declaration of variables, yet once compiled, it will look quite similar to the result of the code in Example 5-6. Now, if we want to consider a new payment type, instead of manually creating a new metric, we need to add it to the payment_types list, declared at the top of the code.

Let's discuss the Jinja nuances that we can find in Example 5-7:

{% ... %}

As a recap, this is used for statements. In this case, we've used it in two distinct places, different from Example 5-6:

set payment_types= ['cash','credit']
This declares the payment_types variable, to be used later in the code. In this case, it's a list with two elements, cash and credit.

for payment_type in payment_types
Here, we iterate the different payment_types declared at the top. Row by row, we will start building our code dynamically.

{{ ... }}
This is used for expressions to print to the template output. In our example, we've used it for {{ payment_type }}, namely, to concatenate with the amount string to generate the final metric name per payment type. Also, we've used the actual metric computation on the expression: when payment_type = '{{ payment_type }}' and status = 'success'.

{# ... #}
Used for comments, this allows you to document your code inline.

Whitespaces
This is another small but important detail in the code. You can control them by using a hyphen on either side of the Jinja delimiter {%- ... -%}, which will trim the whitespace between the Jinja delimiter on that side of the expression.

We recommend exploring dedicated courses or referring to the official Jinja template design documentation (*https://oreil.ly/U2gye*) for a comprehensive understanding of Jinja. These resources can provide valuable insights and help you deepen your knowledge of Jinja's capabilities.

Using SQL Macros

Macros are reusable pieces of code used to automate tasks and processes in a dbt project. They increase productivity by allowing you to automate repetitive or complex tasks, such as queries, data manipulation, and data visualization. After you develop your macros, you can call and trigger them in various ways, including manually, automatically, or in response to user input.

In a dbt project, a macro is typically defined in a separate file, inside the *macros* directory, and written using Jinja syntax. Separating macros from your models allows your macros to be utilized in multiple models and other files within the project. It also allows macros to be customized using variables and expressions, enabling your macro to adapt based on the arguments sent from the specific model.

To use a macro in a dbt project, you will typically call the macro and pass any necessary arguments or options using Jinja syntax. Macros can also interact with other dbt features, such as views, and other macros, to create more complex and robust solutions. For example, you might use a macro to automate refreshing a data model, to filter or transform data in specific ways, or to generate reports or charts based on the data.

Let's try to create our first macro. Our initial use case is simple: create a macro that sums two numbers. Remember, your macro needs to use Jinja syntax. First, create a macro file in your dbt project in the *macros* directory, named *macro_sum_two_values.sql*. Example 5-8 shows what your code should look like.

Example 5-8. macro_sum_two_values.sql

```
{% macro sum(x, y) -%}
    select {{ x + y }}
{%- endmacro %}
```

Let's test it now. Then, in a new file inside your dbt project, you can use the macro by calling it with the desired values for x and y, as shown in Example 5-9.

Example 5-9. Trigger the macro inside macro_sum_two_values.sql

```
{{ sum(13, 89) }}
```

Example 5-9 will present the result of the macro (102) into the output window at the point where the macro is being triggered. You can also pass variables or expressions as arguments to the macro rather than hardcoded values. Look at Example 5-10, which must produce the same output as the previous example.

Example 5-10. Trigger the macro inside macro_sum_two_values.sql, defining the variables on top

```
{% set x = 13 %}
{% set y = 89 %}
{{ sum(x, y) }}
```

Using macros in a dbt project with Jinja allows you to reuse code and customize your models flexibly and powerfully. But now, let's use macros in an example. Using the jaffle_shop database, the first use case we want to deal with is a macro to centralize the payment types configuration to avoid defining it in every model, as we did earlier in the new version of *int_payment_type_amount_per_order.sql*. To accomplish that, in the *macros* directory, create a new file named *get_payment_types.sql* and copy the Example 5-11 code.

Example 5-11. get_payment_types.sql macro

```
{% macro get_payment_types() %}
    {{ return(["cash", "credit"]) }}
{% endmacro %}
```

Then, in your *int_payment_type_amount_per_order.sql* model, replace the payment_types variable being declared at the top with the code from Example 5-12.

Example 5-12. int_payment_type_amount_per_order.sql payment_types variable declaration calling the get_payment_types() macro

```
{%- set payment_types= get_payment_types() -%}
```

Now you can use your macro for other use cases, but consider the following:

- Typically, macros take arguments, so although Example 5-11 is a macro, it doesn't represent a typical one that you will build. Arguments refer to the values passed to a macro when it is called or executed. These arguments can be used to modify the behavior of the macro, such as by specifying input data sources, defining custom configuration settings, or setting certain parameters or flags.

- In Example 5-11, we've used the return function to return a list—without this function, the macro would return a string.

Looking at what you did, the macro in Example 5-11 doesn't seems to be very powerful or static. How could we optimize it so we avoid relying on manual inputs? We can do the following to overcome these issues:

- Understand the source data where we can dynamically pull the payment types.
- Rethink the macro with a modular mindset.

We can use the following query from Example 5-13 to overcome the first point.

Example 5-13. Get distinct payment types query

```
select
    distinct payment_type
from {{ ref('stg_stripe_order_payments') }}
order by 1
```

As you can see, if you run the query, it has distinct payment types, so to make a macro from it, copy the code from Example 5-14 into your *get_payment_types.sql* file.

Example 5-14. New version to make `get_payment_types` more dynamic and scalable

```
{% macro get_payment_types() %}
    {% set payment_type_query %}
    select
        distinct payment_type
    from {{ ref('stg_stripe_order_payments') }}
    order by 1
    {% endset %}

    {% set results = run_query(payment_type_query) %}

    {% if execute %}
    {# Return the first column #}
    {% set results_list = results.columns[0].values() %}
    {% else %}
    {% set results_list = [] %}
    {% endif %}

    {{ return(results_list) }}

{% endmacro %}
```

Let's see what we did:

1. At the top we declared the query `payment_type_query`.
2. Right after that, we executed using the `run_query` function and stored the output inside the `results` variable.

3. Then, we checked whether Jinja is in the **execute** mode—meaning SQL is being executed—and if so, we stored the results of the first column of the dataset in `results_list`. This first column is the one that will have the distinct values.

4. Finally, we returned the `results_list` variable to be used in our models.

Now, if we compile the *int_payment_type_amount_per_order.sql* model again, nothing should change. However, you have implemented a more scalable code. At this time, no manual input is required once a new payment type arises. But we can do even more with modularity. Imagine that you want to use a similar pattern elsewhere in your dbt project (for example, payment methods). In that case, we could do something like Example 5-15.

Example 5-15. Reusing our code multiple times for different scenarios

```
{# Generic macro to give a column name and table, outputs
the distinct fields of the given column name #}
{% macro get_column_values(column_name, table_name) %}

{% set relation_query %}
    select distinct
    {{ column_name }}
    from {{ table_name }}
    order by 1
{% endset %}

{% set results = run_query(relation_query) %}

{% if execute %}
{# Return the first column #}
{% set results_list = results.columns[0].values() %}
{% else %}
{% set results_list = [] %}
{% endif %}

{{ return(results_list) }}

{% endmacro %}

{# Macro to get the distinct payment_types #}
{% macro get_payment_types() %}

{{ return(get_column_values('payment_type', ref('stg_stripe_order_payments'))) }}

{% endmacro %}

{# Macro to get the distinct payment_methods #}
{% macro get_payment_methods() %}

{{ return(get_column_values('payment_method', ref('stg_stripe_order_payments'))) }}
```

```
{% endmacro %}
```

By analyzing this code, we can see three macros. The first, `get_column_values()`, receives the `column_name` and `table_name` as arguments and will dynamically generate a query to execute it, returning the distinct values of the `column_name` provided. Next, we've implemented two separate calls to that macro that will retrieve the distinct `payment_types` with the `get_payment_types()` macro, and the distinct payment_methods with the `get_payment_methods()` macro. Note also that the macro filename was changed to *get_distinct_by_column.sql* to make it more transparent, considering its purpose.

The preceding example presents an interesting demonstration of how to use macros, but they can be useful in many more instances. Another good example is to have a macro that dynamically validates that we are in a development or deployment environment and then automatically filters our dataset. To do that, in the *macros* directory, create a new macro named *limit_dataset_if_not_deploy_env.sql* and copy the code from Example 5-16.

Example 5-16. `limit_dataset_if_not_deploy_env` macro

```
{# Macro that considering the target name,
limits the amount of data queried for the nbr_months_of_data defined #}
{% macro limit_dataset_if_not_deploy_env(column_name, nbr_months_of_data) %}
-- limit the amount of data queried if not in the deploy environment.
{% if target.name != 'deploy' %}
where {{ column_name }} > DATE_SUB(CURRENT_DATE(), INTERVAL {{ nbr_months_of_data }}
  MONTH)
{% endif %}
{% endmacro %}
```

Then, in the `fct_orders` model, include the code from Example 5-17 at the bottom after the left join.

Example 5-17. Call `limit_dataset_if_not_deploy_env` macro from `fct_orders`

```
with orders as (
    select * from {{ ref('stg_jaffle_shop_orders' )}}
),

payment_type_orders as (
    select * from {{ ref('int_payment_type_amount_per_order' )}}
)

select
    ord.order_id,
    ord.customer_id,
```

```
        ord.order_date,
        pto.cash_amount,
        pto.credit_amount,
        pto.total_amount,
        case
            when status = 'completed'
            then 1
            else 0
        end as is_order_completed

from orders as ord
left join payment_type_orders as pto ON ord.order_id = pto.order_id
-- Add macro here
{{- limit_dataset_if_not_deploy_env('order_date', 3) }}
```

Now compile the code. If you are in the development environment, your
fct_orders.sql model should show a new filter, where order_date > DATE_SUB
(CURRENT_DATE(), INTERVAL 3 MONTH). In other words, the filter allows your code
to distinguish between the environments: if not the deployment environment, work
only with the last three months of data; otherwise, gather the whole dataset. Looking
at only *N* months in your development environment will substantially reduce the
overhead in your data platform, while at the same time, you still have a good subset of
data to work with while developing and testing your code. If this is not the case, you
can increase for 12, 24, or even 36 months.

Finally, it's important to mention dbt's adaptability in the ability to customize its core
macros. These macros serve some of dbt's core functionalities, offering predefined
templates for common tasks. One standout example is the generate_schema_name
macro. This macro is responsible for crafting schema names for your dbt models.
What's truly remarkable is that you can arrange it to align seamlessly with your
project's unique naming conventions. Imagine effortlessly generating schema names
that mirror your organization's data structure.

Customizing these core macros isn't just a technical feat. It's a game-changer in how
you exert dbt's capabilities, unlocking the potential to craft a data transformation
process that aligns precisely with your project's needs.

In conclusion, using macros in a dbt project can be a robust and efficient way to
automate and customize your data models and processes. Macros allow you to easily
reuse code and adapt your models to different contexts and requirements. Using Jinja
syntax, you can create flexible and easy-to-maintain macros that can be called and
triggered in various ways. Overall, macros can help you increase your productivity
and create more robust and scalable data models.

dbt Packages

Packages are a way to organize and share code and resources, such as models and macros, that have already been written, within a dbt project. They allow you to structure your project into logical units and to reuse code and resources across multiple models and files.

In a dbt project, packages are defined inside the *packages.yml* file, installed inside the *dbt_packages* directory, and are structured using a hierarchy of directories and files. Each package can contain models, tests, macros, and other resources that are related to a specific topic or functionality.

Packages can be used in many ways in a dbt project. For example, you might use packages to do the following:

Organize your project into logical units
>   Packages can help you structure your project in an intuitive and easy way to understand grouping together related models, tests, and other resources.

Reuse code and resources
>   Packages allow you to reuse code and resources across multiple models and files, saving time and reducing maintenance overhead.

Encapsulate functionality
>   Packages can help you encapsulate specific functionality and hide the implementation details from other parts of the project, making your project more modular and easier to understand.

Share code and resources with others
>   Packages can be shared with other users or projects, which allows you to leverage the work of others and be part of the community by contributing your own code.

Overall, packages are a valuable feature of dbt that can help you to organize, reuse, and share code and resources in your project. You can install dbt packages from three distinct places: a public packages hub, Git, or a local directory. In this section, we will cover how to install packages and show some examples of their usage. We will use one of the most common packages, dbt_utils, but note that there are a lot of great packages out there. You can find plenty of them at the dbt Hub (*https://hub.getdbt.com*) or import them directly from GitHub.

Installing Packages

Installing a package in a dbt project is a straightforward process that can help you leverage the work of others and add new functionalities to your project. We already gave an overview earlier, but let's discuss installing packages further.

The step-by-step guide to installing a package is as follows:

1. Create a *packages.yml* file if you don't already have it. This file is where you will configure the dbt packages that need to be installed in your dbt project.

2. Add the package to your *packages.yml* file: in your dbt project, open the file and add an entry for the package you want to install. Keep in mind that before installing a package, it is important to ensure that your dbt project meets any requirements or dependencies that the package may have. These may include specific versions of dbt or other packages, and system or software requirements.

3. Install the package by running the **dbt deps** command in your terminal. This will install the package and its dependencies in your dbt project.

4. Test the package to ensure it is working correctly. You can run the **dbt test** command and verify that the package's models and tests pass.

Let's try installing one of the most common packages available: dbt_utils (*https://oreil.ly/W-rZN*), which you can find at the dbt Hub (*https://hub.getdbt.com*). Typically, using the public packages hub will give you all the configurations that need to be inside your *packages.yml* file for a specific dbt package, resulting in a smoother installation. So, to install dbt_utils, copy the config from Example 5-18 into your *packages.yml* file.

Example 5-18. dbt_utils package configuration

```
packages:
  - package: dbt-labs/dbt_utils
    version: 1.1.1
```

Save your YAML file and run **dbt deps** in your CLI. Everything should be fine if you get a success message, as shown in Figure 5-7. Later in the chapter, we will use dbt_utils to see if everything is running as expected.

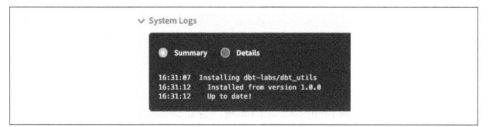

Figure 5-7. Success message on logs, after dbt_utils installation

If you receive a package incompatibility issue with your dbt version, ensure you're running a version of dbt that's compatible with the package you want to use. Check the package's documentation or repository for information on the supported dbt versions. You can also update the package version to be compatible with your dbt version. Finally, alternative packages that provide similar functionality and are compatible with your dbt version can be a solution.

Exploring the dbt_utils Package

First things first, let's meet the package that we will use for our examples: `dbt_utils`. This package is developed and maintained by dbt Labs, the creators of the dbt. It contains a collection of utility functions, macros, and other resources that are useful to extend and enhance the functionality of a dbt project.

Here are some examples of the types of resources included in the `dbt_utils` package:

- Helper functions used to perform common tasks, such as generating lists of columns, formatting dates and timestamps, and handling null values
- Custom data types used to represent data more expressively and flexibly, such as arrays, ranges, and intervals
- Debugging and testing tools for your dbt projects, such as logging functions and test frameworks
- Macros and models for performing a wide range of tasks, such as data manipulation, visualization, and testing

In conclusion, `dbt_utils` is a helpful package for dbt users who want to extend and customize their projects in various ways. It is constantly being updated and expanded to include new features and resources.

Using Packages Inside Macros and Models

In a dbt project, you can use packages inside macros to access other macros, models, tests, and other resources defined in the package. This allows you to reuse code and resources across multiple models and files, modularize your project, and, therefore, have DRY-er code.

Once the package is installed, as we outlined in "Installing Packages" on page 242, you can access its macros by using the package name as a prefix, following a specific syntax, as shown in Example 5-19.

Example 5-19. Sample macro call

```
{{ package.my_macro() }}
```

Using `dbt_utils`, we can generate a series of numbers or dates in a database that can be useful for various use cases. But let's take a look at a practical example. Let's experiment with the `date_spine()` macro. Copy the code from Example 5-20 and execute it.

Example 5-20. `date_spine` macro inside `dbt_utils`

```
{{ dbt_utils.date_spine(
    datepart="day",
    start_date="cast('2023-01-01' as date)",
    end_date="cast('2023-02-01' as date)"
    )
}}
```

The output expected is a list of dates between January 1, 2023 and, but not including, February 1, 2023. The `date_spine` macro is an effective and flexible function that can help you work with dates, generate sequences of dates, or perform other tasks that involve dates, such as creating a `dim_date` dimension in your analytics model.

Another use case is to use your installed packages directly in your developed models. For example, suppose you want to compute the percentage that the `cash_amount` has in a specific order, yet you need to ensure that for orders when the `total_amount` is 0, your code will not break, reporting a division-by-zero error. You can certainly do this logic by yourself, but `dbt_utils` already has a built-in function that handles it. Let's take a look at the code in Example 5-21.

Example 5-21. `safe_divide` macro inside `dbt_utils`

```
select
    order_id,
    customer_id,
    cash_amount,
    total_amount,
    {{ dbt_utils.safe_divide('cash_amount', 'total_amount') }}
from {{ ref('fct_orders') }}
```

This code uses the `safe_divide` macro to divide the numerator, `cash_amount`, by the denominator, `total_amount`, and to store the result in a variable called `result`. If the denominator is 0 or null, the `safe_divide` macro will return `null` instead of raising an error.

The `safe_divide` macro is great for performing division operations in a dbt project, especially when working with data that may contain null or 0 values. It can save time and reduce maintenance overhead by eliminating the need to manually check for null or 0 values.

dbt packages are a versatile tool to help you build better and more efficient data transformation pipelines. In this chapter, we've covered `dbt_utils`, which offers a collection of useful macros and functions that streamline common data modeling tasks, making it a valuable addition to your toolkit. Another interesting package is `dbt_expectations` (*https://oreil.ly/p0Gmi*), which empowers you to define, document, and test your data expectations, ensuring data quality and reliability. Additionally, `dbt_date` (*https://oreil.ly/LFm4q*) simplifies date-related calculations and manipulations in your data models. By leveraging these packages and others, you can simplify your code sharing and collaboration, reduce duplication of effort, and create more scalable and maintainable data models.

dbt Semantic Layer

In data analytics, a *semantic layer* plays a key role, acting as a bridge between raw data and meaningful insights. This logical abstraction is a decisive translator, simplifying complex data structures and facilitating a common understanding of data throughout an organization. Doing so transforms complex database setups into a user-friendly language that empowers a diverse audience, from data analysts to business leaders, to access and understand data effortlessly. Beyond simplification, the semantic layer also provides data integrity and reliability, guaranteeing that data is understandable and trustworthy.

The essence of the dbt semantic layer distinguishes it fundamentally from conventional semantic layers. In many semantic layers, users delineate connections within the data by explicitly specifying the left and right join keys. However, the dbt semantic layer specification adopts a unique approach by introducing *entities*. These entities enable us to automatically infer data connections, the graph's edges, within the layer. For instance, consider a customer table with a `customer_id` as its primary key and an orders table with a `customer_id` entity as a foreign key—this can form a relationship, or, more precisely, an edge in our data graph. This innovation significantly reduces the need for manual logic maintenance, as a graph usually has fewer nodes than edges.

The beauty of this approach lies in its simplicity and efficiency. It encapsulates semantic logic in an exceptionally DRY manner, facilitates a broader array of metric and dimension combinations, and results in cleaner SQL. These advantages make it easier for data teams to oversee, evolve, and leverage their data models.

At the core of the dbt semantic layer lie two essential components: semantic models and metrics. *Semantic models* are the foundational building blocks, comprising three key elements: entities, dimensions, and measures for creating a metric. These components empower MetricFlow, the framework powering our semantic layer, to construct queries for defining metrics.

Metrics, on the other hand, are the tools we employ to measure and analyze our data. They operate atop the semantic models, enabling the creation of sophisticated and elaborate definitions built upon reusable components.

As previously mentioned, the semantic layer relies on three fundamental concepts to create metrics: entities, dimensions, and measures.

An *entity* refers to an independent and identifiable object within a specific context. In the language of databases, entities typically correspond to tables, serving as the core subjects of our data collection efforts. Entities represent real-world concepts within a business, containing, for example, customers or orders. In our semantic models, entities are represented using ID columns, which function as join keys to connect with other semantic models in the semantic graph.

Entities are essential in helping the Semantic Engine understand the relationships among tables or datasets. This enables the engine to comprehend how data is interconnected, ensuring that when a query is made concerning a specific entity, the engine knows where to retrieve the relevant information.

On the other hand, *dimensions* provide context to measures by serving as categorical attributes that allow the breakdown of the data in different ways during the analysis. Dimensions typically describe the characteristics associated with other elements within the model.

Dimensions are configured to empower users to explore and analyze data from diverse perspectives. The Semantic Engine utilizes these dimensions to tailor queries according to user preferences.

Finally, *measures* are the quantifiable data points that are the primary focus of analysis, representing the metrics we intend to examine. Measures are often subject to aggregation, and in many cases, a fundamental role of a BI tool is to aggregate these measures across various dimensions. The definition of measures ensures that calculations maintain consistency across all queries and reports, eliminating any semantic ambiguity.

Let's illustrate how to build a dbt semantic layer. We'll keep using the example of customers and orders entities. We want to measure the total amount paid (`total_amount`) and have a split for what was paid in cash (`cash_amount`) and what was paid in credit (`credit_amount`). Finally, we also want to have the total number of orders made (`order_count`) and the number of customers with orders (`custom` ers_with_orders). We also want to know the capacity to slide per day (order_date) and whether orders completed or not (is_order_completed).

Considering these requirements, the full semantic model is shown in Example 5-22. You can add it to the respective YAML file previously created, _core_models.yml, or create a new one for the semantic model.

Example 5-22. YAML file configuration for the semantic model

```
semantic_models:
  - name: orders
    description: |
      Order fact table. This table is at the order grain with one row per order.
    model: ref('fct_orders')

    entities:
      - name: order_id
        type: primary
      - name: customer
        type: foreign
        expr: customer_id
    dimensions:
      - name: order_date
        type: time
        type_params:
          time_granularity: day
      - name: is_order_completed
        type: categorical
    measures:
      - name: total_amount
        description: Total amount paid by the customer with successful payment
          status.
        agg: sum
      - name: order_count
        expr: 1
        agg: sum
      - name: cash_amount
        description: Total amount paid in cash by the customer with successful
          payment status.
        agg: sum
      - name: credit_amount
        description: Total amount paid in credit by the customer with successful
          payment status.
        agg: sum
      - name: customers_with_orders
        description: Distinct count of customers placing orders
        agg: count_distinct
        expr: customer_id
```

Moving to the last stage, all the components covered previously require the involvement of a Semantic Engine to operationalize them. This engine plays a fundamental role in interpreting the provided data and constructing analytical queries in accordance with those definitions. For example, even after meticulously specifying all the aspects of customer orders, we still depend on an engine to parse the semantic model and generate a query that calculates the desired metrics. Within the domain of dbt, this function is fulfilled by MetricFlow.

The Semantic Engine concept is analogous to a dbt Documentation Engine. When you create a YAML file for a model, it remains inert by itself, lacking significant functionality. However, the dbt Documentation Engine transforms this data into practical tools, including a documentation website, dbt tests, alert systems, data contracts, and more. Similarly, MetricFlow operates as a dbt Semantic Engine, leveraging its capacity to interpret semantic data and generate valuable outcomes, particularly standardized and reusable analytical queries.

To use MetricFlow for the generation of analytical queries, the initial step consists of establishing metrics based on the semantic model you've meticulously constructed. You can define metrics in the same YAML files as your semantic models or create a new file.

To illustrate the process of metrics creation, let's first clarify the specific metrics we intend to develop. To maintain simplicity while retaining interest, it's worthwhile to include a metric that calculates the total amount of orders (order_total). Furthermore, we can create another metric that tracks the count of orders placed (order_count). Finally, we'll explore a metric that, based on the number count of orders placed, filters the metric itself, revealing what portion of the orders placed were completed. Example 5-23 provides a YAML file demonstrating the proper configuration of these metrics.

Example 5-23. Metrics YAML file configuration

```
metrics:
  - name: order_total
    description: Sum of total order amount.
    type: simple
    label: Order Total
    type_params:
      measure: total_amount
  - name: order_count
    description: Count of orders.
    label: Orders
    type: simple
    type_params:
      measure: order_count
  - name: completed_orders
    description: Count of orders that were delivered
```

```
label: Delivered Orders
type: simple
type_params:
  measure: order_count
filter: |
  {{ Dimension('order_id__is_order_completed') }} = true
```

As an example, to get MetricFlow working on `order_total`, use the CLI command `mf query --metric order_total`. MetricFlow will interpret this definition alongside the measure's definition (outlined in the semantic model) to produce the query in Example 5-24.

Example 5-24. Order total query

```
SELECT SUM(total_amount) as order_total
FROM fct_orders
```

> While this chapter aims to showcase the workings of the semantic layer within dbt, note that there may be better choices for organization-wide deployment than `mf query`. For broader and more robust usage across your organization, consider utilizing the APIs provided by dbt. Additionally, we recommend referring to the "Set Up the dbt Semantic Layer" page (*https://oreil.ly/UaZbt*) for the most up-to-date and accurate installation instructions for the semantic layer and MetricFlow, as it is regularly updated with the latest information and developments.

Having established a dbt semantic layer, you've effectively created an abstraction layer over your data. Regardless of any modifications made to the orders dataset, anyone seeking the total order amount can easily access the `order_total` metric. This empowers users to analyze the orders data according to their specific requirements.

Summary

In this chapter, we've dug into advanced topics in the world of dbt, expanding our understanding of this transformative tool. We explored the power of dbt models and materializations, uncovering how they enable us to manage complex data transformations while ensuring efficient performance optimization. Using dynamic SQL with Jinja has allowed us to create dynamic and reusable queries that adapt to changing requirements, thus enhancing the agility of our data processes.

Moving beyond the fundamentals, we presented SQL macros, unlocking a new level of automation and reusability in our codebase. Through insightful examples, we saw how SQL macros can drastically streamline our code and bring consistency to our data transformations.

Moreover, the concept of dbt packages emerged as a cornerstone of collaboration and knowledge sharing in our data ecosystem. We discussed how dbt packages allow us to encapsulate logic, best practices, and reusable code, fostering a culture of collaboration and accelerating development cycles.

Finally, we've demonstrated how the dbt semantic layer can enhance your analytics solution by providing an abstraction layer over your data. This layer ensures consistency and exactness across all reports and analyses because the business logic is centralized and verified within the semantic layer, minimizing the risk of disparities or mistakes. Furthermore, as the database expands or undergoes modifications, having a semantic layer allows you to make adjustments in a single location, eliminating the need to update numerous reports or queries individually.

As we conclude this chapter, we've embarked on a journey through various advanced dbt topics, equipping ourselves with the knowledge and tools required to optimize our data processes. These advanced concepts elevate our data transformations and empower us to elevate our data analytics to unprecedented heights. Armed with these insights, we've competently navigated the complexities of data challenges while promoting innovation in our data-driven endeavors.

However, it's important to note that while this has been a comprehensive guide to dbt, the dbt universe is vast and continually evolving. Several additional topics are worth exploring, such as advanced deployment techniques like blue/green, canary, or shadow deployments. Additionally, digging into the usage of Write-Audit-Process (WAP) patterns can provide teams with greater control over data quality and traceability. Also, exploring how dbt interfaces with other tools in the data ecosystem would be valuable, as well as understanding how to work with multiproject organizations. Indeed, dbt is a dynamic and expansive world; there's always more to learn and discover on this exciting data journey.

## CHAPTER 6

Building an End-to-End Analytics Engineering Use Case

Welcome to the last chapter of our book on analytics engineering with dbt and SQL. In the previous chapters, we have covered various concepts, techniques, and best practices for turning raw data into actionable insights using analytics engineering. Now it's time to pull these topics all together and embark on a practical journey to construct an end-to-end analytics engineering use case.

In this chapter, we will look at designing, implementing, and deploying a comprehensive analytics solution from start to finish. We will leverage the full potential of dbt and SQL to build a robust and scalable analytics infrastructure and also use data modeling for both operational and analytical purposes.

Our main goal is to show how the principles and methods covered in this book can be practically applied to solve real-world data problems. By combining the knowledge acquired in the previous chapters, we will build an analytics engine that spans all phases of the data lifecycle, from data ingestion and transformation to modeling and reporting. Throughout the chapter, we'll address common challenges that arise during implementation and provide guidance on how to effectively overcome them.

Problem Definition: An Omnichannel Analytics Case

In this challenge, our goal is to enhance the customer experience by providing seamless and personalized interactions across multiple channels. To achieve this, we need a comprehensive dataset that captures valuable customer insights. We require customer information, including names, email addresses, and phone numbers, to build a robust customer profile. It is essential to track customer interactions across channels, such as our website, mobile app, and customer support, to understand their preferences and needs.

We also need to gather order details, including order dates, total amounts, and payment methods, to analyze order patterns and identify opportunities for cross-selling or upselling. Furthermore, including product information like product names, categories, and prices will enable us to tailor our marketing efforts and promotions effectively. By analyzing this dataset, we can uncover valuable insights, optimize our omnichannel strategy, enhance customer satisfaction, and drive business growth.

Operational Data Modeling

In our pursuit of a holistic approach we begin our journey with the operational step. In this way, we aim to create a solid foundation for subsequent steps. Our approach involves using the carefully documented requirements for a management database, which will guide us. In line with industry best practices, we will diligently follow the three essential steps—conceptual, logical, and physical modeling—to meticulously build our database.

Keep in mind, we are opting for a breadth-first strategy that covers all the steps but does not go deep in terms of detail. Thus, consider this an academic exercise with simplified requirements, intended to equip you with a better understanding of the processes of building an operational database, and not a comprehensive one.

Conceptual Model

As we previously described, the first step, consisting of the conceptual modeling phase, allows us to conceptualize and define the overall structure and relationships within the database. This involves identifying the key entities, their attributes, and their associations. Through careful analysis and collaboration with stakeholders, we will capture the essence of the management system and translate it into a concise and comprehensive conceptual model (Figure 6-1).

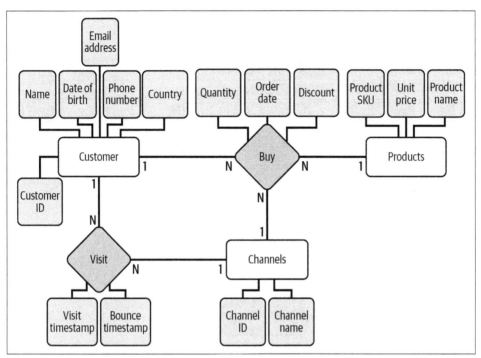

Figure 6-1. Conceptual diagram for our operational database

In the conceptual model in Figure 6-1, we can observe three entities, Customer, Channel, and Products, with two key relationships, Buy and Visit. The first relationship enables us to track purchases of customers of certain products in certain channels. (Keep in mind, we need the channels for understanding performance across them.) The second relationship allows us to track interactions across channels. For each entity and relationship, we have defined a few attributes to make it a richer database.

Logical Model

As we previously mentioned, to convert the conceptual ERD exercise into a logical schema, we create a structured representation of entities, attributes, and their relationships. This schema acts as a foundation for implementing the database in a specific system. We turn the entities into tables, with their attributes becoming table columns. Relationships are handled differently based on the type: for N:1 relationships, we use foreign keys to connect tables, and for M:N relationships, we create a separate table to represent the connection. By following these steps, we ensure data integrity and efficient management of the database, almost normalizing implicitly our conceptual model.

If we apply the previous rules to our concept, we should be able to come up with something similar to Figure 6-2.

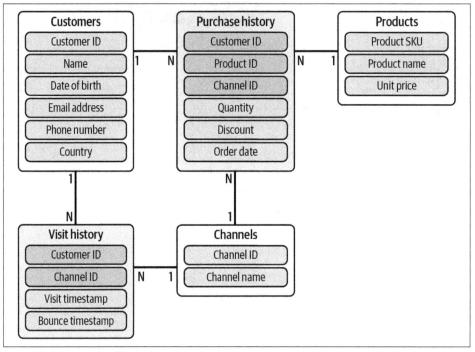

Figure 6-2. Logical schema for our operational database

As you can see, we now have five tables: three of them represent the primary entities (Customers, Products, and Channels), while the remaining two tables represent the relationships. However, for the sake of simplicity, we have renamed the two relation tables from Buy and Visit to Purchase history and Visit history, respectively.

Physical Model

While the logical model primarily deals with the conceptual representation of the database, the physical model delves into the practical aspects of data management, assuming we have chosen a certain database engine. In our case, it will be MySQL. Thus, we need to translate the logical model into specific storage configurations, as per MySQL best practices and limitations.

Figure 6-3 shows our ERD diagram, representing a MySQL data types and constraints.

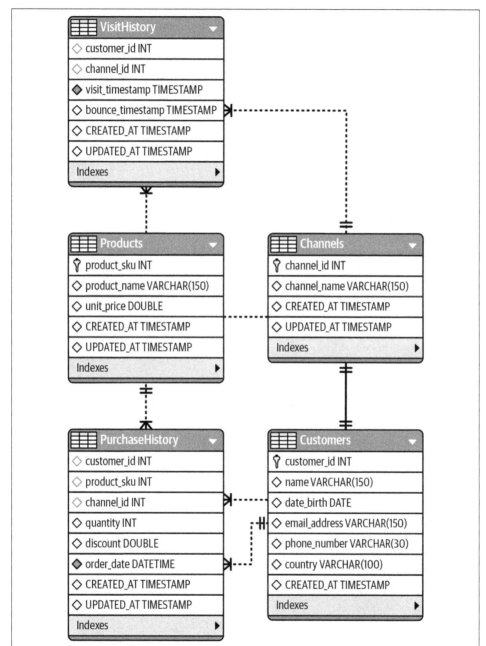

Figure 6-3. Physical diagram for our operational database in MySQL

Now we can translate the previous model to a set of DDL scripts, starting by creating a new MySQL database to store our table structures (Example 6-1).

Example 6-1. Creating the primary tables

```
CREATE DATABASE IF NOT EXISTS OMNI_MANAGEMENT;
USE OMNI_MANAGEMENT;
```

In Example 6-2, we now handle the DDL code to create the three primary tables: customers, products, and channels.

Example 6-2. Creating our operational database

```
CREATE TABLE IF NOT EXISTS customers (
    customer_id INT PRIMARY KEY AUTO_INCREMENT,
    name VARCHAR(150),
    date_birth DATE,
    email_address VARCHAR(150),
    phone_number VARCHAR(30),
    country VARCHAR(100),
    CREATED_AT TIMESTAMP DEFAULT CURRENT_TIMESTAMP,
    UPDATED_AT TIMESTAMP DEFAULT CURRENT_TIMESTAMP ON UPDATE CURRENT_TIMESTAMP
);

CREATE TABLE IF NOT EXISTS products (
    product_sku INTEGER PRIMARY KEY AUTO_INCREMENT,
    product_name VARCHAR(150),
    unit_price DOUBLE,
    CREATED_AT TIMESTAMP DEFAULT CURRENT_TIMESTAMP,
    UPDATED_AT TIMESTAMP DEFAULT CURRENT_TIMESTAMP ON UPDATE CURRENT_TIMESTAMP
);

CREATE TABLE IF NOT EXISTS channels (
    channel_id INTEGER PRIMARY KEY AUTO_INCREMENT,
    channel_name VARCHAR(150),
    CREATED_AT TIMESTAMP DEFAULT CURRENT_TIMESTAMP,
    UPDATED_AT TIMESTAMP DEFAULT CURRENT_TIMESTAMP ON UPDATE CURRENT_TIMESTAMP
);
```

The customers table has columns such as customer_id, name, date_birth, email_address, phone_number, and country. The customer_id column acts as the primary key, uniquely identifying each customer. It is set to automatically increment its value for every new customer added. The other columns store relevant information about the customer.

The products and channels tables follow a similar approach. However, products consists of columns such as product_sku, product_name, and unit_price, whereas channels contains only channel_id and channel_name.

All tables' creation code includes the IF NOT EXISTS clause available in MySQL, which ensures that the tables are created only if they do not already exist in the database. This helps prevent any errors or conflicts when executing the code multiple times.

We are using both CREATED_AT and UPDATED_AT columns in all our tables as this is a best practice. By adding these, often called *audit columns*, we make our database ready for incremental extractions of data in the future. This is also required for many CDC tools that handle this incremental extraction for us.

We can now create the relationship tables, as seen in Example 6-3.

Example 6-3. Creating the relationship tables

```
CREATE TABLE IF NOT EXISTS purchaseHistory (
    customer_id INTEGER,
    product_sku INTEGER,
    channel_id INTEGER,
    quantity INT,
    discount DOUBLE DEFAULT 0,
    order_date DATETIME NOT NULL,
    CREATED_AT TIMESTAMP DEFAULT CURRENT_TIMESTAMP,
    UPDATED_AT TIMESTAMP DEFAULT CURRENT_TIMESTAMP ON UPDATE CURRENT_TIMESTAMP,
    FOREIGN KEY (channel_id) REFERENCES channels(channel_id),
    FOREIGN KEY (product_sku) REFERENCES products(product_sku),
    FOREIGN KEY (customer_id) REFERENCES customers(customer_id)
);

CREATE TABLE IF NOT EXISTS visitHistory (
    customer_id INTEGER,
    channel_id INTEGER,
    visit_timestamp TIMESTAMP NOT NULL,
    bounce_timestamp TIMESTAMP NULL,
    CREATED_AT TIMESTAMP DEFAULT CURRENT_TIMESTAMP,
    UPDATED_AT TIMESTAMP DEFAULT CURRENT_TIMESTAMP ON UPDATE CURRENT_TIMESTAMP,
    FOREIGN KEY (channel_id) REFERENCES channels(channel_id),
    FOREIGN KEY (customer_id) REFERENCES customers(customer_id)
);
```

The purchaseHistory table, which is probably the heart of our purchase relationship, has columns such as customer_id, product_sku, channel_id, quantity, discount, and order_date. The customer_id, product_sku, and channel_id columns represent the foreign keys referencing the respective primary keys in the customers, products, and channels tables. These foreign keys establish relationships among the tables. The quantity column stores the quantity of products purchased, while the discount column holds the discount applied to the purchase (with a default value of 0 if not specified, assuming this is the norm). The order_date column records the date and time of the purchase and is marked NOT NULL, meaning it must always have a value.

The `visitHistory` table is similar to `PurchaseHistory` and contains columns such as `customer_id`, `channel_id`, `visit_timestamp`, and `bounce_timestamp`. The `customer_id` and `channel_id` columns serve as foreign keys referencing the primary keys of the `customers` and `channels` tables. The `visit_timestamp` column captures the timestamp indicating when a customer visited a particular channel, while the `bounce_timestamp` records the timestamp if the visit resulted in a bounce (departure from the channel without any further action).

The `FOREIGN KEY` constraints enforce referential integrity, ensuring that the values in the foreign-key columns correspond to existing values in the referenced tables (`customers`, `products`, and `channels`). This helps maintain the integrity and consistency of the data within the database.

Modeling an operational database is a valuable aspect of an analyst's skill set, even if they are not always directly responsible for designing the raw database structures. Understanding the principles and considerations underlying operational database modeling gives analysts a holistic perspective on the entire data pipeline. This knowledge helps them understand the origin and structure of the data they are working with, which in turn enables them to work more effectively with the data engineers responsible for the operational layer.

While it is not the job of analysts and analytics engineers to design these databases from scratch, with knowledge of operational modeling, they can navigate the intricacies of the data sources and ensure that the data is structured and organized to meet their analytical needs. In addition, this understanding aids in troubleshooting and optimizing data pipelines, as analytics engineers can identify potential problems or opportunities for improvement within the operational database layer. In essence, familiarity with operational database modeling improves analytical skills and contributes to more efficient and collaborative data-driven workflows.

High-Level Data Architecture

We have designed a lean data architecture to support the initial requirements of our omnichannel use case. We will start by developing a Python script to extract the data from MySQL, clean a few data types, and then send the data to our BigQuery project. Figure 6-4 illustrates our target solution.

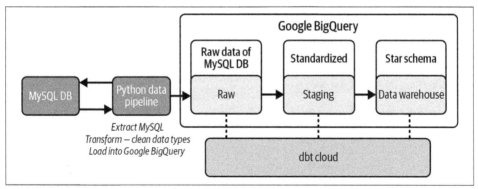

Figure 6-4. Diagram for our lean data architecture to support our use case

Once the data lands on the raw environment, we will leverage dbt to transform our data and build the required models that will compose our star schema. Last but not least, we will analyze data in BigQuery by running SQL queries against our star schema data model.

To extract the data from MySQL and load it to BigQuery, we have decided to simulate an ETL job (Example 6-4). The orchestrator code block containing a single function, `data_pipeline_mysql_to_bq`, performs a few steps: extracting data from a MySQL database, transforming it, and loading it into our target dataset in BigQuery. The code starts by importing the necessary modules, including `mysql.connector` for MySQL database connectivity and `pandas` for data manipulation. Another key library, *pandas_bq*, is also used later in our code structure.

The `data_pipeline_mysql_to_bq` function takes keyword arguments (`**kwargs`) to receive configuration details required for the pipeline. In Python, `**kwargs` is a special syntax used to pass a variable number of keyword arguments to a function as a dictionary-like object Inside the function, a connection is established with the MySQL database using the provided connection details.

To automate the table extraction, given that we want all the tables in our source database, we create a simple routine using the `information_schema` of MySQL. This is a virtual database that provides access to metadata about the database server, databases, tables, columns, indexes, privileges, and other important information. It is a system schema that is automatically created and maintained by MySQL. We leverage the `information_schema` to get all the table names in our database, and the result is stored in a DataFrame named `df_tables`.

After this step, we initiate the core of our pipeline, calling an extraction, a transformation, and a load function to simulate the three steps in an ETL job. The code snippets in Example 6-4 illustrate how we create these functions.

Example 6-4. Loading data into BigQuery

```
import mysql.connector as connection
import pandas as pd

def data_pipeline_mysql_to_bq(**kwargs):

    mysql_host = kwargs.get('mysql_host')
    mysql_database = kwargs.get('mysql_database')
    mysql_user = kwargs.get('mysql_user')
    mysql_password = kwargs.get('mysql_password')
    bq_project_id = kwargs.get('bq_project_id')
    dataset = kwargs.get('dataset')

    try:
        mydb = connection.connect(host=mysql_host\
                        , database = mysql_database\
                        , user=mysql_user\
                        , passwd=mysql_password\
                        ,use_pure=True)

        all_tables = "Select table_name from information_schema.tables
                    where table_schema = '{}'".format(mysql_database)
        df_tables = pd.read_sql(all_tables,mydb,
                    parse_dates={'Date': {'format': '%Y-%m-%d'}})

        for table in df_tables.TABLE_NAME:
            table_name = table

            # Extract table data from MySQL
            df_table_data = extract_table_from_mysql(table_name, mydb)

            # Transform table data from MySQL
            df_table_data = transform_data_from_table(df_table_data)

            # Load data to BigQuery
            load_data_into_bigquery(bq_project_id,
                            dataset,table_name,df_table_data)

            # Show confirmation message
            print("Ingested table {}".format(table_name))

        mydb.close() #close the connection
    except Exception as e:
        mydb.close()
        print(str(e))
```

In Example 6-5, we define the `extract_table_from_mysql` function that simulates the extraction step in an ETL job. This function is responsible for retrieving data from a specified table in a MySQL database. It takes two parameters: `table_name`, which represents the name of the table to be extracted, and `my_sql_connection`, which represents the connection object or connection details for the MySQL database.

To perform the extraction, the function constructs a SQL query by concatenating the table name with the `select * from` statement. This is a very simple way to extract all the rows and works well in our example; however, you might want to extract this data incrementally by filtering records where `updated_at` or `created_at` are greater than the last extraction date (which you can store in a metadata table).

Next, the function utilizes the `pd.read_sql` function from the *pandas* library to execute the extraction query. It passes the query and the MySQL connection object (`my_sql_connection`) as arguments. The function reads the data from the specified table and loads it into a pandas DataFrame named `df_table_data`. Finally, it returns the extracted DataFrame, which contains the data retrieved from the MySQL table.

Example 6-5. Loading data into BigQuery—extraction

```
'''
    Simulate the extraction step in an ETL job
'''
def extract_table_from_mysql(table_name, my_sql_connection):
    # Extract data from mysql table
    extraction_query = 'select * from ' + table_name
    df_table_data = pd.read_sql(extraction_query,my_sql_connection)
    return df_table_data
```

In Example 6-6, we define the `transform_data_from_table` function that represents the transformation step in an ETL job. This function is responsible for performing a specific transformation on a DataFrame called `df_table_data`. In this case, we do something simple: clean the dates in the DataFrame by converting them to strings to avoid conflicts with the *pandas_bq* library. To achieve this, the function identifies the columns with an object data type (string columns) by using the `select_dtypes` method. It then iterates over these columns and checks the data type of the first value in each column by converting it to a string representation.

If the data type is identified as `<class datetime.date>`, indicating that the column contains date values, the function proceeds to convert each date value to a string format. This is done by mapping each value to its string representation by using a `lambda` function. After performing the transformation, the function returns the modified DataFrame with the cleaned dates.

Example 6-6. Loading data into BigQuery—transformation

```
'''
    Simulate the transformation step in an ETL job
'''
```

```
def transform_data_from_table(df_table_data):
    # Clean dates - convert to string
    object_cols = df_table_data.select_dtypes(include=['object']).columns
    for column in object_cols:
        dtype = str(type(df_table_data[column].values[0]))
        if dtype == "<class 'datetime.date'>":
            df_table_data[column] = df_table_data[column].map(lambda x: str(x))
    return df_table_data
```

In Example 6-7, we define the `load_data_into_bigquery` method, which provides a convenient way to load data from a pandas DataFrame into a specified BigQuery table by using the *pandas_gbq* library. It ensures that the existing table is replaced with the new data, allowing seamless data transfer and update within the BigQuery environment.

The function takes four parameters: `bq_project_id` represents the project ID of the BigQuery project, while `dataset` and `table_name` specify the target dataset and table in BigQuery, respectively. The `df_table_data` parameter is a pandas DataFrame that contains the data to be loaded.

Example 6-7. Loading data into BigQuery—load

```
'''
    Simulate the load step in an ETL job
'''
def load_data_into_bigquery(bq_project_id, dataset,table_name,df_table_data):
    import pandas_gbq as pdbq
    full_table_name_bg = "{}.{}".format(dataset,table_name)
    pdbq.to_gbq(df_table_data,full_table_name_bg,project_id=bq_project_id,
      if_exists='replace')
```

In Example 6-8, we execute the data pipeline by calling the `data_pipe line_mysql_to_bq` function with the specified keyword arguments. The code creates a dictionary named `kwargs` that holds the required keyword arguments for the function. This is a convenient way to pass multiple parameters in Python without having to add them all to the method signature. The `kwargs` dictionary includes values such as the BigQuery project ID, dataset name, MySQL connection details (host, username, password), and the name of the MySQL database containing the data to be transferred. However, the actual values for the BigQuery project ID, MySQL host information, username, and password need to be replaced with the appropriate values.

We call the function `data_pipeline_mysql_to_bq` by providing the `kwargs` dictionary contents as keyword arguments. This triggers the data pipeline that moves data from the specified MySQL database to the target BigQuery table.

Example 6-8. Loading data into BigQuery—call orchestrator

```
# Call main function

kwargs = {
    # BigQuery connection details
    'bq_project_id': <ADD_YOUR_BQ_PROJECT_ID>,
    'dataset': 'omnichannel_raw',
    # MySQL connection details
    'mysql_host': <ADD_YOUR_HOST_INFO>,
    'mysql_user': <ADD_YOUR_MYSQL_USER>,
    'mysql_password': <ADD_YOUR_MYSQL_PASSWORD>,
    'mysql_database': 'OMNI_MANAGEMENT'
}

data_pipeline_mysql_to_bq(**kwargs)
```

We should now have our raw data loaded into our target dataset on BigQuery, ready
to be transformed into a dimensional model, using dbt as a tool to do so.

Analytical Data Modeling

As we saw earlier in this book, analytical data modeling uses a systematic approach
encompassing several crucial steps to create a compelling and meaningful representation of your business processes. The first step is identifying and understanding
the business processes driving your organization. This involves mapping out the key
operational activities, data flows, and interdependencies among departments. By fully
understanding your business processes, you can pinpoint the critical touchpoints
where data is generated, transformed, and utilized.

Once you have a clear picture of your business processes, the next step is identifying the facts and dimensions in your dimensional data model. Facts represent the
measurable and quantifiable data points you want to analyze, such as sales figures,
customer orders, or website traffic. On the other hand, dimensions provide the necessary context for these facts. They define the various attributes and characteristics that
describe the facts. Identifying these facts and dimensions is essential for structuring
your data model effectively.

Once you have identified the facts and dimensions, the next step is to identify
the attributes for each dimension. Attributes provide additional detail and enable a
more profound analysis of the data. They describe specific characteristics or properties associated with each dimension. Using an example of the product dimension,
attributes could include product color, size, weight, and price. Similarly, if we want a
customer dimension, attributes might encompass demographic information such as
age, gender, and location. By identifying relevant attributes, you enhance the richness
and depth of your data model, enabling more insightful analysis.

Defining the granularity of business facts is the final step in analytical data modeling. *Granularity* refers to the level of detail at which you capture and analyze your business facts. Balancing capturing enough detail for meaningful analysis and avoiding unnecessary data complexity is essential. For instance, in retail sales analysis, the granularity could be defined at the transaction level, capturing individual customer purchases. In the alternative, we can have other higher-level granularities, such as daily, weekly, or monthly aggregates. The choice of granularity depends on your analytical objectives, data availability, and the level of detail necessary to derive valuable insights.

By following these steps in analytical data modeling, you establish a solid foundation for creating a data model that accurately represents your business, captures the essential facts and dimensions, includes relevant attributes, and defines an appropriate level of granularity. A well-designed data model allows you to unlock the power of your data, gain valuable insights, and make informed decisions to drive business growth and success.

Identify the Business Processes

In the search to develop an effective analytical data model, the initial phase is to identify the business processes within the organization. After engaging in discussions with key stakeholders and conducting in-depth interviews, it becomes clear that one of the primary objectives is to track sales performance across channels. This critical piece of information will provide valuable insights into revenue generation and the effectiveness of various sales channels.

Exploring the organization's goals, another significant requirement is also discovered: tracking visits and bounce rates per channel. This objective aims to shed light on customer engagement and website performance across channels. By measuring the number of visits and bounce rates, the organization could identify which channels are driving traffic, as well as areas for improvement to reduce bounce rates and increase user engagement.

Understanding the importance of these metrics, we recognize a need to focus on two distinct business processes: sales tracking and website performance analysis. The sales tracking process would capture and analyze sales data generated through various channels, such as mobile, mobile app, or Instagram. This process would provide a comprehensive view of sales performance, enabling the organization to make data-driven decisions regarding channel optimization and sales forecasting.

Simultaneously, the website performance analysis process would gather data on website visits and bounce rates across various channels. This would require implementing robust tracking mechanisms, such as web analytics tools, to monitor and measure user behavior on the organization's website. By examining channel-specific visit patterns and bounce rates, the organization could identify trends, optimize user experience, and enhance website performance to improve overall customer engagement.

Thus, identifying these two vital business processes—sales tracking and website performance analysis—emerged as a key milestone in the analytical data modeling journey. With this knowledge, we will become adequately equipped to proceed to the next phase, where we will dive deeper into understanding the data flows, interdependencies, and specific data points associated with these processes, shaping a comprehensive dimensional data model that aligns with the organization's objectives and requirements.

Identify Facts and Dimensions in the Dimensional Data Model

Based on the identified business processes of sales tracking and website performance analysis, we have inferred the need for four dimensions and two corresponding fact tables. Let's detail each of them.

The first dimension is channels (dim_channels). This dimension represents the various sales and marketing channels through which the organization operates. The common channels identified are website, Instagram, and mobile app channels. By analyzing sales data across channels, the organization gains insights into the performance and effectiveness of each channel in generating revenue.

The second dimension is products (dim_products). This dimension focuses on the organization's product offerings. By including the product dimension, the organization is able to analyze sales patterns across product categories and identify top-selling products or areas for improvement.

The third dimension is customers (dim_customers). This dimension captures information about the organization's customer base. The organization can gain insights into customer preferences, behavior, and purchasing patterns by analyzing sales data based on customer attributes.

The fourth and final dimension is the date (dim_date). This dimension allows for the analysis of sales and website performance over time. Analyzing data based on the date dimension allows the organization to identify trends, seasonality, and any temporal patterns that may impact sales or website performance.

Now let's move on to the fact tables. The first fact table identified is the purchase history (fct_purchase_history). This table serves as the central point where the purchase transactions are captured and associated with the relevant dimensions—channels, products, customers, and date. It allows for detailed sales data analysis, enabling the organization to understand the correlation between sales and the dimensions. With the purchase history fact table, the organization gains insights into sales performance across channels, product categories, customer segments, and time periods.

The second fact table is the visits history table (`fct_visit_history`). Unlike the purchase history, this table focuses on website performance analysis. It captures data related to website visits and is primarily associated with the dimensions of channels, customers, and date. By analyzing visit history, the organization can understand customer engagement, track traffic patterns across channels, and measure the effectiveness of different marketing campaigns or website features.

With these dimensions and fact tables identified, we have established the foundation for your dimensional data model. This model allows you to efficiently analyze and derive insights from sales data across various dimensions, as well as track website performance metrics associated with different channels, customers, and time periods. As you proceed with the data modeling process, we will further refine and define the attributes within each dimension and establish the relationships and hierarchies necessary for comprehensive analysis, but for now, we already have conditions to design our star schema (Figure 6-5).

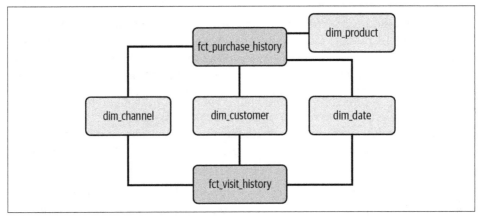

Figure 6-5. Use case star schema model

The star schema incorporates four primary dimensions: channels, products, customers, and date. These dimensions serve as the pillars of analysis, providing valuable context to the data.

> Three of the dimensions—`dim_channels`, `dim_customers`, and `dim_date`—are conformed dimensions. *Conformed dimensions* are shared across multiple fact tables, ensuring consistency and facilitating seamless integration among various analytical perspectives.

Identify the Attributes for Dimensions

With the dimensions identified, it is time to detail each identified attribute within the dimension. The data model gains depth and completeness by incorporating these attributes with their respective dimensions. These attributes enrich the analysis and enable more granular insights, empowering decision-makers to derive valuable information from the data.

When considering the channels dimension (`dim_channels`), several attributes were identified. First, the channel surrogate key (`sk_channel`) provides a unique identifier within the data model for each channel. Alongside it, the channel natural key (`nk_channel_id`), which represents the key from the source system, ensures seamless integration with external data sources. Additionally, the channel name attribute (`dsc_channel_name`) captures the descriptive name of each channel, enabling easy identification and understanding within the data model. This last one is potentially the most interesting for analytics.

Moving on to the products dimension (`dim_products`), multiple key attributes were identified. The product surrogate key (`sk_product`) serves as a unique identifier for each product within the data model. Similarly, the product natural key (`nk_product_sku`) captures the key from the source system, allowing for consistent linking of product-related data. The product name attribute (`dsc_product_name`) provides a descriptive name for each product, helping with clarity and comprehension. Finally, the product unit price attribute (`mtr_unit_price`) records the price of each product, facilitating price analysis and revenue calculations.

In the customers dimension (`dim_customers`), different attributes help provide a wide view of customer-related information. The customer surrogate key (`sk_customer`) is a unique identifier for each customer within the data model. The customer natural key (`nk_customer_id`) keeps the key from the source system, allowing seamless integration with external data sources. Additionally, attributes such as customer name (`dsc_name`), birth date (`dt_date_birth`), email address (`dsc_email_address`), phone number (`dsc_phone_number`), and country (`dsc_country`) capture important details related to individual customers. These attributes enable customer segmentation, personalized marketing, and in-depth customer behavior and demographics analysis.

Finally, the date dimension (`dim_date`) includes a range of date-related attributes. These attributes enhance the understanding and analysis of temporal data. The date attribute itself captures the specific date. Attributes such as month, quarter, and year provide higher-level temporal information, facilitating aggregated analysis. By including these attributes, the data model enables comprehensive time-based analysis and pattern recognition.

Surrogate keys are artificial identifiers assigned to records within a database table. They provide uniqueness, stability, and improved performance in data operations. Surrogate keys are independent of the data itself, ensuring that each record has a unique identifier and remains stable even if natural key values change. They simplify joins between tables, enhance data integration, and facilitate efficient indexing and querying.

Define the Granularity for Business Facts

Having completed the earlier phases of analytical data modeling, we now move on to the last vital step, namely, identifying the granularity of our future business facts. The granularity refers to the level of detail at which data is captured and analyzed within the dimensional data model. Determining the appropriate granularity is essential to ensuring that the data model effectively supports the analytical requirements and objectives of the organization.

To define the granularity of our business facts, it is necessary to consider the specific needs of the analysis and strike a balance between capturing sufficient detail and avoiding excessive complexity. The chosen granularity should provide enough information for meaningful analysis while maintaining data manageability and performance.

In the context of sales data, the granularity identified is determined at the transaction level, capturing individual customer purchases: `fct_purchase_history`. This level of granularity allows for detailed analysis of sales patterns, such as examining individual transactions, identifying trends in customer behavior, and conducting product-level analysis.

For the other requirement, website performance analysis, the granularity is selected at the visit level, gathering individual customer visits and the channel from which they came into the platform: `fct_visit_history`. With this detail, the organization can understand customer engagement, track traffic patterns across channels, and measure the effectiveness of distinct marketing campaigns or website features.

Alternatively, with the level of granularities defined, other units of analysis that are less granular can be determined, such as daily, weekly, or monthly aggregates. Aggregating the data allows for a more concise representation while providing valuable insights. This approach reduces data volume and simplifies analysis, making identifying broader trends, seasonal patterns, or overall performance across multiple dimensions easier.

By carefully defining the granularity of our business facts, the organization can ensure that the dimensional data model hits the right balance between capturing sufficient detail and maintaining data manageability and performance. This step sets the stage for meaningful analysis, enabling stakeholders to derive valuable insights and make informed decisions based on the data.

As we conclude this phase, we have successfully navigated the essential stages of analytical data modeling, including identifying business processes, facts, dimensions, and attributes, as well as defining the granularity of business facts. These foundational steps provide a solid framework for developing a comprehensive and effective dimensional data model that empowers data-driven decision making within the organization. In the next section, we will get our hands dirty and develop our models using dbt, but always with the foundation defined by analytical data modeling.

Creating Our Data Warehouse with dbt

With the analytical data modeling phase complete, it is time to venture into developing our data warehouse. The data warehouse serves as the central repository for structured and integrated data, supporting robust reporting, analysis, and decision-making processes within the organization.

Overall, data warehouse development begins by establishing the necessary infrastructure. Long story short, we already did that earlier, in "High-Level Data Architecture" on page 260, by setting up our BigQuery. At this stage, we only need to set up our dbt project and connect it to BigQuery and GitHub. In "Setting Up dbt Cloud with BigQuery and GitHub" on page 140, we present a comprehensive step-by-step guide explaining how to do all the initial setup, so we will skip this phase in this section.

Our main goal in this section is to develop all the dbt models crafted during the analytical data modeling phase, which serves as the blueprint for the design and construction of our data warehouse. In parallel with the models, we will also develop all the parametrization YAML files to ensure we leverage the ref() and source() functions and ultimately make our code DRY-er. In line with the stated goal, another step needs to be performed along with developing the YAML files: building our staging models area. These will be the seed for our dimensions and facts.

In addition to developing the data models, it is essential to establish consistent naming conventions within the data warehouse. These naming conventions provide a standardized approach to naming tables, columns, and other database objects, ensuring clarity and consistency across the data infrastructure. Table 6-1 presents the naming conventions used to build the data warehouse with dbt.

Table 6-1. Naming conventions

Convention	Field type	Description
stg	Table/CTE	Staging tables or CTE
dim	Table	Dimension tables
fct	Table	Fact tables

Convention	Field type	Description
nk	Column	Natural keys
sk	Column	Surrogate keys
mtr	Column	Metric columns (numeric values)
dsc	Column	Description columns (text values)
dt	Column	Date and time columns

To build our first models, we must ensure that our dbt project is set up and that we have the proper folder structure. During this part of the use case, we will keep it simple and build only *staging* and *marts* directories. So once you have your dbt project initialized, create the specified folders. The models folders directory should look like Example 6-9.

Example 6-9. Omnichannel data warehouse, models directory

```
root/
├ models/
│  ├ staging/
│  ├ marts/
├ dbt_project.yml
```

Now that we have built our initial project and folders, the next step is creating our staging YAML files. As per the segregation of YAML files best practices we discussed in "YAML Files" on page 168, we will have one YAML file for sources and another for models. For building our staging layer, let's, for now, focus only on our source YAML file. This file must be inside the *staging* directory and should look like Example 6-10.

Example 6-10. _omnichannel_raw_sources.yml file configuration

```
version: 2

sources:
  - name: omnichannel
    database: analytics-engineering-book
    schema: omnichannel_raw
    tables:
      - name: Channels
      - name: Customers
      - name: Products
      - name: VisitHistory
      - name: PurchaseHistory
```

The use of this file will allow you to leverage the source() function to work with the raw data available in your data platform. Five tables were specified under the omnichannel_raw schema: Channels, Customers, Products, VisitHistory, and

PurchaseHistory. These correspond to the relevant source tables used to make our staging layer, and dbt will interact with these to build the staging data models.

Let's kick off construction of our staging models. The primary idea here is to have one staging model for each source table—Channels, Customers, Products, VisitHistory, and PurchaseHistory. Keep in mind that each new staging model needs to be created inside the *staging* directory.

Examples 6-11 through 6-15 show the code snippets to build each one of our staging models.

Example 6-11. stg_channels

```
with raw_channels AS
(
    SELECT
        channel_id,
        channel_name,
        CREATED_AT,
        UPDATED_AT
    FROM {{ source("omnichannel","Channels")}}
)

SELECT
    *
FROM raw_channels
```

Example 6-12. stg_customers

```
with raw_customers AS
(
    SELECT
        customer_id,
        name,
        date_birth,
        email_address,
        phone_number,
        country,
        CREATED_AT,
        UPDATED_AT
    FROM {{ source("omnichannel","Customers")}}
)

SELECT
    *
FROM raw_customers
```

Example 6-13. stg_products

```
with raw_products AS
(
    SELECT
        product_sku,
        product_name,
        unit_price,
        CREATED_AT,
        UPDATED_AT
    FROM {{ source("omnichannel","Products")}}
)

SELECT
    *
FROM raw_products
```

Example 6-14. stg_purchase_history

```
with raw_purchase_history AS
(
    SELECT
        customer_id,
        product_sku,
        channel_id,
        quantity,
        discount,
        order_date
    FROM {{ source("omnichannel","PurchaseHistory")}}
)

SELECT
    *
FROM raw_purchase_history
```

Example 6-15. stg_visit_history

```
with raw_visit_history AS
(
    SELECT
        customer_id,
        channel_id,
        visit_timestamp,
        bounce_timestamp,
        created_at,
        updated_at
    FROM {{ source("omnichannel","VisitHistory")}}
)

SELECT
```

```
          *
FROM raw_visit_history
```

In summary, each of these dbt models extracts data from the respective source tables and stages it in separate CTEs. These staging tables serve as intermediate storage for further data transformations before loading the data into the final destination tables of the data warehouse.

After successfully creating the staging models, the next phase is to set the YAML file for the staging layer. The staging layer YAML file will serve as a configuration file that references the staging models and specifies their execution order and dependencies. This file provides a clear and structured view of the staging layer's setup, allowing for consistent integration and management of the staging models within the overall data modeling process. Example 6-16 shows how the YAML file should look in your staging layer.

Example 6-16. _omnichannel_raw_models.yml file configuration

```
version: 2

models:
    - name: stg_customers
    - name: stg_channels
    - name: stg_products
    - name: stg_purchase_history
    - name: stg_visit_history
```

Once the staging layer YAML file is in place, it's time to move forward with building the dimension models. *Dimension models* are an essential component of the data warehouse, representing the business entities and their attributes. These models capture the descriptive information that provides context to the fact data and allows for deeper analysis. Dimension tables, such as channels, products, customers, and date, will be constructed based on the previously defined dimensions and their attributes, derived from "Identify Facts and Dimensions in the Dimensional Data Model" on page 267 and "Identify the Attributes for Dimensions" on page 269. These tables are populated with the relevant data from the staging layer, which ensures consistency and accuracy.

Let's proceed with our dimension model creation. Create the respective models in Examples 6-17 through 6-20 in your *marts* directory.

Example 6-17. dim_channels

```
with stg_dim_channels AS
(
    SELECT
```

```
        channel_id AS nk_channel_id,
        channel_name AS dsc_channel_name,
        created_at AS dt_created_at,
        updated_at AS dt_updated_at
    FROM {{ ref("stg_channels")}}
)

SELECT
    {{ dbt_utils.generate_surrogate_key( ["nk_channel_id"] )}} AS sk_channel,
    *
FROM stg_dim_channels
```

Example 6-18. dim_customers

```
with stg_dim_customers AS
(
    SELECT
        customer_id AS nk_customer_id,
        name AS dsc_name,
        date_birth AS dt_date_birth,
        email_address AS dsc_email_address,
        phone_number AS dsc_phone_number,
        country AS dsc_country,
        created_at AS dt_created_at,
        updated_at AS dt_updated_at
    FROM {{ ref("stg_customers")}}
)

SELECT
    {{ dbt_utils.generate_surrogate_key( ["nk_customer_id"] )}} AS sk_customer,
    *
FROM stg_dim_customers
```

Example 6-19. dim_products

```
with stg_dim_products AS
(
    SELECT
        product_sku AS nk_product_sku,
        product_name AS dsc_product_name,
        unit_price AS mtr_unit_price,
        created_at AS dt_created_at,
        updated_at AS dt_updated_at
    FROM {{ ref("stg_products")}}
)

SELECT
    {{ dbt_utils.generate_surrogate_key( ["nk_product_sku"] )}} AS sk_product,
    *
FROM stg_dim_products
```

Example 6-20. dim_date

```
{{ dbt_date.get_date_dimension("2022-01-01", "2024-12-31") }}
```

In summary, each code block defines a dbt model for a specific dimension table. The first three models, dim_channels, dim_customers, and dim_products, retrieve data from the corresponding staging tables and transform it into the desired structure for the dimension tables. In each one of the models, we've included the surrogate keys generation from the natural key. To do that, we've resorted to the dbt_utils package, specifically the generate_surrogate_key() function. This function takes an array of column names as an argument, representing the dimension table's natural keys (or business keys), and generates a surrogate key column based on those columns.

The last dimension, dim_date, is different since it doesn't arrive from the staging layer. Instead, it is entirely produced using the get_date_dimension() function from the dbt_date package. The get_date_dimension() function handles the generation of the date dimension table, including creating all the necessary columns and the data for each based on the specified date range. In our case, we choose the data range from 2022-01-01 to 2024-12-31.

Finally, remember that we are now using packages. To successfully build our project at this stage, we need to install them, so add the Example 6-21 configurations to your *dbt_packages.yml* file. Then execute **dbt deps** and **dbt build** commands and look at your data platform to check that we have the new dimensions created.

Example 6-21. packages.yml file configuration

```
packages:
  - package: dbt-labs/dbt_utils
    version: 1.1.1
  - package: calogica/dbt_date
    version: [">=0.7.0", "<0.8.0"]
```

The final step is the creation of the models from fact tables that were earlier identified as necessary to analyze the new business processes. These tables are an integral part of a data warehouse and represent the measurable, numerical data that captures the business events or transactions.

Examples 6-22 and 6-23 represent the new fact tables to be developed. Create them inside the *marts* directory.

Example 6-22. fct_purchase_history

```
with stg_fct_purchase_history AS
(
    SELECT
```

```
            customer_id AS nk_customer_id,
            product_sku AS nk_product_sku,
            channel_id AS nk_channel_id,
            quantity AS mtr_quantity,
            discount AS mtr_discount,
            CAST(order_date AS DATE) AS dt_order_date
        FROM {{ ref("stg_purchase_history")}}
    )

    SELECT
        COALESCE(dcust.sk_customer, '-1') AS sk_customer,
        COALESCE(dchan.sk_channel, '-1') AS sk_channel,
        COALESCE(dprod.sk_product, '-1') AS sk_product,
        fct.dt_order_date AS sk_order_date,
        fct.mtr_quantity,
        fct.mtr_discount,
        dprod.mtr_unit_price,
        ROUND(fct.mtr_quantity * dprod.mtr_unit_price,2) AS mtr_total_amount_gross,
        ROUND(fct.mtr_quantity *
                dprod.mtr_unit_price *
                (1 - fct.mtr_discount),2) AS mtr_total_amount_net
    FROM stg_fct_purchase_history AS fct
    LEFT JOIN {{ ref("dim_customers")}} AS dcust
                        ON fct.nk_customer_id = dcust.nk_customer_id
    LEFT JOIN {{ ref("dim_channels")}} AS dchan
                        ON fct.nk_channel_id = dchan.nk_channel_id
    LEFT JOIN {{ ref("dim_products")}} AS dprod
                        ON fct.nk_product_sku = dprod.nk_product_sku
```

fct_purchase_history aims to answer to the first business process identified, namely, to track sales performance across channels. Next, we gather sales data from the stg_purchase_history model and join it with the respective channel, customer, and product dimensions to capture the respective surrogate key, using the COALESCE() function to handle cases where the natural key does not match a dimension table entry. By including the relationship between this fact and the respective dimensions, the organization would be equipped with valuable insights from revenue generation and the effectiveness of various sales channels per customer and product.

To fully meet the requirements, two additional calculated metrics, mtr_total _amount_gross and mtr_total_amount_net, are computed based on the product quantity bought (mtr_quantity), the unit price of each product (mtr_unit_price), and the applied discount (mtr_discount).

In summary, Example 6-22 demonstrates the process of transforming the staging data into a structured fact table that captures relevant purchase history information. By joining dimension tables and performing calculations, the fact table provides a consolidated view of purchase data, enabling valuable insights and analysis.

Moving to the last fact table, let's have a look at Example 6-23.

Example 6-23. fct_visit_history

```
with stg_fct_visit_history AS
(
    SELECT
        customer_id AS nk_customer_id,
        channel_id AS nk_channel_id,
        CAST(visit_timestamp AS DATE) AS sk_date_visit,
        CAST(bounce_timestamp AS DATE) AS sk_date_bounce,
        CAST(visit_timestamp AS DATETIME) AS dt_visit_timestamp,
        CAST(bounce_timestamp AS DATETIME) AS dt_bounce_timestamp
    FROM {{ ref("stg_visit_history")}}
)

SELECT
    COALESCE(dcust.sk_customer, '-1') AS sk_customer,
    COALESCE(dchan.sk_channel, '-1') AS sk_channel,
    fct.sk_date_visit,
    fct.sk_date_bounce,
    fct.dt_visit_timestamp,
    fct.dt_bounce_timestamp,
    DATE_DIFF(dt_bounce_timestamp,dt_visit_timestamp
                , MINUTE) AS mtr_length_of_stay_minutes
FROM stg_fct_visit_history AS fct
LEFT JOIN {{ ref("dim_customers")}} AS dcust
                ON fct.nk_customer_id = dcust.nk_customer_id
LEFT JOIN {{ ref("dim_channels")}} AS dchan
                ON fct.nk_channel_id = dchan.nk_channel_id
```

fct_visit_history answers to the other business process identified: tracking visits and bounce rates per channel to shed light on customer engagement and website performance across channels. To create it, we gather visit data from the stg_visit _history model and join it with the customers and channels dimensions to catch the respective surrogate key, using the COALESCE() function to handle cases where the natural key does not match with a dimension table entry. With this fact and dimension relationship established, the organization will be able to identify the channels that are driving more traffic. An additional calculated metric was added, mtr_length_of_stay_minutes, to understand the length of stay of a particular visit. This calculated metric leverages the DATE_DIFF() function to compute the difference between the bounce and visit date, aiming to support the organization in identifying areas for improvement to reduce bounce rates and increase user engagement.

In conclusion, the fct_visit_history fact table transforms the staging data into a structured fact table that captures relevant visit history information. By joining with dimension tables and performing calculations, as we did for both facts, the fct_visit_history table provides a compact view of visit data, enabling valuable insights and analysis.

In the next section, we will continue our journey and develop tests and documentation and finally deploy to production. These will be the last steps inside dbt, aiming to guarantee the data model's reliability, usability, and ongoing availability and support data-driven decision making within the organization.

Tests, Documentation, and Deployment with dbt

As the development of our data warehouse nears completion, it's crucial to ensure the accuracy, reliability, and usability of the implemented data models. This section focuses on testing, documentation, and going live with your data warehouse.

As previously noted, when using dbt, tests and documentation should be created while developing models. We took that approach, but opted to split it into two parts for clarity. This division allows for a clearer understanding of what we accomplished within dbt for model development, as well as our processes for testing and documentation.

As a brief summary, testing is essential in validating the data model's functionality and integrity. Testing verifies the relationships between dimension and fact tables, checking data consistency, and validating the accuracy of calculated metrics. By conducting tests, you can identify and rectify any issues or discrepancies in the data, thus ensuring the reliability of your analytical outputs.

It is important to perform both singular and generic tests. Singular tests target specific aspects of the data models, such as verifying the accuracy of a specific metric calculation or validating the relationships between a particular dimension and fact table. These tests provide focused insights into individual components of the data models.

On the other hand, generic tests cover a broader range of scenarios and monitor the overall behavior of the data models. These tests aim to ensure that the data models function correctly across various dimensions, time periods, and user interactions. Generic tests help uncover potential issues that might arise during real-world usage and provide confidence in the data models' ability to handle various scenarios.

Simultaneously, documenting the data models and related processes is required for knowledge transfer, collaboration, and future maintenance. Documenting the data models involves capturing information about the purpose, structure, relationships, and assumptions underlying the models. It includes details on the source systems, transformation logic, business rules applied, and any other relevant information.

To document the data models, it is recommended to update the corresponding YAML files with comprehensive explanations and metadata. YAML files serve as a centralized location for the configuration and documentation of dbt models, making it easier to track changes and understand the purpose and usage of each model. Documenting the YAML files ensures that future team members and stakeholders have a clear understanding of the data models and can effectively work with them.

Once testing and documentation are complete, the final step in this section is to prepare for the go-live of your data warehouse. This involves deploying the data models to the production environment, ensuring data pipelines are established, and setting up scheduled data updates. It's important to monitor the data warehouse's performance, availability, and data quality during this phase. Conducting thorough testing in a production-like environment and obtaining end-user feedback can help identify any remaining issues before the data warehouse is fully operational.

Let's start with the tests. Our first batch of tests will focus on generic tests. The first use case is to ensure for all dimensions that the surrogate key is unique and doesn't have null values. For the second use case, we must also grant that every surrogate key in a fact table exists in the specified dimension. Let's first create the respective YAML file in the marts layer, using the Example 6-24 code block to achieve all we've stated.

Example 6-24. _omnichannel_marts.yml file configuration

```
version: 2

models:
  - name: dim_customers
    columns:
      - name: sk_customer
        tests:
          - unique
          - not_null

  - name: dim_channels
    columns:
      - name: sk_channel
        tests:
          - unique
          - not_null

  - name: dim_date
    columns:
      - name: date_day
        tests:
          - unique
          - not_null

  - name: dim_products
```

```
      columns:
        - name: sk_product
          tests:
            - unique
            - not_null

  - name: fct_purchase_history
    columns:
      - name: sk_customer
        tests:
          - relationships:
              to: ref('dim_customers')
              field: sk_customer
      - name: sk_channel
        tests:
          - relationships:
              to: ref('dim_channels')
              field: sk_channel
      - name: sk_product
        tests:
          - relationships:
              to: ref('dim_products')
              field: sk_product

  - name: fct_visit_history
    columns:
      - name: sk_customer
        tests:
          - relationships:
              to: ref('dim_customers')
              field: sk_customer
      - name: sk_channel
        tests:
          - relationships:
              to: ref('dim_channels')
              field: sk_channel
```

Let's now execute our **dbt test** command to see if all tests executed successfully. Everything went well if logs are as shown in Figure 6-6.

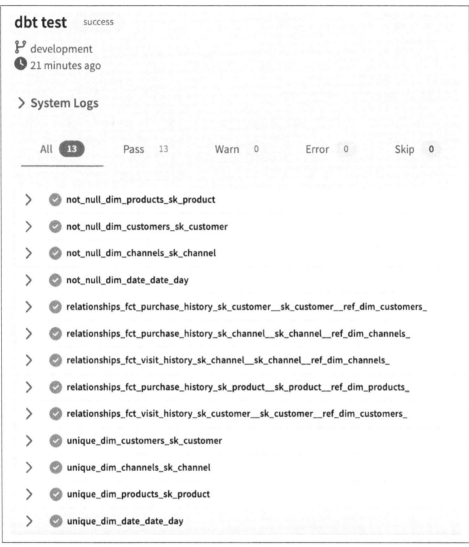

Figure 6-6. Logs for generic tests

Now let's go to our second iteration of tests and develop some singular tests. Here we will focus on our fact table metrics. The first singular use case is to make sure our mtr_total_amount_gross metric from fct_purchase_history has only positive values. For that, let's create a new test, *assert_mtr_total_amount_gross_is_positive.sql*, in the *tests* folder with the code in Example 6-25.

Example 6-25. assert_mtr_total_amount_gross_is_positive.sql

```
select
    sk_customer,
    sk_channel,
    sk_product,
    sum(mtr_total_amount_gross) as mtr_total_amount_gross
from {{ ref('fct_purchase_history') }}
group by 1, 2, 3
having mtr_total_amount_gross < 0
```

The next test we want to do is to confirm that mtr_unit_price is always lower or equal to mtr_total_amount_gross. Note that the same test could not be applied to mtr_total_amount_net since a discount was also applied. To develop this test, first, create the file *assert_mtr_unit_price_is_equal_or_lower_than_mtr_total_amount_gross.sql* and paste the code in Example 6-26.

Example 6-26.
assert_mtr_unit_price_is_equal_or_lower_than_mtr_total_amount_gross.sql

```
select
    sk_customer,
    sk_channel,
    sk_product,
    sum(mtr_total_amount_gross) AS mtr_total_amount_gross,
    sum(mtr_unit_price) AS mtr_unit_price
from {{ ref('fct_purchase_history') }}
group by 1, 2, 3
having mtr_unit_price > mtr_total_amount_gross
```

With all the singular tests created, we can now execute them and check the output. To avoid executing all the tests, including the generic ones, execute the **dbt test --select test_type:singular** command. This command will execute the tests from the type singular, ignoring any that are generic. Figure 6-7 shows the expected log output.

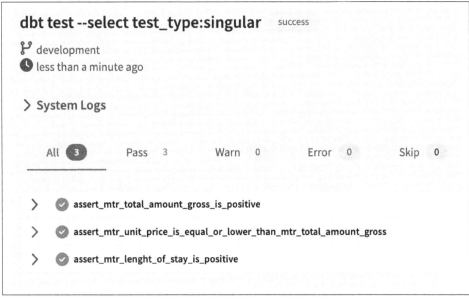

Figure 6-7. Logs for singular tests

The last singular test we want to do is to confirm that, in `fct_visit_history`, the `mtr_length_of_stay_minutes` metric is always positive. This test will tell us if we have records with a bouncing date that is earlier than the visit date, which can never happen. To perform it, create the *assert_mtr_length_of_stay_is_positive.sql* file with the code in Example 6-27.

Example 6-27. *assert_mtr_length_of_stay_is_positive.sql*

```
select
    sk_customer,
    sk_channel,
    sum(mtr_length_of_stay_minutes) as mtr_length_of_stay_minutes
from {{ ref('fct_visit_history') }}
group by 1, 2
having mtr_length_of_stay_minutes < 0
```

By implementing tests, you can validate the integrity of the data, verify calculations and transformations, and ensure compliance to defined business rules. dbt offers a complete testing framework that allows you to conduct both singular and generic tests, covering various aspects of your data models.

With all the tests successfully executed, we now move on to the next vital aspect of the data warehouse development process: documentation. In dbt, a good portion of the documentation is done using the same YAML files we use to configure our models or do our tests. Let's use the marts layer to document all the tables and columns. Let's refer to the _omnichannel_marts.yml file and replace it with the code in Example 6-28. As a note, we document only the columns used for the generic tests to make the example cleaner, yet the premise is the same for all other columns.

Example 6-28. _omnichannel_marts.yml file configuration with documentation

```
version: 2

models:
  - name: dim_customers
    description: All customers' details. Includes anonymous users who used guest
    checkout.
    columns:
      - name: sk_customer
        description: Surrogate key of the customer dimension.
        tests:
          - unique
          - not_null

  - name: dim_channels
    description: Channels data. Allows you to analyze linked facts from the channels
    perspective.
    columns:
      - name: sk_channel
        description: Surrogate key of the channel dimension.
        tests:
          - unique
          - not_null

  - name: dim_date
    description: Date data. Allows you to analyze linked facts from the date
    perspective.
    columns:
      - name: date_day
        description: Surrogate key of the date dimension. The naming convention
        wasn't added here.
        tests:
          - unique
          - not_null

  - name: dim_products
    description: Products data. Allows you to analyze linked facts from the products
    perspective.
    columns:
      - name: sk_product
        description: Surrogate key of the product dimension.
```

```
      tests:
        - unique
        - not_null


  - name: fct_purchase_history
    description: Customer orders history.
    columns:
      - name: sk_customer
        description: Surrogate key for the customer dimension.
        tests:
          - relationships:
              to: ref('dim_customers')
              field: sk_customer
      - name: sk_channel
        description: Surrogate key for the channel dimension.
        tests:
          - relationships:
              to: ref('dim_channels')
              field: sk_channel
      - name: sk_product
        description: Surrogate key for the product dimension.
        tests:
          - relationships:
              to: ref('dim_products')
              field: sk_product

  - name: fct_visit_history
    description: Customer visits history.
    columns:
      - name: sk_customer
        description: Surrogate key for the customer dimension.
        tests:
          - relationships:
              to: ref('dim_customers')
              field: sk_customer
      - name: sk_channel
        description: Surrogate key for the channel dimension.
        tests:
          - relationships:
              to: ref('dim_channels')
              field: sk_channel
```

With the YAML file updated, execute **dbt docs generate**, and let's have a look at the new documentation available. For example, if your fct_purchase_history page looks similar to Figure 6-8, you are good to go.

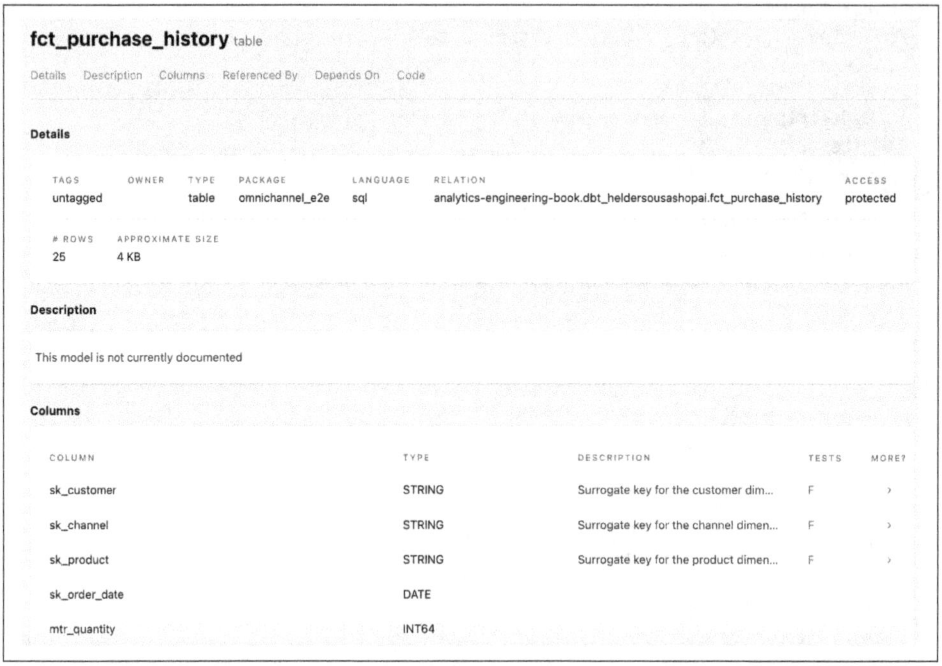

fct_purchase_history table

Details   Description   Columns   Referenced By   Depends On   Code

Details

TAGS	OWNER	TYPE	PACKAGE	LANGUAGE	RELATION		ACCESS
untagged		table	omnichannel_e2e	sql	analytics-engineering-book.dbt_heldersousashopai.fct_purchase_history		protected

# ROWS	APPROXIMATE SIZE
25	4 KB

Description

This model is not currently documented

Columns

COLUMN	TYPE	DESCRIPTION	TESTS	MORE?
sk_customer	STRING	Surrogate key for the customer dim...	F	›
sk_channel	STRING	Surrogate key for the channel dimen...	F	›
sk_product	STRING	Surrogate key for the product dimen...	F	›
sk_order_date	DATE			
mtr_quantity	INT64			

Figure 6-8. fct_purchase_history documentation page

And that's it. The final step is deploying what we've been doing into the production environment. For that, we need to create an environment in dbt, similar to the one presented in Figure 6-9.

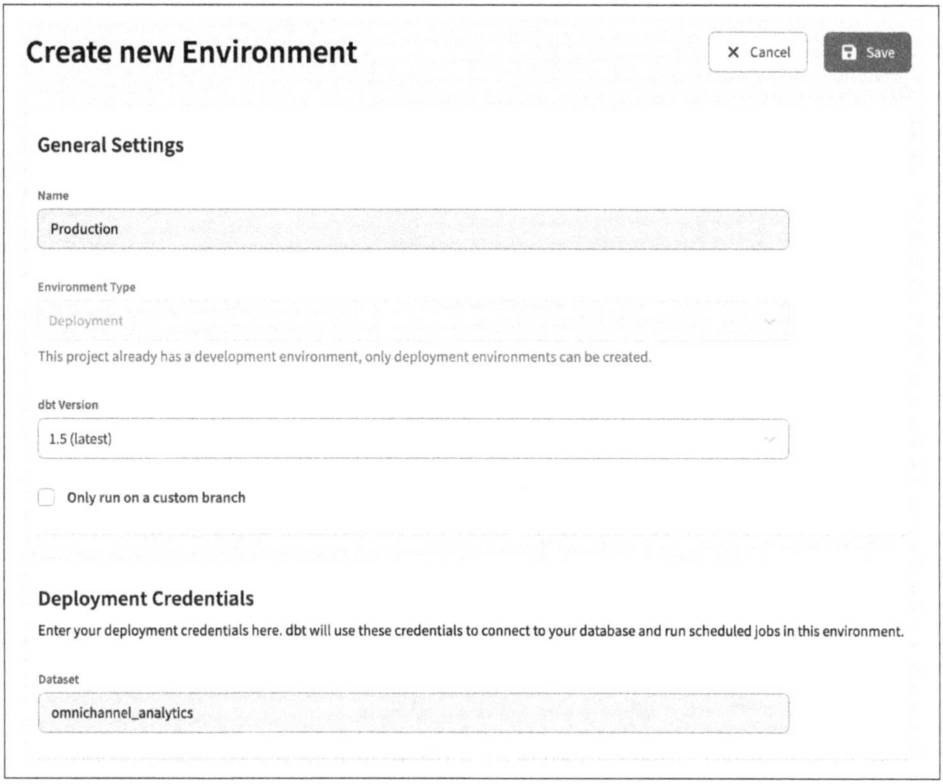

Figure 6-9. Creating a production environment

Note that we named our production dataset `omnichannel_analytics`. We'll use this dataset in "Data Analytics with SQL" on page 291. After creating the environment, it is time to configure our job. To make it straightforward, in Create Job, provide the Job name, set the environment to Production (the one that you've just created), check the box "Generate docs on run," and finally, in the Commands section, include the command **dbt test** below the `dbt build` command. Leave all the rest by default.

After the job creation, manually execute the job, and let's check the logs. It is a good indicator if they are similar to Figure 6-10.

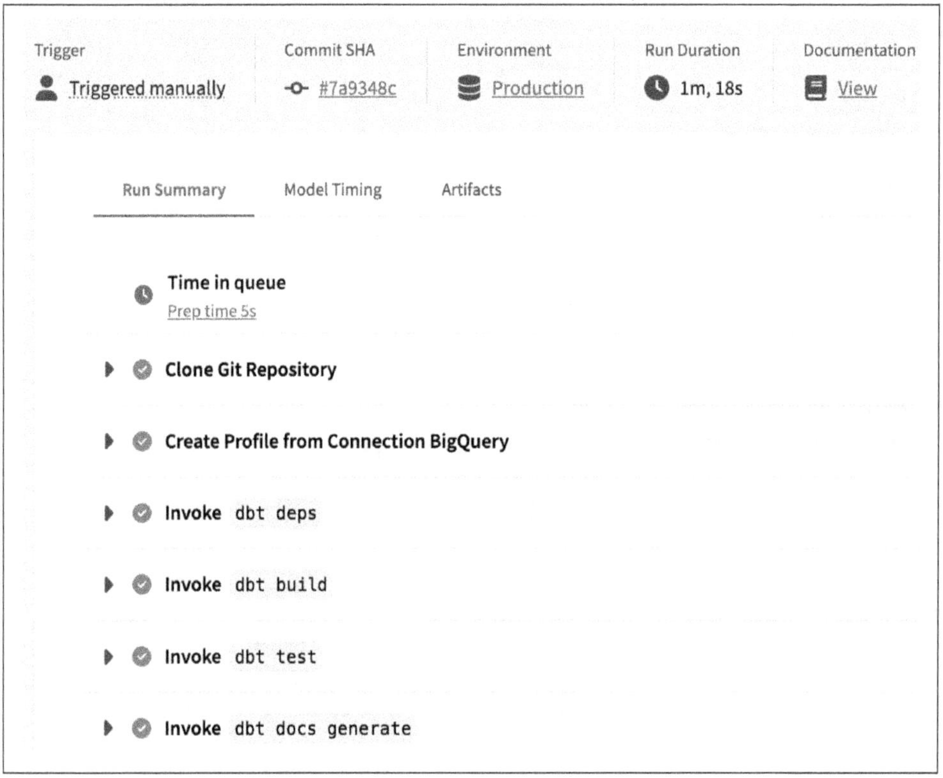

Figure 6-10. Job execution log

Let's have a look at our data platform, which in our case is BigQuery, and check if everything ran successfully. The models in BigQuery should be the ones presented in Figure 6-11.

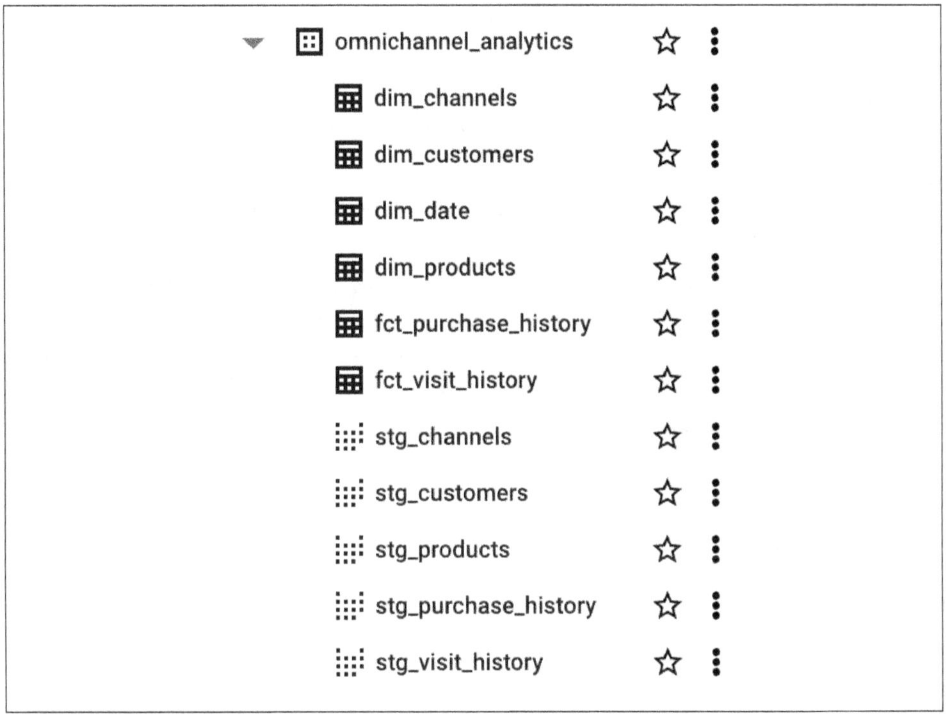

Figure 6-11. Models in BigQuery

In conclusion, the final part of building a data warehouse focused on testing, documentation, and the go-live process. You could ensure your data warehouse's accuracy, reliability, and usability by conducting extensive tests, documenting the data models, and preparing for production deployment. In the next section, we will dive into data analytics with SQL, taking our data warehouse to the next level.

Data Analytics with SQL

With our star schema model completed, we can now start the analytics discovery phase and develop queries to answer specific business questions. As previously mentioned, this type of data modeling technique makes it easy to select specific metrics from fact tables and enrich them with attributes that come from dimensions.

In Example 6-29, we start by creating a query for "Total amount sold per quarter with discount." In it, we fetch data from two tables, fct_purchase_history and `dim_date`, and perform calculations on the retrieved data. This query aims to obtain information about the sum of total amounts for each quarter of the year.

Example 6-29. Total amount sold per quarter with discount

```
SELECT dd.year_number,
      dd.quarter_of_year,
      ROUND(SUM(fct.mtr_total_amount_net),2) as sum_total_amount_with_discount
FROM `omnichannel_analytics`.`fct_purchase_history` fct
LEFT JOIN `omnichannel_analytics`.`dim_date` dd
                        on dd.date_day = fct.sk_order_date
GROUP BY dd.year_number,dd.quarter_of_year
```

By analyzing the results of running this query (Figure 6-12), we could conclude that the second quarter of 2023 was the best, while the worst was the first quarter of 2024.

Row	year_number ▼	quarter_of_year ▼	sum_total_amount_with_discount ▼
1	2023	3	279.96
2	2022	2	559.96
3	2022	3	452.94
4	2023	4	313.95
5	2023	1	373.96
6	2022	4	219.96
7	2022	1	277.95
8	2023	2	870.94
9	2024	1	149.99

Figure 6-12. Analytical query for obtaining total amount sold per quarter with discount

In Example 6-30, we calculate the average length of stay (in minutes) for each channel by using our star schema model. It selects the channel name (`dc.dsc_channel_name`) and the average length of stay in minutes, which is calculated with the function `ROUND(AVG(mtr_length_of_stay_minutes),2)`. The `dc.dsc_channel_name` refers to the `channel_name` attribute from the `dim_channels` dimension table.

The `ROUND(AVG(mtr_length_of_stay_minutes),2)` calculates the average length of stay in minutes by using the `AVG` function on the `mtr_length_of_stay_minutes` column from the `fct_visit_history` fact table. The `ROUND()` function is used to round the result to two decimal places. The alias `avg_length_of_stay_minutes` is assigned to the calculated average value.

Example 6-30. Average time spent per visit on each channel

```
SELECT dc.dsc_channel_name,
    ROUND(AVG(mtr_length_of_stay_minutes),2) as avg_length_of_stay_minutes
FROM `omnichannel_analytics.fct_visit_history` fct
LEFT JOIN `omnichannel_analytics.dim_channels` dc
on fct.sk_channel = dc.sk_channel
GROUP BY dc.dsc_channel_name
```

By analyzing the results of running this query (Figure 6-13), we could conclude that users spend more time on the website than on the mobile app or the company's Instagram account.

Row	dsc_channel_name ▼	avg_length_of_stay_minutes ▼
1	Instagram	5.0
2	Mobile App	5.0
3	Website	8.33

Figure 6-13. Analytical query for obtaining average time spent per visit on each channel

In Example 6-31, we take our model to an advanced use case. We are now interested in getting the top three products per channel. As we have three distinct channels, namely mobile app, website, and Instagram, we are interested in obtaining nine rows, three for each of the top three best sellers per channel.

To do so, we leverage the structural benefits of CTEs and start with a base query that will return the sum_total_amount per product and channel. With it, we can now create a second CTE, starting from the previous one, and rank the total amount descending per channel, which means the performance order of each product across channels. To obtain this rank, we default to window functions, specifically the RANK() function, which will score the rows based on the previously mentioned rule.

Example 6-31. Top three products per channel

```
WITH base_cte AS (
    SELECT dp.dsc_product_name,
        dc.dsc_channel_name,
        ROUND(SUM(fct.mtr_total_amount_net),2) as sum_total_amount
    FROM `omnichannel_analytics`.`fct_purchase_history` fct
    LEFT JOIN `omnichannel_analytics`.`dim_products` dp
                        on dp.sk_product = fct.sk_product
    LEFT JOIN `omnichannel_analytics`.`dim_channels` dc
                        on dc.sk_channel = fct.sk_channel
    GROUP BY dc.dsc_channel_name, dp.dsc_product_name
),
ranked_cte AS(
```

```
SELECT base_cte.dsc_product_name,
    base_cte.dsc_channel_name,
    base_cte.sum_total_amount,
    RANK() OVER(PARTITION BY dsc_channel_name
                ORDER BY sum_total_amount DESC) AS rank_total_amount
FROM base_cte
)
SELECT *
FROM ranked_cte
WHERE rank_total_amount <= 3
```

By analyzing the results of running this query (Figure 6-14), we conclude that our top performer for mobile app is the Men Bomber Jacket with Detachable Hood with €389.97 in sales, for website it's Leather Crossbody Handbag with €449.97 in sales, and for Instagram it's Unisex Running Sneakers with €271.97 in sales.

Row	dsc_product_name ▼	dsc_channel_name ▼	sum_total_amount	rank_total_amount
1	Men Bomber Jacket with Detachable Hood	Mobile App	389.97	1
2	Women Oversized Cat Eye Sunglasses	Mobile App	242.97	2
3	Men Stainless Steel Chronograph Watch	Mobile App	199.99	3
4	Leather Crossbody Handbag	Website	449.97	1
5	Men Stainless Steel Chronograph Watch	Website	399.98	2
6	Men Genuine Leather Ankle Boots	Website	219.98	3
7	Unisex Running Sneakers	Instagram	271.97	1
8	Women Elegant Floral Print Dress	Instagram	143.98	2
9	Men Bomber Jacket with Detachable Hood	Instagram	129.99	3

Figure 6-14. Analytical query for obtaining the top three products per channel

In Example 6-32, we conclude our roadshow through supporting business questions with SQL by leveraging our recently created star schema data model to perform an analysis of the top customers in 2023 on our mobile app. Once again, we leverage CTEs to structure our query correctly, but instead of window functions, this time we combine the ORDER BY clause with the LIMIT modifier to get the top three buyers in terms of money spent on purchases.

Example 6-32. Top three customers in 2023 on the mobile app

```
WITH base_cte AS (
    SELECT dcu.dsc_name,
        dcu.dsc_email_address,
        dc.dsc_channel_name,
        ROUND(SUM(fct.mtr_total_amount_net),2) as sum_total_amount
    FROM `omnichannel_analytics`.`fct_purchase_history` fct
    LEFT JOIN `omnichannel_analytics`.`dim_customers` dcu
                    on dcu.sk_customer = fct.sk_customer
```

```
    LEFT JOIN `omnichannel_analytics`.`dim_channels` dc
                        on dc.sk_channel = fct.sk_channel
    WHERE dc.dsc_channel_name = 'Mobile App'
    GROUP BY dc.dsc_channel_name, dcu.dsc_name, dcu.dsc_email_address
    ORDER BY sum_total_amount DESC
)
SELECT *
FROM base_cte
LIMIT 3
```

By analyzing the results of running this query (Figure 6-15), we conclude that our top buyer is Sophia Garcia with €389.97 spent. We can send an email to her at *sophia.garcia@emailaddress.com*, thanking her for being such a special customer.

Row	dsc_name ▾	dsc_email_address ▾	dsc_channel_name ▾	sum_total_amount
1	Sophia Garcia	sophia.garcia@emailaddress.com	Mobile App	389.97
2	Emma Johnson	emma.johnson@emailaddress.com	Mobile App	382.94
3	John Smith	john.smith@emailaddress.com	Mobile App	219.98

Figure 6-15. Analytical query for obtaining the top customers for a mobile app

By demonstrating these queries, we aim to highlight the inherent simplicity and effectiveness of using a star schema to answer complex business questions. By using this schema design, organizations can gain valuable insights and make data-driven decisions more efficiently.

While the preceding queries demonstrate the simplicity of each query, the real power lies in the ability to combine them with CTEs. This strategic use of CTEs allows queries to be optimized and organized in a structured and easy-to-understand manner. By using CTEs, analysts can streamline their workflows, improve code readability, and facilitate the reuse of intermediate results.

Also, implementing window functions brings an extra layer of efficiency to data analysis. Using window functions, analysts can efficiently calculate aggregated results across specific data partitions or windows, providing valuable insights into trends, rankings, and comparative analyzes. Analysts can efficiently derive meaningful conclusions from large datasets by using these functions, accelerating the decision-making process.

By writing this section, we intend to encapsulate the significance of the topics covered in this book. It emphasizes the importance of having a solid command of SQL, proficient data modeling skills, and a comprehensive understanding of the technical landscape surrounding data technologies like dbt to grow your analytics engineering skills. Acquiring these competencies enables professionals to effectively navigate the vast quantities of data generated within businesses or personal projects.

Conclusion

The landscape of analytics engineering is as vast and varied as the limits of human imagination. Just as Tony Stark harnessed cutting-edge technology to transform into Iron Man, we are empowered by databases, SQL, and dbt that make us not just spectators but active heroes in the data-driven age. Like Stark's array of armor, these tools provide us with the flexibility, strength, and precision to face the most intricate of challenges head-on.

Databases and SQL have always been our foundational pillars in data-driven strategies, providing stability and reliability. However, as the demands and complexities have grown, analytics has expanded to integrate complex data modeling practices. This transition goes beyond just mechanics, emphasizing crafting business narratives, anticipating analytical trends, and forward planning for future requirements.

dbt has emerged as a transformative element in this dynamic landscape. More than just a complement to SQL, it redefines how we approach collaboration, testing, and documentation. With dbt, the processing of raw and fragmented data becomes more refined, leading to actionable models that support informed decision making.

Analytical engineering blends both traditional practices and innovative advancements. While there are established principles of data modeling, rigorous testing, and transparent documentation, tools like dbt introduce fresh approaches and possibilities. Every challenge faced is a learning opportunity for both those stepping into this field and those with experience. Each database and query offers a unique perspective and a potential solution.

Just as Holmes weaves labyrinthine stories from fragmentary evidence, analytics engineers can create compelling data models from highly fragmented data points. The tools at their disposal aren't just mechanical, but empower them to anticipate analytic trends, align data models with business needs, and, like Holmes, become storytellers of the data-driven age. In this context, dbt is their Watson, fostering collaboration and efficiency, much like the famous detective's trusty companion. The parallels to Holmes are striking, as both have made it their mission to uncover secrets hidden in cryptic cases or complex datasets. It's our hope that through this book's chapters, you've gained insights and a clearer understanding of this evolving discipline.

Index

D

About the Authors

Rui Machado is the vice president of technology at Fraudio and has a background in information technologies and data science. He has over a decade of experience in the architecture and implementation of data warehouses, data lakes, and decision support systems in industries such as retail, ecommerce, supply chain, healthcare, and social networks. He has led engineering and analytics teams at companies including Jumia, Nike, Facebook, Talkdesk, and Feedzai, while advising others on technology, data platforms, and strategies. He is also the cofounder and CEO of ShopAI. He has previously collaborated with Synfusion in publishing three technical books on Powershell, SSIS, and BizTalk Server.

LinkedIn profile: *https://www.linkedin.com/in/rpmachado*

Hélder Russa is a data engineering lead with a background in information technologies and data science. He has over 10 years of professional experience in computer science, with an emphasis on evolving and maintaining data solutions applied to decision making. Nowadays, he works as the head of data engineering at Jumia, contributing to the strategy definition, design, and implementation of multiple Jumia data platforms. Since 2018, he has been a cofounder, managing partner, and data architect of ShopAI, a company specializing in deep learning that uses images to optimize webshop searches.

LinkedIn profile: *https://www.linkedin.com/in/hrussa*

Colophon

The animal on the cover of *Analytics Engineering with SQL and dbt* is a sperm whale (*Physeter macrocephalus*), the largest toothed predator on earth. They are found in all of the world's oceans, but tend to prefer deep, offshore waters, inhabiting regions from the icy Arctic and Antarctic to tropical and temperate zones.

The sperm whale's most prominent feature is its enormous, block-shaped head, which can account for up to a third of its dark gray or brownish body. Stretching to lengths of up to 60 feet and weighing around 50 tons, sperm whales are often covered with scars and scratches earned from battles over their 70-year lifespan.

Sperm whales hold the record for the deepest and longest dives of any mammal, descending to astonishing depths of over 10,000 feet and staying submerged for up to 90 minutes. Their ability to collapse their lungs to avoid nitrogen absorption and their unique blood composition aids in tolerating extreme pressure. Sperm whales have a unique and complex social structure, living in family groups called pods led by a dominant female and communicating through a series of clicks, which are believed to be among the loudest sounds produced by any animal.

This whale gets its name from the spermaceti organ within its large head that contains a waxy substance—spermaceti oil—that was historically used in cosmetics, textiles, and candles. While they were historically targets of whaling, today, conservation efforts strive to protect and understand these creatures, recognizing their vital role in the marine ecosystem. Many of the animals on O'Reilly covers are endangered; all of them are important to the world.

The color illustration is by Karen Montgomery, based on an antique line engraving from *British Quadrupeds*. The series design is by Edie Freedman, Ellie Volckhausen, and Karen Montgomery. The cover fonts are Gilroy Semibold and Guardian Sans. The text font is Adobe Minion Pro; the heading font is Adobe Myriad Condensed; and the code font is Dalton Maag's Ubuntu Mono.

Printed in the USA
CPSIA information can be obtained
at www.ICGtesting.com
JSHW061511220124
55856JS00020B/94

9 781098 142384